LITERARY VOICE

SUNY Series,
The Margins of Literature

Mihai I. Spariosu, Editor

LITERARY VOICE

The Calling of Jonah

Donald Wesling
and
Tadeusz Sławek

STATE UNIVERSITY OF NEW YORK PRESS

Cover Art: *Jonah Cast Up*. Marble, 40.6 x 21.6 x 37.6 cm. Eastern Mediterranean, probably Asia Minor, Early Christian, ca. 260–275.

Production by Ruth Fisher
Marketing by Dana E. Yanulavich

Published by
State University of New York Press, Albany

Printed in the United States of America

For information, address the State University of New York Press, State University Plaza, Albany, NY 12246

Library of Congress Cataloging-in-Publication Data
Wesling, Donald.
Literary voice : the calling of Jonah / Donald Wesling and Tadeusz Sławek.
p. cm. — (SUNY series, the margins of literature)
Includes bibliographical references and index.
ISBN 0-7914-2627-0 (alk. paper). — ISBN 0-7914-2628-9 (pbk. : alk. paper)
1. Criticism. 2. Style, Literary. 3. Bible. O.T. Jonah—Criticism, interpretation, etc. I. Sławek, Tadeusz. II. Title, III. Series.
PN81.W447 1995
801′ .95—dc20 94-45743
CIP

10 9 8 7 6 5 4 3 2 1

To Walter J. Ong

Who wrote of voice that "It is essential for language, but extends beyond language to the direct, inarticulate expression of emotion. . . . It is archaic, yet as up-to-date today as ever, combining freely and creatively with the most advanced technologies." (Foreword to Paul Zumthor, *Oral Poetry: An Introduction* [1990]).

AND

To the Memory of Michel de Certeau

Who said of self that it is "in reality plural, social in its very constitution. Its activities follow out dialogues that have begun well before one sets oneself to speak." (Interview with Guitta Pessis-Pasternak in *Le Monde*, 19–20 January, 1986).

CONTENTS

PREFACE

In this book we take up Jonah's *calling*, his teaching profession; also his receiving and giving of commands. Errant Jonah, who absconds when Yahweh calls on him to preach, is type figure for all philosophers of voice and professors of literature. Jonah's perverse detour results in illumination, not for him, but for the people of Nineveh whom he warns, and for readers of the Bible.

Jacques Derrida has ably analyzed the writing that is in speaking, but this reply to his work analyzes the speaking that is in writing. Our book defends and illustrates literary voice against modern philosophy's critique of the spoken, and in the light of Mikhail Bakhtin's dialogism and Henri Meschonnic's studies on subjectivity in rhythmic language. We find literary voice to be maximal (not as value, but as limiting case) in bardic speech, where the author speaks for the nation (Adam Mickiewicz's Polish epic); and this full voice stands between the two minimums of *the body* (grunts and sighs and birdsong), and on the other side *the material text* (loss of logic, narrative, and social tones in Nietzsche and in the American Language poets). The current moment's skepticism is not an auspicious one for anything like a bounded self or subject, but propositions of subject may be necessary for literature and for politics. With the aid of dozens of examples in four languages, we define for the many-voiced speaking subject a small, believable ground from which to maneuver.

The concept of 'literary voice' has always been hovering at the margins of literature. Many elements of a synthesis have been in detached motion, but oddly, no scholar has faced this topic for sustained study before now. Our book develops the meanings of terms that have been around for some time, such as *the speaking subject*. The book also adds key terms to the lexicon of literary study: *minimal articulation, regional intentionality, detonation, literary voice*. By developing such terms, we argue on behalf of new possibilities inherent in the idea of an impersonal, "syncopated" subject: a construction of human identity which, while operating in the sphere of the conscious, remains in vital relationship with the unconscious and paralogic.

During the academic year 1989 to 1990, Tadeusz Sławek held a fellowship at University of California, San Diego from the American

Council of Learned Societies. He lived with his family five minutes away from Donald Wesling and his family in Pacific Beach, California. Each Saturday morning we would walk to Ingrid's German Deli on Garnet Avenue or to an open-air restaurant on the boardwalk facing the ocean. We would discuss the ambitious plan of this book for several hours, then separately during the week would write segments of chapters. By June 1990 when Tadeusz Sławek returned to Poland, we had the makings of a book.

Our focal idea about literary voice has found one example in our own work. Collaborating as a method of writing underlines, indeed exaggerates, the impossibility of knowing who is speaking. Since our definition of literary voice is the impossibility of knowing who is speaking, we hope to have performed what we have defined.

Thanks are due to Debra Bronstein, Thomas K. Dunseath, Jon Snyder, Mihai Spariosu, and Andrew Wright, who corrected errors and challenged arguments. We would also thank the American Council of Learned Societies (for Tadeusz Sławek's fellowship); and at UC San Diego the Research Committee (for support of word processing), and Stanley Chodorow, Dean of Arts and Humanities (for help with Donald Wesling's travel to Poland).

Acknowledgment is due to those who granted permission to reprint excerpts from the following copyright material:

Samuel Beckett's *Stories and Texts for Nothing* (New York: Grove Press, 1967), by permission of Grove/Atlantic, Inc.

An article by Gabriella Bedetti, "Henri Meschonnic: Rhythm as Pure Historicity," *New Literary History* 23, 2 (Spring 1992), by permission of the editor of *New Literary History*.

Paul Celan's poem cycle *Die Niemandsrose* (Frankfurt am Main: S. Fischer Verlag, 1963), by permission of S. Fischer Verlag. Copyright 1963 by S. Fischer Verlag, Frankfurt am Main.

John Clare, excerpts from four poems in *John Clare* (Oxford Authors), ed. Eric Robinson and David Powell (Oxford: Oxford University Press, 1984), by permission of the Curtis Brown Group Ltd., London. Copyright 1984 by Eric Robinson.

Donald Davie's poem "Or, Solitude," from *Donald Davie: Collected Poems* (Chicago: University of Chicago Press, 1991), by permission of University of Chicago Press. Copyright 1991 by Donald Davie.

Robert Frost's poem "Provide, Provide," *The Poetry of Robert Frost* (New York: Henry Holt, Co., Inc., 1949), by permission of Henry Holt, Co., Inc. Copyright 1936 by Robert Frost.

William Gibson's novel *Neuromancer* (New York: Ace Books, 1984), by permission of The Putnam Berkley Group. Copyright 1984 by William Gibson.

Thomas Gray's poem "The Bard," *Selected Poems of Thomas Gray and William Collins*, ed. Arthur Johnson (Columbia, SC: University of South Carolina Press, 1967), by permission of University of South Carolina Press.

Michael Hamburger's translation of five poems by Paul Celan, from *Poems of Paul Celan* (London: Anvil Press Poetry, 1988), by permission of Anvil Press.

Lyn Hejinian, *My Life* (Los Angeles: Sun & Moon Press, 1991), pp. 41-42, copyright 1991, 1987, 1980 by Lyn Hejinian; reprinted by permission of Sun & Moon Press.

Vachel Lindsay, "Litany of the Heroes" and "The Congo" in *Collected Poems of Vachel Lindsay* (New York: Macmillan Publishing Company, 1925), by permission of Simon & Schuster. Copyright 1923 by Macmillan Publishing Company, renewed 1951 by Elizabeth C. Lindsay.

An article by Anne Mack and J. J. Rome, "The Alphabet, Spelt from Silliman's Leaves . . .," *South Atlantic Quarterly* 89, 4 (Fall 1990), by permission of the editor of *South Atlantic Quarterly*, published by Duke University Press.

Kenneth Mackenzie's translation of Adam Mickiewicz's *Pan Tadeusz* (London: Everyman's Library, 1966), by permission of Everyman's Library, David Campbell Publishers, Ltd., London.

Henri Meschonnic's scholarly study *La Rime et la vie* (Paris: Editions Verdier, 1989), and his book of poems, *Voyageurs de la voix* (Paris: Editions Verdier, 1985), by permission of Editions Verdier, Paris.

Henri Meschonnic's Interview with Gabriella Bedetti, published in *Diacritics* (Fall 1988), by permission of the editor of *Diacritics*, published by The Johns Hopkins University Press.

Adam Mickiewicz's *Pan Tadeusz* and his Sonnets from the Caucasus, from *Dziela Adama Mickiewicza*, ed. J. Krzysanowski (Warsaw: Czytelnik, 1955), by permission of Spoldzielnia Wydawnicza Czytelnik, Warsaw.

Cyprian Norwid's three poems from Norwid's *Dziela Zebrane*, 1 (Warsaw: Panstwowy Instytut Wydawniczy, 1966), and from *Dziela Wszystkie*, 3 (Warsaw: Panstwowy Instytut Wydawniczy, 1971), by permission of Panstwowy Instytut Wydawniczy, Warsaw.

George Rapall Noyes's translation of Adam Mickiewicz's sonnet, "View of the Mountains from the Kozlov Steppes," *Poems by Adam Mickiewicz* (New York: Polish Institute of Arts and Sciences in America, 1944), by permission of the Polish Institute of Arts and Sciences in America.

Michael Palmer's poem "Notes for Echo Lake 8 . . . .," *Notes for Echo Lake* (San Francisco: North Point Press, 1981), by permission of Michael Palmer to whom rights have reverted.

Dennis Potter's play *The Singing Detective* (New York: Vintage Books, 1988), by permission for the US and Canada and elsewhere except the British Commonwealth from Vintage Books, a Division of Random House, Inc.; by permission for British Commonwealth from Faber and Faber, Ltd., London. Copyright 1988 by Dennis Potter.

J. H. Prynne, one poem from *Wound Response* (1974) and one poem from *Down Where Changed*, as reprinted in *Poems* (Edinburgh and London: Agneau 2, 1982), pp. 223 and 307, by permission of J. H. Prynne to whom rights have reverted. Copyright 1974, 1979, 1982 by J. H. Prynne.

Avital Ronell's *The Telephone Book: Technology, Schizophrenia, Electric Speech* (Lincoln & London: University of Nebraska Press, 1989), by permission of University of Nebraska Press.

Ron Silliman's poem *Tjanting* (Berkeley, CA: The Figures Press, 1981), by permission of Ron Silliman to whom rights have reverted.

CHAPTER 1. Toward a Philosophy of Literary Voice

Person as Voice: Thinking about a Metaphor

This is a book about a concept with its own profile and history. Our focus is human selfhood and subjectivity, as understood through the guise of voice. Voice is mask, grid, metaphor, a phenomenon of delay and remove. Difference, deferral is inevitable, even within one person's makeup, for full self-presence is strictly impossible. We know that, if we *think* of the sound and sense of our own voices, even as we speak our individual given names, we hear ourselves ever so slightly as another. (A further step away, worthy of study, but not here, is when a jazz clarinet or sax becomes the lyrical stand-in for the singing human voice, guise of a guise.) In newspaper language, the metaphor of voice is absolutely equated, conflated with the person. Philosophically this is an error, but it testifies to a need which the present study may analyze but never uproot. For voice is in fact a metaphor of enormous prestige in political and literary culture, an idealism that moves across nearly all geopolitical borders. Studying the person through and by means of the guise, we hope to penetrate ordinary usage and thus to tease apart the tenor (person) and the vehicle (voice) of the metaphor, to see what logical products may be created. Guise means something about person, and about why person needs guise. To begin by looking at guise and not directly at person will, we trust, release unusual energies. Voice as person is a special kind of metaphor—synecdoche, part for whole. But this need not mean a reduction in logical terms. It may indeed mean an expansion of the understanding of person, by means of movement into detours and inner foldings, mappings of outer battlements and inward sounding corridors of selfhood. We may also move into volatile border states of noise just before literature comes into being and just after, on the other side, it has phased out into nonsense.

The verbs *defect, substitute, deviate*: in setting up the inquiry thus, thinking about the metaphor of person as voice, we are repeating Jonah's errancy, refusing to answer the call. Jonah is not only our figure for resistance to vocation, reluctant prophecy, the teacher who needs instruction; he is also a role model for scholarly method and, to expand this to its proper dimensions, for an ethics of scholarship. Resisting the arrogance of an apocalyptic scholarship that would eliminate Jonah's fear and self-suspicion, Henri Meschonnic ends his book on Jonah as an "errant signifier" saying "Jonah, that's me. That's to say, you."[1] Peter Dews ends his book about post-structuralism's logics of disintegration by denouncing an "inability to provide anything other than a repudiation of the philosophy of the subject," and by affirming what any philosophy of voice must needs affirm, "that critique is not a question of the arbitrary and coercive espousal of premisses and precepts, but rather a commitment to that coherence of thought which alone ensures its emancipatory power."[2] In the present post-post-structuralist moment, the order of the day is the finding of a logic of integration which would deliver a human subject not held captive by the limitations of a discredited philosophy of consciousness.

Perhaps this is why so many excellent studies have recently converged on the issue of voice: not only the Franco-American and central European appropriation of the dialogism of Mikhail Bakhtin, but in addition many French and French-influenced and homegrown Anglo-American descriptions of what Eric Griffiths calls "printed voice." In this integrationist moment, we are beyond the stage of David Carroll's 1980s book, *The Subject in Question*, beyond the necessary thoroughgoing skepticisms of Jacques Derrida's sixties antiphonocentrism, and ready to be "For the Subject," as Geoffrey Hartman says in his dedication to *Saving the Text* (1981).[3] But what subject, and according to what logics? How preserve a critical and political dimension within the metacritique, while still admiring Jonah's strange disgust at a prophecy that has no instant result in agency, his unwillingness, as Meschonnic says (81), to play God's game? Only a cogent theory of the relation of the subject to the social will support a philosophy of voice as a metaphor of person. Beyond even this, as a difficulty quite sufficient by itself for study, is the question of the sacred, raised by Jonah when he runs away and refuses Yahweh (act of commission and escape) and raised by Jonah when he holds his tongue (silent act of omission and escape). Meschonnic (81): "Job recognizes that God is right. Jonah is quiet. The book ends on Jonah's silence, his non-response to God's question." Could our book dare to do better than Jonah, to complete Jonah? *To answer*? Never. Yahweh hasn't talked to us—directly. (To be exact, Yahweh never talked to the anonymous author of the Book of Jonah, either.) Still, we come up against the edges of sacred voice at several points, because no comprehensive study should omit theology or, in our day, the scholarship of Henri Meschonnic on the Jewish side and of Jesuits Walter J. Ong and Michel de Certeau.

Three Elements of a Comprehensive Philosophy of Literary Voice

A History/Theory of the Relation of Voice to Person

Such a history/theory would also be an account of the relation of person to the voice that is in the text, on the page. Our own account says that voice is the undecidable as between person and text. Literary voice simultaneously affirms writing and puts it into question. This is our way of rephrasing the truly constructive point, first to our knowledge made by Meschonnic, that those marks of orality we call "voice" may be found equally in speaking and in writing. If that is the case, then the speaking-writing opposition which has so dominated thinking in this field, and which has put speaking over writing, can be surpassed by thought. The issue for the present book is the correct definition of the speaking that is in writing.

A naturalized and entirely conventional usage is to call the voice the "self," by an unproblematized synecdoche of the ephemeral part, sounds on the breath, for the person or the group of persons. Our way, by contrast, is to keep pressing the to-us-unanswerable question, Who is speaking? To ask the question in historical and phenomenological contexts will reduce the possible number of replies from infinity to something usually countable, usually nearby.

Who is speaking? is preeminently a question of our own period of literary speculation, the period of communications technology and advanced methods of voice simulation, voice reproduction. Our inability to be certain in this matter tends to define us in our modern and postmodern era. Dennis Potter, author of *The Singing Detective*, a six-part television series for the BBC, says: "One of the reasons I choose to write 'drama' rather than prose fiction is precisely to avoid the question which has so damaged, or intellectually denuded, the contemporary novel: '*Who is saying this?*'" Potter believes that "the masking of the Self is an essential part of the trade. Even, or especially, when 'using' the circumstances, pleasures and dilemmas of one's own life."[4] So far from stating that he wants a definitive answer to the question of Who, far from wanting certitude, he is looking for ways to increase and diversify the baffles and masks. Potter rejects a fussy, popular-psychology questioning of the Who behind the story, because he resists anyone's reducing a play to an expressive event, a personal hangup. This critique of expressivity is perhaps the crucial motive for scholarly questioning of literary voice in our period and for authorial dismissal of voice as a metaphor of person.

To write such a critique does not only mean a withdrawal from the concept of 'art as expression', but it necessarily implies a discussion of certain important philosophical issues, as the very concept of 'expression', as Gilles Deleuze convinces us, is formed as a hub of most significant philosophical notions such as 'being' (*être*), 'knowledge' (*connaître*), and 'production' (*produire*).[5] Signalling here only a necessity of a much more detailed analysis of expression, suffice it to say that a critique of expressive self involves two very important areas. First, it must allow space for the events which are not directly or causally linked with an individual, which have not been, so to speak, mastered by the subject, and which yet enter the individual without being integrated or submitted to any order imposed upon them by the subject. What it practically means is that the correlation both between the subject and the world and between the "corporal" and "spiritual" orders within the subject itself has been shaken and weakened. Thus, there are events in one sphere which now do not quite "correspond." (Deleuze [304] writes that it is precisely expression which establishes a link between the spiritual and corporal series in humankind to any value or symbol in the other, the "flat" events which we have no better terms for than *chance* or *incident*.) In other words, a critique of expressivity must signify the end of the romantic, individualistic tradition of "correspondences" which sees the poet as the central unit capturing and then expressing the system of relations. In fine, whereas romanticism made an individual responsible for inscribing each occurrence into the general pattern of correspondence between the physical and historical on the one hand and the spiritual and transcendental on the other, now the subject does not regulate the mechanisms of general relatedness but is a part of it. One does not "express" phenomena but takes down notes and minutes of chance operations.

Thus, John Cage is right when he claims that his intention in preparing some of his musical pieces was to put "the stories, the incidental sounds from the environment . . . together in an unplanned way . . . to suggest that all things are related, and that this complexity is more evident when it is not oversimplified by an idea of relationship in one person's mind."[6] Second, a critique of expressive self puts a question mark next to such important notions as 'similitude' and 'analogy'. The expressive self operates on the principle that, (a) its acts are recognizable as carrying marks of their maker, and (b) that each act allows us to recapture the totality of the self. In terms of traditional metaphors, one has to recall Deleuze's point about two crucial metaphors of expressivity, one of the "mirror" (*"qui reflète ou réfléchit une image"*), and the other of a "germ" (*qui exprime l'arbre tout entier*) [Deleuze, 69, 163]. Thus, the self which does not define itself along the lines of expressivity cannot or at least cannot always "recognize" itself in its own product; neither can it claim that anyone, including the self itself, can get access to the "totality" of self through the "stylistic" analysis of the self's products. Consequently, there creeps in a noticeable rift between *ratio essendi, ratio cognoscendi,* and *ratio agendi* which, in turn, implies that a subject is no longer describable in terms of Leibnitzean monad.

One has only to mention dadaist and surrealist practices of collage making or *écriture automatique* to see how the aleatory appears as an integral part of the subject's product, the part which cannot be recognized as "resembling," "depicting" or "explaining" the subject. John Cage's operation on the book of *I Ching* is another good example of such procedures.[7]

Ours is a critique of expressivity, authorship, bardship, because it is a critique of presence. Jacques Derrida's famous attack on phonocentrism is our starting point. Elimination of the old philosophical subject and implied critique of intention and agency were the main legacies of Derrida's work in the sixties, primarily *Speech and Phenomena* and *Of Grammatology*. However, Derrida's absolute dismissal of the sound stratum of writing, and of the speech that is in writing, printed voice, seems now an overplayed hand. The tactful reassertion of voice as sound, voice as person, in Geoffrey Hartman's Derrida-influenced book *Saving the Text* (1981) gave support for our own sense that there was something to be rescued from the general devastation of antiphonocentrism at the very least, an error to be defended. On the other hand we are conscious that Hartman has himself been criticized for giving back, in that book's analyses of Tennyson, what he took away from the philosophy of consciousness in his general statements.

The fundamental premises of the philosophy of the subject are self-constitution, self-boundedness, and self-property. The critique of this Cartesian-Kantian-Hegelian (and Capitalist) self-isolated subject has been thoroughgoing in the Marxist, deconstructive, and poststructuralist semiotic traditions. But there are other possible and workable notions of the subject, and we develop and exemplify these. In the process, we write a critique of the expressive self and of self-presence, entering into an existing body of inquiry that seeks new forms of subjectivity and, we hope, extending its terms. (Whereas early in his career Michel Foucault argued for scholarly elimination of author study so as to widen research to historical discourses, later on he used this very term, *new forms of subjectivity*.)

Ours is an intersubjective account that makes much of the role of alterity, the equal-to-self role of others in the constitution of subjectivity. Utterance is on the borderline between at least two consciousnesses where all dialogic discourse takes place. This, Mikhail Bakhtin's lesson about dialogue, answerability, unfinalizability is in process of being tested in many kinds of examples of voice and bids fair to being the most complete theory of human communication to have emerged in the twentieth century.

The power and comprehensiveness of Bakhtin's dialogism may well mark the end of an entire era in Western thought about voice as person, person as voice. Walter J. Ong is right to argue that the era has its origins in the century of Ramus and what Ong calls the "decay of dialogue" with Guttenberg and the new forms of writing, reading, listening. These new forms, emergent in the late middle ages, tend to obliterate older collective modes of thought and earlier technologies of speaking, writing, reading. They permit, indeed encourage, that "ideology of the aesthetic" (Terry Eagleton's term) emergent in early modern Europe, particularly in Descartes, wherein separate selves separately experience the world and art. The seventeenth century is a crucial turning point, and we (like Jonathan Goldberg in his book on voice) see a remarkable new sophistication about the borrowing and citational echo effects in the poets of the seventeenth century, including the devotional poets. Writers in the era of the Restoration, such as Hobbes and Locke, begin to theorize self as property in a new way in the notion of possessive individualism. To have a notion of social contract means ceding some selfhood, some voice in the sense of representation and power, in order to found a state force which will keep brutishness at bay. One literary version of the new nationhood ideology is the bardic, many of whose origins or reinvigorations lie in the mid-eighteenth century. In the bardic is propounded a poetics of self and nation at a moment when the nation is being expanded (England) or attacked (Poland), and when the poet can speak expansively, expressively, with an I that is claimed to be a We. (That is why the bardic is in our own era unfashionable—the self expanded to represent the nation seems monstrous, a ridiculous claim.)[8]

This seventeenth and eighteenth-century moment also evokes the greatest explosion in the West of what Bakhtin called "inner speech." George Steiner documented the rise of this type of consciousness in the coming of the novel, the proliferation of letter writing, the development of genres like memoirs, travel narratives, picturesque journeys. All these drive voice down into the interior self.[9] The culmination rather than the reversal of this trend is of course romanticism, when European history arrives at what early science, colonialism, proto-Capitalist acquisitiveness, and Cartesian self-study were all, it now seems, conducing toward—possession of an inner generative self, genius, an infinitely rich personality. Romantic philosophy and poetry explore the jostling of the humanism of the one against the humanism of the many, in the recent terms of historicist Roy Harvey Pearce, with the richness of singular self gaining preference. And as M. H. Abrams, Walter Jackson Bate, and others have shown, romantic criticism put the generative self at the center of systems of literary commentary. Within the public sphere of the two revolutions, industrial and political, there emerged promethean individuals, and also apertures for democratic individuals and indeed for the coming into power of a new middle class and the coming into consciousness of a new working class that identified itself as a group after 1789. Remaining with England only, we can record the coming of vote as voice in 1832; schooling as voice in the new education acts from the middle of the century to the end; extension of the vote to women during World War I. Heroic modernism in literature and painting develops lines already started in romanticism, chastening, diversifying, extending notions of self—only in Gertrude Stein and a few isolated figures, still unincorporated, anticipating the postmodern by spreading hints of self all over the flat surface of language.

Consider now the public sphere of eastern and central Europe in the 1990s, where many groups claim voice in the political sense: voice as vote, voice as nation, voice as ethnic group, voice as language. These imaginary communities, in Benedict Anderson's phrase, are finding an assertion of self and group after many years of submitting to the voice of authority. Just now, inner speech is in recession and political speech is a desperate life or death issue; but it is likely that, at any punctual moment shown in these paragraphs' quick survey, the same may well have seemed true for contemporaries with an interest in literature and in social justice.

A Theory of Communicative Context

Voice as person, person as voice, we have seen, is logically at the core of this topic, and yet this remains partial. Any cogent method must describe and exemplify a large network of interrelationships of enunciation. Every voice, including prayer, needs an ear, imagines an addressee. The audience is, as Walter J. Ong has insisted, always a fiction, and particularly with the temporal and spatial distances required by printed voice. So voice is projecting an audience, to an audience—also the audience is plainly influencing content and tone. Thus in some sense uttering is also answering and listening is also helping to sculpt matter and tone of discourse. Bakhtin's work of the twenties on answerability is one source of such speculation. Another crucial achievement here is Jürgen Habermas's extended labor toward a sociology of communication—on the influence of a public sphere on communicative action. For Habermas, speaker and hearer, as partners, both simultaneously occupy the level of intersubjectivity and the level of objects (or state of affairs). This valuable inclusiveness is not to be found in accounts of communication which would foreground the metaphysics of power or desire, accounts which omit the relation to the other which is constitutive of subjectivity. An exception would be Jacques Lacan's reading of therapeutic communication, where without its being politicized we do find a theory of how interactive speaking forms and deforms selfhood from the earliest childhood moments.

Describing the reader's state of apprehension and actual practices will be part of any comprehensive account of literary voice. There will be many states and many practices, perhaps as many as readers, and yet the printed voice is there as a guide or grid to reading, a specific form of words. If there is plural reception, there would also appear to be plural enunciation, as in the kinds of questions Michel de Certeau asks as a reader of the devotional works of St. Teresa of Avila, "Who are you? Who else lives in you? To whom do you talk?" Mystical writing sponsors a plural enunciation to a single divine interlocutor, which is then overheard or overread by others.[10]

As a diagram to think with, to judge comprehensiveness, let us imagine a schema of critical theories that bear on communicative context. The schema is a more explicit version of M. H. Abrams' well-known triangle, here a clock with positions filled in for multicultural discussion of critical theories by Wai-lim Yip.[11] The compass points are North=World (things, events); East=Author (as individual); South=Work (the relative autonomy of the artwork); and West=Reader (norms of the reading public, cognitive practices of reading as a skill). At forty-five degrees from each of these cardinal points on the circle are four categories of literary theory, namely:

1. Between world and author: theories of perception of objects, author-centered theories of poetics.
2. Between author and work: theories of perception into art, form matching perception, mediumistic theories.

3. Between work and reader: theories of communication, function and effect, social and linguistic contract, communicative strategies, reception theory, hermeneutics.
4. Between reader and world: theories of historical relevance, mode of production theories, historical discrepancies in perception.

In the middle of the circle, subject to lines of force running from all points on the circumference, are a number of topics such as national resources, technological level, psychological features, societal norms, cultural factors, aesthetic theories, linguistic modes. That a valid literature and literary theory may be constructed from any of the eight positions on the outside of the circle is clear; names and schools of writers can be ranged on and between the cardinal compass points. Mikhail Bakhtin's dialogism and Jürgen Habermas's theory of communicative action do not fit at any one compass point like other writers' ideas in the twentieth century. Bakhtin in particular moves between all points, existing in the middle of the circle with equal ability to move in all directions. Bakhtin's dialogism, with voices that are strongly marked by class and sociolect, retains issues in ideology. Western scholars, not only Slavists, looking to complete formal stylistics with a more communitarian-based stylistics, begin to find Bakhtin more adequate than, say, Roman Jakobson. What primarily distinguishes Bakhtin is his commitment to elaboration of the premise of the speaking subject as an answerable subject.

A Stylistics Based on Speech Orientation

In order to theorize the whole issue, a responsible philosophy of voice should bring back for analysis the following elements of printed voice, all of which have often been relegated to the sphere of the merely instrumental: the sound stratum of the text; questions of idiolect, dialect, sociolect; ordinary conversational language; and the visual configuration of the text, including the graphological and typological form, and also the processual patterns of the hands in sign language.

Sound made equal and made nonequal in meter, rhyme, and rhythm at all levels from syllable all the way up to whole text—those formal, phonic linguistic issues are not faced by Derrida, are indeed dismissed by him. But those who would revise and extend grammatology pay close attention to these devices—as in Garrett Stewart's focus on the double meanings literary works get from word junctures, in a recent book with a thesis in its title, insisting that *Reading Voices* (1990). Henri Meschonnic, in *Critique du rythme* (1982) treats rhythm as a privileged category, the place in the text where the free choice of the self is on display and in rapport with the social, eluding the false opposition of signifier and signified. Another rich field of exploration is the role of sound as sound, sound as repetition, in religious glossolalia, studied by Michel de Certeau as a phenomenon of vocal utopia.[12] Intonation, for example in Jamaican or African-American writing that moves into and out of dialect, provides crucial interpretive information that is given over primarily by sound, though of course a writer's choices are also lexical, syntactical. When we study code switching in represented talk we put voice back into its cultural matrix. Printed voice must also include the fullest possible reference to visual configurations which give the reader an inducement to read a text as a unity, to recognize emphases, and to know when it is over. American sign language, which is not a spelling out of alphabet with fingers, is a privileged case for theory of voice, because it unquestionably is a language with a grammar and a syntax and has no phonic component whatever. Sign language is voice without sound, the purest instance of voice as person we can imagine, engaged daily by hundreds of thousands, and with its own literary technologies, sign systems, devices, emphases.

Whether as spoken evanescent sound or visual voice, the issue here comes down to a location in the human body, in physiology, in pulsions and compulsions that preexist, or accompany, language. This too has been relegated and needs to be repossessed, as it is most thoughtfully in David Appelbaum's philosophy of phatic and physical and preliterary voice. Our own way of conceiving this will be to bracket our study by developing two modes of the minimal. Maximal voice, which we treat in our middle chapters, has highly overdetermined meanings—meaning grafted onto meaning—and is thus literary voice as such. Minimal voice in our first sense (as noise) is exclamation, birdsong, babble, phatic utterance, phonic material that seems on the way to being articulate speech. Minimal voice in our second sense (as nonsense), in the final chapter, is the deliberate minimal of the avant-garde where language is used to mime breakdown of language, so to force the reader to look at each word, syllable, stanza, sentence, paragraph, or other structural or semantic feature as itself in all its strangeness and materiality. The first minimal is that of the not yet of the speaking subject, and the second minimal is the no longer. Innovation in critical inquiry as in literary creation sometimes occurs, when one inspects those places where stable constructions of person and genre break down. But to study only those places is not to be comprehensive. Language and voice as person need the body both for production and for reception, but to treat these as limited to or trapped within the body would betray the primary Bakhtinian axiom, which we take as our own: *we are dialogue on the boundaries between consciousnesses.*

There is now a larger fellowship of many scholars writing on related topics, and our affiliated inquiry is a work of synthesis, development, exemplification, refocusing, specification. Our book treats materials from ancient Greece and biblical culture, from early modern literature and philosophy, from the heyday of the bardic as a type of national voice in Enlightenment and romanticism, and from modernist and postmodernist literary culture. As to method, we have set out to complete a phenomenology with a historical stylistics and a sociology of voice. Theoretical and comparatist, we develop exemplary readings across many geopolitical and generic boundaries. Our book tries to live up to its title by arguing theoretical, theological, historical, and current pedagogical pertinences for the figure of errant, dissatisfied Jonah.

Across this gridwork, we develop our four leading ideas for the following reasons:

> Speaking subject: Because we can no longer say subject as such, subject with a locked-inside consciousness that is bounded, self-possessed. Because we want to analyze propositions of subject which liberate and empower and propositions of subject which enslave.
>
> Minimal Articulation: Because we want to test versions and elisions and syncopations of subject, vulnerable or perverse or excited or momentary states of experience, fragments of subjectivity where sound has not come all the way over to concept, where the vox confusa of animals or the body has not reached vox articulata but still has human meanings.
>
> Regional Intentionality: Because we can no longer say "within the bubble of consciousness of the biographical individual," and yet, until we reach the furthest limit of avant-garde decentering and of electronic networking, we still refer to intention and agency, making assumptions about the social and other placement of person, of voice, knowing we can never finally specify a single place.
>
> Indeterminate voice: Because we want to indicate an avant-garde literary language that is not reducible to person, but forces the reader into a furious hunt for continuity, individuality, centeredness, bounding outline, social tones of voice, most of which attributes have been eliminated in postmodern writing. Because the writing that eliminates or defaces relies on residual hopes for such attributes, in an era when they have been decertified as values.

These four expositions are designed as ways of putting right and filling the gaps in the survey of voice philosophy which follows in the two remaining sections of the present chapter.

The Speaking Subject: Our Most Comprehensive Premise as Derived from Emile Benveniste and Julia Kristeva

> Where would I go, if I could go, who would I be, if I could be, what would I say, if I had a voice, who says this, saying it's me? Answer simply, someone answer simply. It's the same old stranger as ever, for whom alone accusative I exist, in the pit of my inexistence, of his, of ours, there's a simple answer. It's not with thinking he'll find me, but what is he to do, living and bewildered, yes, living, say what he may. Forget me, know me not, yes, that would be the wisest, none better able than he. Why this sudden affability after such a desertion, it's easy to understand, that's what he says, but he doesn't understand. I'm not in his head, nowhere in his old body, and yet I'm there, for him I'm there, with him, hence all the confusion. That should have been enough for him, to have found me absent, but it's not, he wants me there, with a form and a world, like him in spite of him, me who am everything, like him who is nothing. And when he feels me void of existence it's of his he would have me void, and vice versa, mad, mad, he's mad. The truth is he's looking for me to kill me, to have me dead like him, dead like the living.[13]

Who says this, saying it's me? Literary voice is not empirical speech or even, usually, reducible to such familiar anchor points as logical thinking or audible sounding. Hence all the confusion. Samuel Beckett has written about literary voice from within, speaking as, and imitating and personifying literary voice. All writers do this but not, perhaps, with such a theoretically fierce explicitness about the anxious murderous collegiality of the speaking self and the self that is spoken, that detachable shadow.

As to "the self," then, which is it, really, the speaking self or the self that is only (though possibly magnificently) spoken? This question is *unanswerable*. That is the point of this book. It is wiser, therefore, to dismiss the term *self* as emblem for our task, since it stands ambiguously for the speaking and the spoken, and those two are necessarily to be discriminated.

Between the speaking and the spoken, the slash between active and passive voice, is this book's inquiry. The very processual quality of the betweenness is captured in a third term, one we among others have learned from Emile Benveniste and Julia Kristeva, *the speaking subject.* The speaking subject, one of the main tropes and instruments of our inquiry, is not the biographical author, not the old philosophical subject, not in the first instance possessed of gender, race, or class, and not the center of true intentionality. Of course, one fairly soon gets past the first instance, that theoretical fiction, and gender, race, class, and intentionality become separable propositions of subject. Indeed *agent* might be a term preferable to *subject,* in order to rule out connotations of subjectivity we inherit from the more watery forms of romanticism, but *speaking subject* is the term we get from Julia Kristeva's French; we employ it with reservations. Bakhtin's Russian has *govaryashchii ya,* the speaking I, but doubtless that has limitations of its own, and anyway Kristeva's term has a theoretical history and a quite specific set of connotations.

For an entirely adequate preliminary definition of the term, our readers may reread the passage from Beckett. The speaking subject is an in-process, dialogic relationship between whoever speaks and whoever is spoken, theorized in full consciousness that there will be baffles, multiplications of imaginary selves and voices, diacritical distances, slippages of meaning, problems with pronouns. These troubles arise because each of the fraternal internal antagonists, the speaking and the spoken, wishes to interfere with, silence, and finally to kill off the other, even as both must know that the continuous mutual interference is what creates the effect of literature.

How is literature possible? What voice speaks in the works of literature? These questions generate and finally frustrate our study. Like others, we find useful a definition of literature as an activity that ceaselessly puts itself into question. However, this position can perhaps be maintained without accepting the total subversion of the subject. For that is what is at issue: whether the effacement or dispersal of the human subject, that sometimes takes the guise of voice, is necessary or even possible.

To assume a relation between voice and person in literature would be wrong. That assumption of a fundamental humanism is the very thing to be validated. Specifically, could we show the traces of the voice in the author's selection of point of view and in the very play with tense, syntactic weave, punctuation, and prosodies of writing? If we keep the idea of voice, we will have to show with it how and why literary devices can be used to mime spontaneous thinking and ordinary language. (For example, Beckett performs this mime even as he creates theory at the highest level.) An adequate account will have to show how voice itself is a literary concept which designates a falling away from literature toward speech, ordinary language, and everyday life. What we above termed "interference" is just this when viewed from the vantage of the literary discipline. The calling away meets an equal and opposite calling back.

Just here is the convergence of our leading terms, *voice* and *speaking subject*. It bears repeating that Henri Meschonnic has admirably framed the meaning of literary voice by stating that voice may appear both in writing and in speaking. Voice is the indeterminate between writing and speaking. It is a metaphor of and for both writing and speaking. Its status is inherently ambiguous, a hybrid strain. It is the projection of a virtual subject toward a virtual other. The subject and the other may be entirely imagined, but even if the subject or the other results from reportage, the printed voice will be a fiction of communication. Our return to a specialist term, the *speaking subject,* is prompted by a wish to rethink the subject within literary work. There are so many arguments advanced for abandoning the author, collapsing the author into the reader or into the author's society or the words on the page, that authorship may be a contaminated category for now. Yet the printed voice is not usually far from the reach or range of some attributable intentionality, some regional intentionality. Social registers of intonation can and must be read if we are interpreting texts. The speaking subject allows that the voice may not be the author's, but does not allow, except in the extremes of textual voice, that the voice becomes entirely, exhaustively detoned, dissolved into society or world or some other abstraction that can accept the intentionality we used to give to an agent.

The concept of the 'speaking subject' emerged from linguistic theory of a rather restricted sort. At the beginning was Roman Jakobson, whose work in pronouns as shifters was the main linguistic account of subjectivity in language before the 1960s. But Jakobson did not develop his thinking in this field, and the major act of clarification is by Emile Benveniste in two essays of the late fifties, "The Nature of Pronouns" and "Subjectivity in Language." Benveniste saw that persons are constituted by these little words in the form class of grammar, and by parts of the verb in conjugation. Out of Benveniste came several further extensions: Louis Althusser used this in his own study of how subjectivity is "interpellated" in specific ideological contexts; Henry Meschonnic developed his theories of rhythm in poetry as the always-different expression of subjectivity in language; Julia Kristeva pursued the notion of the 'speaking subject,' notably in a crucial article of 1973 that politicizes the concept. Out of Kristeva develop more recent Anglo-American accounts of literature and film, notably Kaja

Silverman's two books and certain psychoanalytic, feminist, and political extensions.[14]

Michel de Certeau has well said that the "self" is "in reality plural, social in its very constitution. Its activities follow out dialogues that have begun well before one sets oneself to speak."[15] He is speaking of dialogues, not scripts; one sets oneself to speak, changing the discourse by entering it. This is, as Kristeva has written, a subject in process (*en procès*: on trial, but also ever in motion), but still a subject. Across her career, Kristeva seems skeptical about centered and bounded subjects, about personal identity; but after the early seventies and her mastery of psychoanalytic tools, she comes more to accept a subject position in beings who suffer and who may be influenced by the talking cure. In her 1970 article "The Ruin of a Poetics," Kristeva shows how Bakhtin in his 1929 book on Dostoevsky transcends the structural-linguistics backgrounds of Russian Formalism. Bakhtin does so by taking *slovo* not as word but as discourse, as speech addressed to someone else. "The word/discourse," says Kristeva, "is . . . distributed over the various instances of discourse that a multiple 'I' can occupy simultaneously." Kristeva's 1973 piece "The Speaking Subject" is the classic exposition of a semiotics that "can establish the heterogeneous logic of signifying practices . . . can lead to a historical typology of signifying practices by the mere fact of recognizing the specific status within them of the speaking subject."[16] What Toril Moi says of Kristeva may be affirmed of others whose work contributes to the exposition of the word as dialogical discourse, in the direct line from Bakhtin: "a difficult balancing act between a position which would deconstruct subjectivity and identity altogether, and one that would try to capture these entities in an essentialist or humanist mould."[17] For better or worse, we admit this of ourselves as well, with this qualification regarding our balancing act: the radical nihilism Moi refers to has never really occurred, except as a theoretical limit, a fear of thinkers who would challenge Nietzsche, Derrida, and the Italian proponent of "weak thought," Gianni Vattimo. Derrida, his German master, and his Italian affiliate would all insist that there is no possible deconstruction of the subject that would be total, only an endless labor of weakening, draining, and diluting the terms of Western thought, which are all that we have.

So our precursors in this body of theory adopt the dialogism of Bakhtin as opposed to that of Jakobson and the formalists and structuralists. In the debates over Moscow-Tartu structuralism in Russia in the sixties, nowhere on either side was there raised a notion corresponding to dialogue as shared differences or of the speaking subject that might have mediated these issues. The establishment Socialist

Realist critics and the innovative Tartu semioticians were both unable to make use of the paradigm shift begun by Bakhtin. This repeated the failure of historical and theoretical knowledge of formalism itself, which lacked all understanding of the speaking subject and the voice within the text, even as it very well mapped the separate devices that made up the printed voice. And the Russian inability to put to use Bakhtin's coherent, successful construction of an integral theory of all human culture in terms of communication is but a local lapse within a larger one. Much in the theory of language, worldwide, would have been different had Bakhtin been known.

In this book we propose a historical-theoretical typology of signifying practices, on the lines Kristeva has suggested, recognizing within these the specific status of the speaking subject. Donne-Descartes, the Bardic in Gray and Mickiewicz and Lindsay, and twentieth-century writers of the textual voice, such as Paul Celan, are the primary examples, and among these the subject positions of race and class are occasionally discussed, but given foreground focus only in the long section of Mickiewicz. We also wish to reckon in our own situation as male speaking subjects from different parts of the world. In view of the immense changes of representation and nationhood in eastern Europe in 1989 and 1990, and in view of advances for various races and for women in the past twenty years, we have registered the ironies for scholarship of our leading term. At the moment of emergence of oppressed or underrepresented groups, including nations in Mickiewicz's sense of fatherland, in greater numbers and power than we have experienced in our lifetime, there is also a scholarly criticism of previous illusions and errors concerning selfhood and voice and representation in both senses of voting and showing forth. Just when the new groups have emerged, scholarly theory would deny them the kind of full faith in voice that previous, more oppressive, generations indulged. It does seem politically important to salvage something for democratic voice from the current hygiene of theory.

Dialogism, Speaking Subject, and the Critique of Existing Theory of Voice

"Where would I go . . . if I had a voice": Samuel Beckett's monologue dramatizes the conflict between the biographical person and the literary person, each trying to reduce the other to matter, a necessary interference—*not one without the other* in literary voice. So Beckett repeats a distinction that has existed in literary theory since classical Greek aesthetics, between *diegesis* and *mimesis*. For Plato in *The*

Republic, diegesis is simple narrative, presumably a biographical voice: mimesis is imitation of the speech of another. (Aristotle applies mimesis to both simple narrative speech and imitative speech, so only Plato sharply draws the distinction.) Plato's distinction has been reworked by T. S. Eliot in "The Three Voices of Poetry" (poet to self, audience; or in dramatic character), and by many others.

New Critics and traditional critics tend to understand voice as unique and personal, while post-structuralists understand it as separate from individual consciousness. With post-structuralists, voice is more related to grammatical categories (Roland Barthes, Gérard Genette), more soaked in citation of previous voices (Jacques Derrida, Jonathan Goldberg), more like a code among many codes (Roland Barthes: the "positional field of the subject," rather similar to our idea of a 'regional intentionality'.) Only among the post-structuralists, and not among the New Critics, except perhaps in their advocacy of a special term, *persona*, as the stand-in for a poem's biographical speaker, is there sufficient distancing from the human person to conceive a speaking subject. And only among a few of the post-structuralists is there sufficient distance, from a Cartesian self-bounded consciousness, to entertain a philosophy of dialogism. Actually then, a small number of theorists, across these many centuries and national traditions, hold the most capacious accounts of voice.

As a tool for thinking, the speaking subject gives subjectivity without subjectivism. As a tool for thinking, the dialogic imagination gives subjectivity a way to be social, determined by communicative context but also determining it. These double-barreled phrases are in fact oxymorons, allowing a centrifugal adjective to pull against a centripetal noun; as tools, they baffle oppositional thinking.

Existing theory of voice, as it superintends its subset literary voice, shows certain limitations when read through a grillwork that understands "voice as having a human, yet nonpersonal referent."[18] To set out these limitations may help to synthesize and reconfigure the field. For the present generation of scholarship, Jacques Derrida's is the constitutive philosophy of voice. His critique of two thousand years of privileging speaking over writing was sustained over several books and articles. Put writing on the level with speaking and see what happens, Derrida proposed; deconstruct the opposition, promote the science of writing with a disciplinary name, *grammatology*. Derrida went to the heart of the topic with a critique of centered selfhood, authorship, originality, and self-presence, all of which had spuriously been connected, he argued, with speaking alone as the traditional way to devalue writing. Derrida is protagonist and sparring partner in our own account of literary voice, as he is in recent studies by, for example,

Geoffrey Hartman, Garrett Stewart, Jonathan Goldberg, David Appelbaum, and Eric Griffiths, precisely because one must either accept his position or get to the other side of it with a refutation or partial correction. To us, his definition of a breaking moment of thought is productive, and yet we see the necessity of certain large, hard nubs of granite that cannot be swept away by the force of his thought. Resisting Derrida in particular points, we nonetheless would now define all theories of voice as before and after grammatology. Even though some of this work, such as post–J. L. Austin speech-act philosophy, is produced chronologically after Derrida's three major books of 1967, it is nonetheless part of the earlier thinking, locatable by its neglect of Derrida's logic.

Before Grammatology

The physiology of literary voice is the least of voice but not nothing. The human voice measures and masters a column of air from the lungs to the lips, taking its energy from the stream that comes from the lungs as we exhale. The mouth takes in both food and air and perfects the sounds which emerge from the larynx, that gate or valve which closes automatically during swallowing. So this human speech, which may be taken down and back to a breath that confounds itself with the very breath of life, may give some reality to the object of memory and desire but is itself hardly noticeable and usually dies on the lips which give it a form. Empirical speech, like all sound, "exists only when it is passing out of existence" (W. J. Ong's words), each previous noise annulled, forgotten. This undulation of the air, whose speech print is so personal that we have not been able to build machines to recognize it, is born in the body but effaces, forgets the body. Empirical speech and the speaking subject are not the same, but those who would train singers and actors, those who would claim referential communication with parrots, those who would treat the speech disorder spasmodic dysphonia with minute doses of deadly botulinum toxin, do not worry about the differences. "The Voice as an Expression of the Whole Person" is the first subhead of the first chapter in Michael McCallion's *Voice Book* (1988), a primer on the splendid voice-training method of F. M. Alexander.[19] None of these physiologies of voice have encountered Derrida; nor has he encountered them as body or as sound, unless we might include them as implied in his crushing demonstration that there is no purely phonetic writing.

A more mediated pedagogy of voice comes to us through intelligent popular studies, which encourage insecure writers to begin

Writing with Power (1981).[20] Peter Elbow's book of this title has a long chapter where he admits that voice is a "mysterious standard" (283), but nonetheless he offers a definition: "Voice, in writing, implies words that capture the sound of an individual on the page. . . . Writing with no voice is dead, mechanical, faceless. It lacks any sound" (287). "Real" voice is "uttered by a person," so the "expression-filled" speaking of announcers, salesmen, and preachers is "an extreme example of voice-but-not-real voice" (292). Elbow seems partly aware that he is using terms as gestures. But since he is writing a practical handbook in order to develop maturity and mastery, he feels it helpful to give writers advice on linguistic individuation in the largest sense, on how to separate real voice from voice. Though Elbow's practical tone and his anecdotes may free up and inspire beginning writers, his voice-person-sound-reality equation has been surpassed. One cannot read this version of traditional pedagogy, through the grill of grammatology, without seeing the irony at the expense of Elbow's mysterious standard.

Also pre-Derridian are certain anthropologies and phenomenologies of voice. In 1963, early in his career, Jack Goody wrote with Ian Watt "The Consequences of Literacy," an influential article whose broad distinctions between nonliterate and literate societies Goody, writing alone, has traced through a series of books: nonliterate societies transmit cultural tradition through face-to-face communication and are thus homeostatic, keeping only those memories that are functional; literate societies transmit cultural traditions in fixed form, so "the past is . . . set apart from the present, [and] historical enquiry becomes possible."[21] Skepticism, syllogism, and logic are the result in the ancient Near East and Ionia. The Goody-Watt article is a thought piece that takes a cut into its material at the highest level of generality, loading its cultural preferences against the "simple" nonliterate cultures which are all taken to be simple in the same way. Maintaining the privilege of the analytical consciousness that comes with writing, which is not a grammatology, they take no interest in the speaking that is in writing or the writing that is in speaking. Don Ihde's *Listening and Voice: A Phenomenology of Sound* (1976) shows fascination for *centers* and *depths*, metaphors of voice open to question, but his ontological inquiry also shows welcome attention to the reader-receiver of musical and literary sounds—an "ethics of listening." Pursuing intersubjective openings, he explores inner speech, gestalts of figure and ground in the auditory field, silence as something more than a lack, temporalities in our reception, and other experiences. Ihde's study is more empirical than Derrida ever gets, because he describes physical sensation. Ihde is also more metaphysical: "The 'darkness' hidden in voiced language is in fact not a weakness of word but its strength. It is the ultimate withdrawing Openness of the silent horizon as full ontological possibility. The relation of voice to inner speech and to the pregnant silence of the face gives way ultimately to the Open horizon of silence."[22] Whatever its excesses, such a way of talking is unquestionably more dialogic than Derrida, more open to voice experience at the ground level of sound, sensation, uncanniness, temporal extension.

Speech act philosophy has not, like the others above here, passed grammatology in silence. The two were on a collision course from the start. Both had their heyday in the sixties and seventies, through the debates of Derrida and John Searle in the pages of *Glyph*. The signal strength of speech act philosophy is that it recognizes and celebrates the effective behavior of an agent who wills, who is speaking to (or at, actually) other agents within a social context involving intention, rules, knowledges. The emphasis is on active verbs. In illocutionary acts the completed utterance finishes an intentional act; in perlocutionary acts, illocutionary utterances have some specific consequences. What is lacking is *interlocutionary* acts, the heteroglossia of specific social discourses which hierarchize ordinary languages and put them into conflict. What is lacking is any sense that the metaphorical side of speaking makes for logical dilemmas and literary opportunities. The speaking and willing person behind speech act philosophy is still the Cartesian subject with full self-presence. Since John Searle's thought is not reconstructed by Derridian attack on presence and phonocentrism, John Searle hopes to pull apart that attack, showing it as contrary to common sense. Alas, a direct-agency account of language has no mechanism to deal with irony as a form of thought, or with the irony of double-voicing and multiple personhood, or with the aporias of the question that organizes our own inquiry: Who is Speaking? We conclude that speech act philosophy would yield a starved and one-dimensional philosophy of literary voice.

The question of voice has been explored in terms of verb rather than in terms of person. Have we only the alternatives of active voice and passive voice, and might the question itself lead to new modes of agency and subjectivity? In passing, in "Differance" Derrida said he was after something like the Greek middle voice. In "To Write: An Intransitive Verb," Roland Barthes asked when and why writing as such became transitive, arguing that modernist writing has its end within itself, radically intransitive, and the middle voice explains, or at least analogizes, the simultaneities of modernist writing as such. By implication, since the issue is never publicly joined, this is a French avant-garde reply to speech act philosophy's hopes for a public language of agency. If agency/patiency, subjecthood/objecthood, activity/passivity has been given to us in modern languages in terms of a choice, the Greek middle voice affords an alternative that would not be binary—a simultaneity of agent with act, cause with effect, and a dissolution of the logic of subject and object. Of course, modern languages afford many examples of phrasings that mime the middle voice: Hayden White cites the sentence from Virginia Woolf, "The yellow rose went there," where *went* means both *traveled* and *belonged*, both active and passive.[23] But (1) is this the actual meaning and use of the Greek middle voice, or a convenient myth of it, a machine for collapsing binary distinctions? (2) Is the person here the same old Cartesian philosophical subject, masking its inability to be dialogic by diverting attention from persons to verb? (3) Can agency in the verb and agency in experience be essentially different in logic, the former a metaphor of the latter? It is too early to say, but until middle-voice philosophy of the verb can answer such questions it cannot claim comprehensiveness, or even pertinence. Perhaps it gives too much away at the outset by framing its inquiry with the explicit elimination of person.

After (and beyond) Grammatology

One clever post-Derridian literary analyst, Eric Griffiths, takes as his method the "illocutionary re-description" of Victorian printed voice in the poems of Tennyson, Browning, Hardy, Meredith, and others. This is consciously to try to get beyond Derrida with the help of his antagonists, cranking down the level of generality by following poems with extreme closeness as, among many other things, speech acts. Even though the speech act terminology functions mostly as a metaphor here, without much of the technical meaning given to illocution by Austin and Searle, the results are impressive because of Griffiths' care for the Victorian poet's every beck and nod of intention, taking voice down even as far as use of periods and commas, of metrical substitutions. Griffiths spends a long first chapter working through objections to Derrida's dismissal of voice as presence, even as he shows himself conditioned by that dismissal.[24] His most stunning point is that spoken utterance must decide between meanings which writing holds together. Writing may mime speech, but also, there and then, may insist on its printed form, keeping those differences in play, so the most capacious readers refuse a choice, and opting for a grammatology Derrida makes a premature choice.

During the 1980s, Anglo-American criticism undertook a similar labor, in empirical studies whose (sometimes attenuated) theoretical frame involves contest with Derrida. The pivotal book, as we have said, was Geoffrey Hartman's *Saving the Text: Literature/Derrida/ Philosophy* (1981), a far more empirical book than may appear, packed full of visual and verbal examples of the rendering and stilling of voice (153). "AND YET: is not writing too much with us?" (xx): Hartman strives to bring back the numinous, wounding, oral dimensions of texts, soundings as making heard and as going in and down, "intolerable ear-fear" (157) that the receiver of voice strives to master. Garrett Stewart has affinities to Hartman. Stewart's *Reading Voices: Literature and the Phonotext* (1990) also studies Joyce and problematizes all roots in an authorizing voice. Stewart like Hartman is an opportunist with the witty pun as tease to the auditory imagination, "sheared lexeme," "phonemic lubriciousness" (148): "This is the para-vocal excitation Derrida wrestles down by too quickly redefining its terms" (248). Jonathan Goldberg's book on poems from Spenser to Milton sets out, with Derrida and Maurice Blanchot in the background, "to show in the Renaissance text voice-as-text, and to show it through a practice of voice terminated" (1). In *Voice Terminal Echo: Postmodernism and English Renaissance Texts* (1986), Goldberg claims to dismiss critical tact and connected argument, and indeed the book has a diamanté style full of paradoxes, parentheses, quick turns, images, puns—nonetheless relentless in its close reading of a small body of text to show the assertion and stilling of voice. This is one way of cutting across the oppositions active/passive, inside/outside, originality/citation, process/ monument. Thus: "Locating 'his' voice in one that anticipates his own and that survives its end, Milton's 'I' [in sonnet 16, "When I consider how my light is spent"] is sustained precisely by being denied. Buried, it has become a monument" (131). Milton's poem cites and refigures Shakespeare's sonnet 15. His voice echoes and terminates Shakespeare's. According to Goldberg's last sentences, echo is "preventive space. Preventing birth. Preventing death. Coming before oneself." This exceeds Derrida not by questioning or qualifying, rather by showing line by line, stanza by stanza, the richness of citation and the dilemmas of latecoming in supremely conscious scholar-poets. Stephen M. Ross's study *Fiction's Inexhaustible Voice: Speech and Writing in Faulkner* (1989) barely mentions Derrida and Bakhtin and shows a residual strong interest in the author's presence and authority. Yet in its detailed readings of Faulkner's display of the paradoxes of phenomenal, mimetic, psychic, and oratorical voice in fictions such as *As I Lay Dying*, its modest evidences address every issue of literary voice. Most empirical of all these studies, Charles O. Hartman's *Jazz Text: Voice and Improvisation in Poetry, Jazz, and Song* (1991) takes little note of current dilemmas of theory even as it is skeptical toward presence as "personalized sound" (4). Hartman's rhythm-following, prosodic readings of jazz and poetry are based on a definition of voice as "a tension between music and statement" (7), and on a prosodic-moral-political faith in improvisation as group dialogue, sharing of solos. To the extent that this is Bakhtinian, this too shows the limitations of grammatology when it comes to hearing, describing, and living with works of art that employ sounds in time.[25]

The act of composing, performing, or hearing music becomes George Steiner's most precious example of the unity and freedom of communication in *Real Presences* (1989), a book with hardly a mention of voice but nonetheless a post-Derridian affiliate of our own inquiry.[26] Steiner's survey of the age of the sign, the "general retreat from the word" (114), is at base an elegiac response to the draining away of presence and intentionality in our recent era's scholarly and artistic nihilism. "This essay argues a wager on transcendence. It argues that there is in the art-act and its reception, that there is in the experience of meaningful form, a presumption of presence" (214). For Steiner, the poets and artists know best: "I have found no deconstructionist among them" (227). He quotes Derrida: "The age of the sign is essentially theological," and where Derrida would say this as a critique of the semantic sign Steiner would say it as one phase of his wager on meaning: "The origin of the axiom of meaning and of the 'God' concept is a shared one" (119). Philosophy seems to be ready to confront the God-concept anew, quite apart from belief, even belief as cautious as Steiner's Pascalian wager.

Jean-Luc Nancy has brandished the fragmentariness of his long essay "On Divine Places" as a rhetorical response to our coming late into a culture that perhaps still has some divine places. Nancy has written of the God concept with tender dissentient respect in *Le partage des voix*:

> To put it another way: there isn't *one* voice of divinity, nor perhaps any divine voice in general: because these 'divine poems' are spoken in language, or rather in the languages of human beings. But *voice as such,* for the divine, is partition and difference [*partage* means "partition," but also "sharing"]. And this difference: is it divine or human? The question is not posed. This difference is the articulation of the divine on and in the human. The human being who's a poet is outside himself, there, but the divine is also there, outside itself: in the partitioning/sharing of voices.[27]

On pages following: "But voice plural and indirect *is* [God's] *voice*, and not a transcription, translation, interpretation (68). . . . What we've called 'logocentrism,' where nature is here confirmed by a 'theologo-centrism,' establishes itself as *at the same time* dedicated to the most powerful of decenterings, to fated and fatal division of *logos* itself. . . . (*We* are sense, in the parting of our voices.)" (82). So the God concept retains a certain usefulness for thinking about ourselves; we put ourselves in parentheses, befitting our partiality and diminution, but we make claims with and emphasize our pronoun. We may imagine that our voices, plural and indirect, are that way because God's voices are already that way. This is a mode of thinking, not, in Nancy, of believing. Heidegger in section 10 of *Being and Time* warned against using "subject"—"*ontologically*, every idea of a 'subject'—unless refined by a previous ontological determination of its basic character—still posits the *subjectum* (*hypokeimenon*) along with it"—and Derrida was able to dismantle Rousseau and Lacan by such a logic of finding hidden metaphysical (and phonic-phonemic) assumptions; but Nancy may succeed in thinking a way behind the difficulty. That is, if logos is already partitioned, and if we are also in our address to meaning, then we cannot be bounded subjects in the manner conceived by the philosophy of consciousness, the bad old thought of presence. And in a doubleness French *partager* can keep in one verb where English needs two, *to partition* is also *to share*. The English analogue is *to articulate*: *to separate/speak forth/connect*.[28]

Apparently we come closer to the center of philosophy of voice when we consider this issue of a dividing that is a connection. This is the issue in Derrida's charge, in "Le facteur de la vérité" in *The Post Card* (English trans. 1987), that Jacques Lacan's exempting the physical letter "from all partition—in the phonematic structure of language" leads to "phallogocentric transcendentalism. Especially if within *metalanguage*, language is centered on the voice, that is, on the ideal sites of the phallus."[29] Lacan, for Derrida, "supposes an interpretation of *phoné* which . . . spares it divisibility. The voice occasions such an interpretation in and of itself: it has the phenomenal characteristics of spontaneity, of self-presence, of the circular return to itself. . . . Things would be quite otherwise if one were attentive to the writing within the voice, that is, before the letter" (464–65). We raise this not to defend Lacan but to allude once again to the terms by which Derrida, fifteen years after his grammatology has emerged, expresses revulsion against sound as such, as if voice may only be a coincidence between a sign and a presence. He is keen to have us be attentive to the writing within the voice, and we shall, but let us also study the voice within writing.

For theologians of voice such as Walter J. Ong and Michel de Certeau, the question of presence is misplaced. For Ong and de Certeau, the partitioned voice of the human believer is never a coincidence nor a noncoincidence between a sign and a presence, but rather a metaphor between two terms, both proper nouns. The other, who may be God or another person or being, is an impossible presence. Communication, especially prayer, is a reaching after an impossible presence. Ong writes: "Voice is the least exterior of sensible phenomena because it emanates not only from the physical but also from the divided psychological interior of man and penetrates to another, physical and psychological interior where . . . it must be re-created in the imagination in order to live."[30] Every human word implies the existence of the other. It also implies that the speaker has a kind of otherness within; voice enters humans easily and literally obliges humans to enter into others, a situation that holds special terrors for some. To use Geoffrey Hartman's term, the print-fixated theorists of poststructuralism have an "ear-fear"; they worry that *the ear is the only organ that can't be closed* to sharing from outside. They have, Ong says, "seldom adverted to the fact that texts must be recycled back through sound to have meaning." By contrast, both Ong and de Certeau have been scholars of the oral-aural components in the history of education, of the practices of everyday life that involve communicative strategies, and of new technologies of language, like writing, print, electronic media, that either impede or expand vocal control. De Certeau's study of speaking in tongues is a study of the *phoné* that does not spare it divisibility. His book on the mystical fable, and his article on mystical writing in St. Teresa, are readings of impossible presence in the unknown addressee, a seventeenth-century rhetorical relationship heavily scripted, rich in complexity, entirely contrary to the version of presence given by Derrida.[31]

Ong and de Certeau are too tactful ever fully to pursue the terms of their debate with post-structuralism on this crucial issue of the presence of the word. Derrida, who may stand as powerful exemplar of philosophy as critique of presence, has such an aversion to foundational assumptions that he must reject the word as sound, which carries and interiorizes those assumptions. In Ong's *The Presence of the Word,* a book exactly contemporary with the emergence of Derrida's *De la grammatologie* in 1967, the issue is joined as precisely a religious one: "Voice is not *peopled* with presences. It itself is the manifestation of presence, and as such has permanent religious possibilities" (168); "the word as sound signals interiority and mystery. . . . It also signals holiness" (314); hearing, of all human senses, "is the most productive of understanding and unity, the most personally human, and in this sense closest to the divine" (324). Ong is right to point out that the French post-structuralists and their adherents have avoided a line of scholarship, in writings of scholars like A. B. Lord, Eric Havelock, and Paul Zumthor, that establishes a history of voice quite separate from the usual hypervisualism and type fixation. If we pursue this line to its conclusion and make explicit what Ong will not, post-structuralist "antiphonocentrism" exhibits *not an analysis but the bias or symptom* of an aural to visual shift. For Ong, the failure to consider language as sound is a regrettable loss of divinity, but also incomplete history and an intellectual fatality. It is enough, here, to make this encounter explicit. In addition, we would like to acknowledge the force of Ong's historical story of a "widespread reorganization of the sensorium" (*Presence*, 21) from sound to sight; most valuable is his documentation that earlier oral modalities are always available, never surpassed, even more readily recuperable in the age of audio tape. Sound, where what's *uttered*, Ong says, is already *outered*, makes up for its evanescence by its instant passage from inner to outer and back.[32]

Recently the question of gaps in the mode of information has been politically inflected by Mark Poster, philosophically inflected by Avital Ronell.[33] Plainly, new technologies have created a radically changed state of affairs for the question of voice, a situation N. Katherine Hayles has begun calling "cyborg subjectivity."[34] When there is an interface between computers and humans to create information, what happens to subjectivity? Is it dispersed into the circuits? Does the body still "contain" the subject in virtual reality of e-mail, or in simulation suits for mental imaging, or in computer-network dating? Are our virtual bodies, in such circuits, *gendered electronically*? Hayles argues that in the dominant and inherited tradition of selfhood, agency is enmeshed with possession; but in the moment of the new intelligence augmentation, agency is access. The subject is the one who knows the authorization codes for entry to the system. In William Gibson's cyberpunk novel *Neuromancer* (1986), a space cowboy is immobilized with wounds but travels around cities within the camera eyes of a bionic woman. He can put jacks behind his ears and travel, mentally and with full physical and spatial sense, a vast network of information. In Ian Watson's *Jonah Kit* (1975), a Russian composer, terribly ill, has his intelligence grafted into that of a Pacific Ocean whale. The human experiences the underwater urges of a creature that swims, and the whale becomes leader of his species, a mammal Christ, who leads all whales to strand themselves on earth's beaches as a protest against ecological damage. Watson's language to describe the whale mind is innovative in the use of physical sensation, an estranging periphrasis: literary voice as another calling of Jonah, another language and linguistics, another guise of self.

Because twentieth-century linguistics has turned from an analysis of language based on the written word to a direct analysis of spoken language, a strict antiphonocentric philosophy might outlaw the whole discipline. But there is another linguistics that constitutes an opposing tradition to Derrida in French philosophy of voice—Henri Meschonnic's orality-philosophy of language, derived not from German phenomenology, Meschonnic's *bête noire*, but from Benveniste and French philology. Meschonnic's principled distinction between the spoken and the oral would seem to short-circuit Derrida's primary reproach to linguistics; Meschonnic proposes, at his most speculative, something considerably beyond Benveniste, nothing less than a historical anthropology of language.

Meschonnic's overall account of voice is so comprehensive that we devote a section to it at the end of this book, following a section on Derrida. Meschonnic gives something like the completion grammatology needs, though to put it that way is unfair. He is in no sense a supplement or answer; rather his work is an alternative route. He spends nearly a hundred pages teasing out the meanings of Derridian *écriture* in *Le signe et le poème* (1975) and ends his study with two damning pages on the paradox of the Derrida effect: "At the precise moment where this theory and this practice of writing is made and received as radically innovative, non-recuperable by tradition . . ., in the movement where it seems to exercise a Nietzschian 'vitality,' it practices the oldest substantialization of the sacred."[35] Meschonnic's book-length negative account of *Le Langage Heidegger* (1990) can also be read as a response to Derrida and all French continuators of the German philosopher's myth of language (German ought to be Greek, Greek is already German!), which leads up to and never recants the politics of the Nazi rectorship, 1933 to 1934 at Freiburg. Meschonnic wrote *Voyageurs de la voix* (1985, Verdier, Paris), unpunctuated poems, the first of which ends "i / left my life through my own mouth when / your sleep made me i begin there where i / interrupt myself": Jonah to the whale, needing the whale as his rescuer and his double ("mon histoire la tienne"), the whale's belly and mouth as his own, the break with God really a beginning.[36] Meschonnic's scholarly book on the Jonah story is an account of translation from the Hebrew into French, his method based on the rhythms of collective oral chanting. His major book *Critique du rythme* (1982) is a further demolition of the dominant poetics of the sign, in this case by means of the argument that rhythm is the subject in writing, an unrealized but persistent dialectical relating of the individual and the social. Here as elsewhere, his is a linguistics of discourse, contrary to the linguistics of the sign from Saussure to Jakobson:

> Structuralism and sensibility-poetics are the illiteracies of the future. Without losing by regression the lesson of the structural-

> ists, that a text is a system, the language of poetry can better situate itself as a rapport between language-knowledge and language, between I and history, that places as already archeological the connexion between poetry and the sacred. Poetry is the politicization of the effects of the sacred. That is why it tropes the spoken, works the spoken to make of the spoken itself the figure of language which language needs to transform itself—without recourse to separatist traditions which would give . . . a solution to contradictions: their rhyme and their reason. The I for all makes itself by all."[37]

According to Gabriella Bedetti's penetrating summary of Meschonnic's essential positions, he shares with Derrida and Foucault the notion that discourse shapes and circumscribes the subject, but he goes further: "The subject also determines the language one uses in the very act of borrowing that language from the social cistern of language . . . [this opens the possibility] for the subject to transform culture's language which is itself transforming the subject." In such a scheme, Bedetti continues, voice cannot be linked to the individual, "nor, if it is to attain to the level of the social, can voice be reduced to language."[38] Thus we have Meschonnic's term *politicization*. History, linguistics, poetics, and rhythm analysis are for him finally populist politics, poetry for all and all for poetry. He is committed to keep power flowing in both directions between discourse and the subject. Meschonnic, conceiving linguistics thus, without committing naivetés about the *phoné,* condemns Heidegger's antisemitism and nazism from its etymology-based myth of language in theory, to its expression in a special philosophical argot and syntax, and calls in question the naive use of speech-act terminology, as Habermas's basis for a language philosophy in the theory of communicative action. As critique and as construct, Meschonnic offers to this date the most comprehensive twentieth-century meditation on literary voice, able to move from technical linguistics to the largest questions of subject, presence, and politics.

To conclude this survey of current studies, we return to our beginning topic of physiology but now in a carefully Derridian work, David Appelbaum's *Voice* (1990).[39] David Appelbaum shows himself fully aware of Derrida's signal failure to acknowledge "the audible, acoustic dimension of vocal experience," and to remedy this he asks a question concerning Derrida's thought: "is the terminal or originary point at which signification abruptly collapses the moment when voice reveals itself resoundingly?" (xiv). The shock of recognition produced by the question Whose voice is this? leads Appelbaum to the hypothesis that every auditor's quandary "liberates the kinaesthetic impulses to participate in and be interrogated by an unsignified and unsignifiable reality" (xiv). His inquiry into minimal articulation, through chapters on cough, laugh, breath, madness, babble, chant, and deafness, finds what he calls "the germ of intention" in subvocal, bodily experiences as these are known culturally, philosophically: "In truth most any laugh comes with its web of syntax" (20). He comes at the end to the violence of voice in the poem: "The violation by phonemic domination calls forth a voiced response in kind. The interval between that voice and its comprehension is always filled with resistance" (117). Framing his poem chapter entirely with the notions of Condillac and Diderot, he is especially good on the stratum of an unsignified and unsignifiable reality in works of literary art, whatever's kinetic, violent, disharmonious. A final chapter on Plato takes up the risks of trying "to elicit a phenomenon of depth" (138) and the need to reckon into any account the human suffering body: "Voice minus suffering equals speech. Speech is a negative whose subtraction is a plus. Unphonemic voice reveals suffering and suffering reveals whence voice comes" (134). Elsewhere: "This voice that escapes the written or spoken page is deeply organic and fraught with the problem of human suffering" (xiv). This voice of ourselves "remains concealed in [Derrida's] study" (xiv), but Appelbaum brings it out of and back to the minimal of the body, without any of philosophy's traditional contempt for the body. David Appelbaum traces minimal articulation phenomenologically to the brink of literature, just the point at which we take up the inquiry.

CHAPTER 2. Fish and Bird: Minimal Articulation

The Idea of the Call

Call evidently marks a distance. Unlike a whisper or a murmur, or even plain *speaking*, it puts space between the calling one and the called not merely to emphasize what separates the two but also to signal a special kind of intimacy. The call implies a familiarity which does not consist in repeated acts of loyalty but, often, in strife and combat. The words called out and at an Other are not mere "terms of endearment," but they refer to the Other's *real name*, the name by which he or she is "called" against his or her will, the name given to the Other by yet another (parental) Other.

The Other, who is the origin of my (but who am I?) name, is the domain of incident, a whole concatenation of incidents which eventually bring the Other to the situation where he or she becomes a name giver. Nowhere is this more striking than in *Tristram Shandy* where the link connecting the name dispenser with the name is particularly knotty and twisted. In the story the priest who is about to baptize the child receives a desemanticized message from the servant girl, and thus the name *Tristram* becomes not a maximum but a minimum carrier of sense. We can detect in Sterne the same telephonicity of the name which Avital Ronell in *The Telephone Book* discovers in the life of Alexander Graham Bell's assistant, Watson: "A measure of desemanticized sound, a quality of language scrambling and general production of background meaning already augurs Watson's receptivity to random noise, undermining any pretensions held out for transcendental signifying or technological power markers."[1] *Random noise* describes the call which reverberates in the name turned inarticulate.

The call brings back the name. All of a sudden the name looms on the public horizon as a denomination to which I have to respond; the call calls me back to my name which no longer hides in the crypt of privacy, and, by doing so, it brings me back to the presence of the name-giving Other. Avital Ronell's "maternalizing call" (20) shows that I have not been aware enough of my name and that this awareness can be yet restored. This restoration, however, can occur only on the strength of inarticulacy with which my (?) name attacks my ear. The name called at me sounds strange, as if it were a mass of unidentified acoustic waves. Such a call thus desemanticizes my name, changes it into white noise and, in this way, restores it to me. I am called to the extent to which I go through the detour of the inarticulate. In Ronell's words: "Whatever the lesson of the mother, which turns into a desemanticized Nietzschean scream, telephonic logic means here, as everywhere, that contact with the Other has been disrupted; but it also means that the break is never absolute" (20).

In the act of calling, my (?) name rings, it resounds with the inarticulate noise, a mechanical rattling of vowels and consonants, which announces that there is someone who is separated from me and who is calling. Not only calling me, but —first of all—calling me back to my name. In the act of calling there are two calls. I am called by the Other and by my name. The telephone calls twice: first, it calls me; second, it calls me back to the reality of my name. Necessarily, before I respond to the Other I have to respond to the latter calling; I go toward the Other by the delay of pondering upon my (?) name; before I relate to the Other I have to listen to my name. In the call the name imposes its presence on me by all available means, like a shout or a scream.

{Enter Jonah. At the beginning, he does not want to listen and to heed the call. Running away to Tarshish he not only evades God's voice but also the call of his name. The name *Jonah* seems possible to be evaded because it operates on a merely personal level on which administration communicates with a subject. The escape is facilitated only because Jonah was not struck with his name, that is, because his name never went through the detour of the inarticulate. By running away without a plan, by relying on chance and incident, Jonah enacts a substitute drama: it is his life which will be ruled by incident, thus becoming inarticulate, rather than his name. The name will be made unreadable, however, in the voice of the "mighty tempest" and "great wind" which, obviously, calls Jonah and for Jonah. When the call of the name reaches us, the name becomes fuzzy. It speaks a language we do not know.}

{The call of the name is transformed into a story, a whirlpool, which wrecks and leaves us on an is(I)land—the call of the name, a story of *The Tempest* and *Robinson Crusoe*. In the 1942 Paul Goodman version of the biblical story, Jonah literally closes his ears against the call of his name, and the angel has "to call three times," and the last call is so loud that "the house quakes." Jonah cannot turn toward God as he is instructed by the shipmaster ("What meanest thou, O sleeper, arise and call upon thou God"); he cannot turn toward the Other because he did not, first, go through the "storm" of his name. He failed to answer the name's call.}

{We can add Ronell summarizing Heidegger to our reading of Jonah and say, "The call befalls you, and you cannot prevent the 'falling' which you are: it throws you. You are thrown—thrown off before any I can constitute itself or any subject can be thrown together" (Ronell, 66). One cannot help being astonished by the accuracy of the metaphor linking calling and falling through the sense of *thrownness*: when you get the call of the name, when it strikes you with the inarticulacy of the tempest and great wind, you regain the name by losing it—you are thrown into the sea (the sailors are the agent of the name), baptised in its waters, thus receiving your name. The call, scream, or shout of the name also tries to undo the work of "translation" (*Ubersetzung*) which passes over what is essential in the name. Heidegger in his *Holzwege* finds that Roman thought has committed a serious and irreparable distortion of Western philosophy, by taking over Greek words without the experience of what is being spoken. Such "undoing" is an example of "Destruction" (*Destruktion*); that is, as a recovery, it has "the positive sense of attempting to break through structures which have become hardened and rigid with the passage of time in order to reclaim Being's revelation." When Jonah is thrown into the sea, his story demonstrates the necessity of the inarticulate and of *Destruktion;* these constitute an indispensable detour on the way toward being able to answer the call of the name.}

It is this mediacy of the name that interests us here; the situation when we cannot react to "our" name immediately because, first, it strikes us as an alien sound. In other words, we cannot be obedient to the call of the name because in its very nature there is a necessity of reluctance on the part of the called who has to delay his or her action on account of not knowing who the name, turned inarticulate, calls—who is the me that is being called. When the name calls, there is a moment of astonishment at my sudden dispersal among sounds which I have, so far, taken to be me but which now seem to be liberated from its signified. When called by the name I have, painstakingly, to recollect elements of me before I start acting. Thus, we can act immediately when we hear our name only when it is not a call, that is, a voice which shatters our certainty and self-assuredness as to our identity.

We can venture a thesis that it is this shatteredness of self (momentary "annihilation of Selfhood" as Blake puts it at the beginning of *Jerusalem*), the space of delay and detour, mediation and thus disobedience, that opens the sphere of ethics in me. It is through such disobedience that subject becomes involved in ethical dilemmas.

What is at stake in this discussion of calling is also the issue of home. The call of the name comes from where the name is no longer *at home*, and yet when the call reaches us, it brings back the notion of home. (Heidegger in Ronell says, "'You just wait!—I'll teach you what we call obedience,' a mother might say to her boy who won't come home," 27.) However, it denies being-at-home, ultimate locatibility, its privileged position of centrality ("does the telephone [call] . . . not fundamentally belong to the structure of not-being-at-home, of a being expropriated from a *chez-soi*?" 51).

{Reenter Jonah. It is the prophet's displacedness which is striking. The call of God, which is at the same time the call of the name, deprives him of house and home. In Paul Goodman's version, the prophet desperately tries to save his being-at-home against the incursion of the call ("Desperately Jonah begins to pile up a barricade of furniture"). For Henri Meschonnic, Jonah becomes a symbol of the errancy of the signifier. Robert Nathan in *Jonah or the Withering Vine* (1924) centers his rendition upon the prophet's longing to get married and settle down. But the name calls and, through its power of the inarticulate, makes Jonah homeless; the one who or which calls is my sense of being suddenly turned inarticulate or senseless. What calls is the suspended meaning of my identity as a being. The caller, says Ronell, "is Dasein in its not-at-homeness" (68). It is not God but Jonah himself who orders the sailors to cast out the transgressor: "And he said unto them, 'take me up and cast me forth into the sea.'"}

In Blake's *Songs* the call and its link with *home* surface dramatically in both poems titled "Nurse's Song." In *Innocence*, the nurse speaks from the position of harmony of being with the world. The inner state of being at rest corresponds with the outer stillness. The latter does not imply silence or immobility but, rather, the congruity which holds between the dominating and protecting authority (the nurse) and its subjects (the children). The laughter of children indicates that "stillness" of the world is a certain fundamental disposition toward the world, the disposition which is interpreted in the categories of being with the world instead of being within oneself. As David Appelbaum observes in his exquisite analysis of laughter, "Only the child's laugh has us forget the ego's eccentric flight; only then is the laugh voiced free from the syntactical constructions of ego."[2] The nurse's condition of being at rest results from her residing on the threshold of ego; it is the intervention of history that makes this dwelling problematic. When, in the second stanza, the nurse calls to the children to come home, she does it turning away from the audible toward the visual (in the first stanza where the situation of remaining at rest is sketched, we remain in the sphere of acoustics ["voices of children are heard," "laughing is heard"]). The appeal is motivated by the sense of time and its passage as observed in the external world where activities are regulated by allotting appropriate time for each operation:

> Then come home, my children, the sun is gone down
> And the dews of night arise;
> Come, come, leave off play, and let us away
> Till the morning appears in the skies.[3]

The call of the nurse (of authority, the protecting and forming voice of the mother) comes from the home which is not the home of being but of "proper" time and chronological history. It is no surprise that the children do not obey this call ("No, no, let us play"); their refusal juxtaposes the astronomical bureaucratic ordering of the day, and the lived time of "the little birds" and "sheep." The nurse realizes that her call must come from the position of "home," that is, "sleep" and "bed," and thus we have the call toward equilibrium, balance of power, and control of desire—the eighteenth-century call for the domination of reason over passion.

The children's power to call back ("No, no, let us play") is performed on behalf of activity ("leaped and shouted and laugh'd") which defies stagnation ("we cannot go to sleep") and turns again toward the acoustic ("And all the hills ecchoed" [sic]). Two processes need to be noticed: first, that the call has to be resisted if it comes as an articulate demand for obedience (it is this space of diversion which is the domain of ethical action); second, that the call will be resisted also when it comes from the inarticulate, when it is the call of the name as sheer sound, because then the resistance will come from the lack of congruity between the phonetic structure and the structure of human subjecthood.

Interestingly enough, the nurse is placed on the boundary between the two calls: she does act as a supervisor and mistress of time who knows that a function of growing up is a loss of "hearing" which implies immersion in the "Single vision and Newton's sleep" (Blake's famous denunciation). (In the *Experience* version of the poem the nurse will become a perfect embodiment of this role of Medusa whose glance or call petrifies its victims). By contrast, the nurse in *Innocence* allows the children to go on playing, thus subverting or suspending the power of her call. This reluctance marks her ethical dimension: ethics is opened by the awareness, the hearing of the call of the Other (even if the call comes from oneself), and its suspension in which it is allowed to reverberate or "echo" in the human being's reflection which is, simultaneously, the time during which human subject coagulates and forms in the space of diversion and delay.

Subjecthood forms round the call of the Other but not in and through immediate answering and fulfilling its demands; mediation is the domain of subject, that is, when the call is heard but not answered yet. Another mode of describing human subjecthood would be to say that it is a collection of methods by which I ponder and philosophize the call. Such a subject is impure because it includes the deposits of the Other, it acts as parasite upon and exploits the Other, and also because it takes time before responding to the call, thus becoming potentially suspect of not taking the Other seriously. But, as we have noticed before, it is exactly this impurity, or suspicion of moral neglect, that makes ethics possible for the subject. If Heidegger becomes unethical in his decision of accepting the rector's post on the instigation of Nazi officials, he is so due to a sudden transgression against the law of mediacy: by responding momentarily, he attempts to reconstitute what is virtually impossible, namely a human subject who could be formed in the act of an immediate response to the call. In this, he also betrays his concept of Dasein, the power of which resided in the element of distance, ever renewing spacing, white margins, which were constitutive of the subject. By responding immediately, the philosopher erases the Da- from his notion of Dasein, returning to the centrality of individual being (*Sein*) and, thus, becoming an easy prey for any totalitarianism ("Jean Luc Nancy links fascism and Nazism precisely to phantasms of immediacy which are opposed to indefinite mediation," Ronell, 9). Where the distance is stretched or the mediations are unusually winding or buried, Ronell's telephonic metaphor is especially apt: for example, "For Freud, the telephone, while exemplifying unconscious transmissions, set off the drama of an unprecedented long distance" (9).

{Reenter Jonah: not only is he God's reluctant messenger, but he is also, in Ronell's terms, an "unconscious transmitter." When asking the sailors to cast him into the sea, he does it both from his own will and as an act of fulfilling God's wish for the plan to be completed; speaking of himself, he voices the absent master's voice. God is an impure Other which dwells in Jonah as "the constituting nonpresence . . . what Freud in Derrida's sense called the unconscious" (Ronell, 85). Jonah tries not to be pulled into the central scheme; he endeavors to evade responding to the call, and thus not to be strangled by the "umbilicus of a telephone cord whose radius he failed to measure" (Ronell, 9). By not obeying, he saves God from turning into a totalitarian, tyrannical father figure.}

If an Other is a forming deposit of the subject, then the distinction between inside and outside must necessarily turn out to be volatile. Rather, what matters when we bring back the problematic of the call is the notion of *beyond*, which emphasizes three main paradoxes of the (telephonic) subject:

1. It locates the subject both here and at the far end, at the farther side of itself: one could formulate a thesis that the subject is always beyond the Other.
2. It promotes the subject as a child of the Other, as a formation later than the Other, and in this respect we could say that the subject comes after the Other.
3. It speaks of the subject as of a form which surpasses its own boundaries, and thus the Other is this realm of the subject where it exceeds itself, where it does not and cannot understand itself.

As Ronell says quoting Borch-Jakobsen: "Being is not a substantive; being is the Word that you are yourself beyond yourself" (72). There is then a desubstantivization of being, its etherealization or vocalization: being turns out to be a communication between beyond me and me that takes place on the territory which we choose to call the "subject." So the notion of the subject does not connect with the intensified and well-defined sense of being, but just the opposite—with the sense of being which is made problematic or, at least, movable, shifted between here and there, near and far away. The Being of the subject revolves round the technology of speaking over long distances. Ronell finds two phrases for this. One claims that in the telephonic concept of the subject we deal with "a megaphone from the beyond" (87), and the second that the beyond "organizes the divinized region from where a technology of long-distance calling takes place" (87). In short, an unproportionateness and unmeasuredness (*beyond*) of voices (*phone*) get amplified (*mega*) and thus, necessarily, ordered, made repeatable and reproducible (*technology*) in a certain territory which we call the "subject."

The terms *unproportionate* and *unmeasured* have been suggested above with a specific reason. First, they draw our attention to the somewhat irregular character of the subject which inevitably goes beyond itself and thus betrays the ideas of proportion and measure the human individual has been associated with especially in the powerful, although misleading, tradition of humanism ("man is a *measure* of all things" claimed Protagoras). Thus, a deviation from such a "mathematical" description of the subject as a steady yardstick of all other phenomena necessarily displaces it from its centralized position of the measure. Second, the two qualifications in question reflect Heidegger's concept of 'rhythm' which, in the Heraclitus seminar, is understood less as a flow or a mere perfectly timed repetition, and more as "coinage, imprint, or distinguishing characteristic" (*Gepräge*) or "chain, fetters" (*Fesseln*). Unproportionateness signifies that the subject cannot be demarcated by means of standard measures (such as body-soul, inside-outside, *thymos-phronesis*), and that it goes beyond these axes of proportion. In his analysis of Trakl's poem Heidegger concentrates on the lines speaking of the absence of measure ("Is there a measure on earth? There is/None.") to emphasize not the general lack of measure but its relegation from earth. The measure is shifted "beyond," and—as the philosopher maintains—"The measure consists in the way in which the god who remains unknown, is revealed as such by the sky." The sky of Heidegger is Ronell's "divinized region from where a technology of long-distance calling stems," and the subject forms when the human being, as being, locates between the "on the earth" and the "beyond." It is not a coincidence that Heidegger links the idea of 'imprint' with that of a 'chain,' as his theory seems to imply the *necessity* of responding to the call which comes from "beyond," a reaction which should be the more immediate the more humans uncover their rootedness in being. The call comes from the divinity, from what imposes its voice upon us and, in the name of our authenticity, makes us obedient listeners.

{Reenter Jonah, whose story delivers two divergent ideas about the human subject. Both stem from the act of listening to the call, but whereas one (Heidegger) emphasizes obedient immediacy of our reaction as the measure of our integrity, the other (Blake, Jonah himself) stresses the need for human rebellion against the caller. The latter idea includes the necessity for some anarchic time of play, which must precede our heeding of the call. We might refer to this first notion of the subject as the "Promethean" (humans are bound by the *rytmos* of voice) and to the second as the "Dionysian" (humans are opened to the dangerous element of anarchy and play, a rejection of divinity which, by this means, prepares the ground for divinity's appearance). In other words, the Heideggerian subject is rhythmic and is founded upon the necessity of listening. But the Blakean subject is syncopated and displaces the beats and accents of the call, producing new rhythms, a jazzy subject about which we could claim what Charles O. Hartman says concerning a sequence of choruses of Lee Konitz: "The shifting accents . . . contribute to the overall sense of syncopation—of rhythmic energy and surprise—in a way that complements the shifting symmetries."[4] Jonah, in his contorted escape from the divine, is a perfect embodiment of such a syncopated subject, which "shifts accents" and is circumscribed by "energy and surprise."}

Apparently it is not by obeying God that we show God exists. The God who "calls out, . . . desires, . . . lacks, . . . calls for the complement or the supplement. . . . The God is at the controls but without knowing what he controls until the Other—still lacking—answers his call" (Ronell, 228). Apparently an ethical dimension is opened by refusal of compliance; this prevents the human being from turning into a robot. The subject is a way of forming one's being in an act of refusal to be an answering machine. The ubiquitous phone answering machine, with its taped message, is one image for the schizophrenic person as radically compliant, as in Ronell's account of Ronald Laing's psychoanalysis. Schizophrenia is immediate response to many clearly perceived voices; sanity is protected by a clouded, obscured understanding that keeps us from instant compliance. So on this reading the subject is what cannot fall victim to insanity; the subject is what is immune to illness, what remains always sane. This does not mean that "I" cannot collapse into insanity, but it emphasizes that there remains a placeless place in which thought shelters itself, which cannot be mapped, which must remain forever a blank spot, and which returns in momentary glimpses of sanity. Such a placeless space is, in Ronell, allotted to the telephone and the metaphysics of the call: "The telephone has no site as its property, which makes it break down the limits of spatiality—that is what makes it uncanny, the inside calling from an internal outside" (Ronell, 82).

{Reenter Jonah. When devoured by the fish (a speechless animal, a synonym of voiceless subjugation; the Polish proverb says that "children and fish have no say"), Jonah speaks precisely in the following two capacities: (1) He is an outsider, an alien body, praying from the inside, and thus, to an external observer, he is an inner voice of the fish suddenly, through a strange kind of magic, allowed to speak; (2) he is thus the inside (of the fish) calling from an internal (a belly) outside; Jonah belongs to the sphere of the outside and does not form an inherent part of the fish's organism. Hence, in a spectacular way, the philosophy of voice, as the most intimate sign of the presence of one's thought and its expression, is radically questioned. The inner voice turns out to be violently borrowed from the outside, or to be more specific, torn out from the world as a nourishment. (A double miracle: philosophical, because it marks the absolute presence and thus unveils the subject, pins it down; and zoological, because a speaking animal is a constant element of circus shows, laboratory tests, and fairy-tale images.) The inner voice, a supposed site of the subject, is shown to be the voice of the Other who has been met and appropriated in an act of violence. Thus the tarnishing of the halo of Western metaphysics: voice is shown to be the domain of refined and sophisticated cannibalism. Voice becomes the spectacle of pleasurable torture where the victim is as pleased as the tormentor, where I eat your voice to go on living, somehow doubling your existence as now you live also in my vocal cords.}

The long-distance calling which constitutes the telephonic, syncopated subject resounds in this unmeasurable space of *beyond*; the association of telephonic voice with death is an obvious next step for thought to take. This association with death is crucial for Heidegger, who writes: "To be able to die means: to accept death as death. Only man dies—and indeed continually, so long as he stays on this earth, as long as he dwells."[5] This marks a fundamental moment in Heidegger's analysis of Dasein, because it is death which gets unveiled as the stakes in the authenticity of human being. This is not a neutral discovery, but an act of certain violence: "Dasein must be *torn* out of its everyday existence before it can be pushed into its authentic, finite existence by going toward its death" (Ronell paraphrasing Heidegger, 57). We speak out of death and, somehow, in the name of death, and only then do we speak in our own voice. For the telephonic subject, however, the subject of immense distances, such a conclusion seems invalid. Accepting death as an ordinary encounter with the uncanny, we claim that even then voice remains entangled in the problematic of the other. Death in Heidegger closes, rather than opens, the beyond—where I speak in my own voice, there is no longer any beyond possible, since such speaking establishes the space of presence. Mikkel Borch-Jacobson comments on Heidegger's philosophy along this telephonic line: "Listen, therefore and receive: listening for, you already owe yourself to the Other, having to respond to him/her and to render to him his due. . . . Listen again, you are not alone, your death is calling you" (quoted in Ronell, 70). Eventually humans may realize that death is not a moment where the movement of voices stops. Humans are moving not towards but out of death; for Heidegger, in Ronell's transposition to telephone metaphors, the scene of death is no "surprise call," but rather a scene of recognition (Ronell, 57). Because I am always another, "I" dies before it is even born due to the fact that it owes itself to the Other. The subject knows that it speaks from beyond itself, it says sane things, philosophizes, lives, thinks, always from the impossible domain of one's own absence which lies already on the side of madness. "Listen well: Being is being guilty; other, dead. You *are* guilty, you *are* Other, you *are* dead" (Borch-Jacobson quoted by Ronell, 72).

As Ronell notices, for Heidegger the question of death links with the problem of madness. In *On the Way towards Language* the philosopher maintains that "the dead one is the madman" (quoted in Ronell, 174). In this work, Heidegger claims that the madman, despite his ability to sense as "no one else does," "does not have the sense of the others." Just here we disagree: the telephonic, syncopated subject retains the ability to sense the Other even at the depth of its own existence, even in clinical cases of madness. The subject as voice is an internal outsider, because it speaks sanity from within madness. The subject is the living dead.

It is not only the horror of Don Siegel's *Invasion of the Body Snatchers*, or George Romero's *Night of the Living Dead*. In H. P. Lovecraft's story, "The Statement of Randolph Carter," research is carried out into "why certain corpses never decay, but rest firm and fat in their tombs for a thousand years."[6]

{Reenter Jonah. Speaking entombed from the belly of a fish, he deals with his own absence. Having disappeared from the surface of the world and descended into the abyss, nonetheless he is still alive. Ronell has described it, though, in different discourse than the Bible: "The subject . . . hooks up with the phenomenon of his own disappearance, located in the belly of the Other" (87).}

In the Lovecraft story, Harley Warren's exploration leads him toward a crypt at an ancient cemetery, which early on becomes a setting for the dream of voice. Its "lethal silence" (Lovecraft, 180), before it reveals itself as the aphonic call of death (like the voice of a conscience it can remain silent and this silence "renders it that much more alien, *other*": Ronell, 63), is juxtaposed to the "mellow tenor voice [of Warren]; a voice singularly unperturbed by our awesome surroundings" (Lovecraft, 181). We should notice two things: first, the mellowness of the voice which bespeaks the firmness of man's decision, of the integrity of his self. Second, the voice is placed in an arrogant position of an element which does not agree, refuses to agree, with other elements of the world. The self, represented by such a voice, is not so much with but, rather, over the world and thus refuses to heed the call which, despite being aphonic, nevertheless clearly signals the message of intensive, although hidden, processes which may be described as that of transformation: "The removal of the slab revealed a black aperture, from which rushed an effluence of miasmal gases so nauseous that we started back in horror" (180).

{Reenter Jonah. The fish swallowing the prophet places him in its belly, the place of digestion, transformation of matter. The inner voice not being, as we have seen, quite inner, now reaches us from a low place, thus negating the noble qualities usually attached to voice as the most immediate sign of one's presence.}

In Lovecraft's tale, the dominating self is strengthened by technology: first "electric lanterns" and then, significantly enough, telephone. It is the latter, as a device of voice carrier, that becomes one of the main protagonists of the story. "The portable telephone outfit" Warren is carrying with him into the crypt secures a connection which, to begin with, inaugurates a praise of technology and, later, is meant to become a channel through which new, epoch-making discovery will be transmitted to the surface. Technology and the dominating self it produces emphasize the solidity and security of the connection based on the principal ability to recognize new things—to avoid surprise and shock by the perfect reliability of the measure. The telephone betrays this double significance of measure: first, it provides a link which is measured in the sense of being exact and well thought out; and second, it literally measures the distance separating the caller and the called ("But I promise to keep you informed over the telephone of every move—you see I've got enough wire here to reach to the center of the earth and back!" [181]). What is at stake in the telephone is that it refuses to go beyond measure and promises to measure the beyond.

Very quickly, however, the telephone is transformed from a merely technological contraption into a magical device, an umbilical cord linking one with the unknown Other, a magical thread which does not allow the self to be alone and, in this way, begins to shatter the premises of the self's domination based on the technological control over itself: "I was alone, yet bound to the unknown depths by those magic strands whose insulated surface lay green beneath the struggling beams of that waning crescent moon" (182).

In Heideggerian terms this move from mere technology to hermeneutics is related to a complicated question of distance, deseverance, and directionality. In short, we can say that a sudden estrangement of a person from the everydayness of telephone as a part of common equipment marks a revelation that proximity and distance are not matters of technically measured remoteness (this is rendered in Heidegger's terminology as *Abstand*), but of "Dasein's essential tendency towards closeness." This remoteness (*Entfernen*) is "estimated proximally by circumspection," which is the only power able to "decide as to the closeness or farness of what is proximally ready-to-hand environmentally."[7] Thus, it implies that parts of equipment which are instruments of closeness (like spectacles or telephones) must, if we wish to define their real role in bringing close, lose their routinely near position, must become magically distant: "Equipment for seeing—and likewise for hearing, such as the telephone receiver—has what we have designated as the inconspicuousness of the proximally ready-to-hand." It follows that the telephone, if it is to regain its function and character of a device which annihilates distances, must, first of all, lose its superficial apparent closeness which, in fact, makes it practically absent from the scene of communication. A telephone receiver has to evolve toward becoming a magic wand. In Lovecraft's story the telephone wire is called "magic strands," for it secures a certain prosthesis-like presence of someone who is not here, but it is also "magic" because it protects its secret powers against the undesirable intervention not so much sheltering the secrets shared by the caller and the called, but enviously guarding the enigmatic operations of its own magic. The descent into the crypt is also a plunge toward the crypt of the telephone whose secret protocols of the magic of communication will remain forever crypt-ic. Hence, the significance of the emphasis (measured by a careful description of its color) of the "insulation" of the telephone cord. Its insulation bespeaks that the messages transmitted inside are protected from any leakage, that they will remain locked in the appropriate channel, but—simultaneously—that they will be forever alienated, isolated, or, to use Lovecraft's expression, "unperturbed" by the surroundings. The merely technological interpretation of the telephone seeks in it a means which blocks the access of madness toward the self; it guards the secrets and isolates, not allowing any room for the plurality of voices.

But Lovecraft's story is the tale of the withdrawal of such an interpretation. Warren, a dominating self of the "mellow tenor voice," begins to turn into a syncopated subject, the subject who speaks "in accents more alarmed and quivering" (182). There is no more talk about voice and its steady, regulated, and controlled flow; instead we deal with a sudden disintegration of the communicative power which gets disseminated into particular grains or elements ("words") of a questionable constitution ("quivering," "shaky whisper") which, ultimately, lead to a decomposition (a significant word in the context of the story) of voice into "frenzied tones" and a dissolution of syntax into a concatenation of expletives: "Carter, it's terrible—monstrous—unbelievable" (182). The wire which was supposed to provide us with security of recognition turns out to be Arladne's thread leading us through the maze of the "monstrous," and the technological interpretation of the telephone is replaced by a hermeneutics which abolishes the precision of the articulate of the magic and cryptography of the secrets of the telephone cord and its insulation with the power of the inarticulate which pulverizes the chronological construction of technology: "Here Warren's whisper swelled into a cry; a cry that gradually rose to a shriek fraught with all the horror of the ages" (183). Despite a still clear semantics of Warren's discourse, the ear of the listener becomes attentive not so much to the words as to the tones of the message ("frenzied tones," "the tone changed again"). Thus, a move from a technological to a hermeneutic interpretation of the telephone implies concentration on the tonalities and shades of voice; it is linked with the attention paid to the static, "clicks," noises, which accompany voice and cause it to become more and more "faint" (183). The fainting of the voice is the drama of the telephone communication. First, it makes voice blurred and unreadable, changes it from a certain whole into an arrangement of fragments ("tones"); second, it activates the unconscious of voice which fainting becomes unaware and loses control over itself, letting to the surface what is normally suppressed and contained in the "mellow tenor."

The maturity of full voice is replaced by a series of uncontrolled vocal utterances which desperately try to call back the Other. Nevertheless, calling—so characteristic of controlled maturity—becomes now only *one* possible manner of regaining the Other, the manner accompanied by "whispering, muttering, screaming" (183). This redefined calling implies that what the caller is struck by ("I sat stupefied") is precisely the thereness of the Other, a sudden discovery of the fact that not only has the Other disappeared, but also the there he vanished into remains not a mere designation of distance but a description of total and insurmountable difference. The there (the Da of Dasein) belongs now to we do not know where, to the territory in which thought fails, and which thus has to threaten the constitution of my very self. This makes for the drama of the syncopated subject: both the prominence of there (where the Other resides, the there of a receiver) and its total annihilation (the there which devours, destroys, the Other made radically unavailable by the there): "Warren! Warren! Answer me—are you there?"

The syncopated subject loses its steady, solid, rhythm precisely due to the oscillating power of *there,* which both promises and denies the Other, thus constituting a subject between these two movements. The area that the syncopated subject acquires access to is a domain in which the Other loses its familiarity, where it ceases to function as a guarantor of the sense of reality (and thus also of myself). The latter there is not striking and paralyzing because it demarcates the perennial silence of the Other, but because it processes the call of the Other, thus turning the stronghold of thought and order into "the unbelievable, unthinkable, almost unmentionable" (Lovecraft, 183). Now the voice of the Other, the voice which constitutes in an essential sense my position as a subject, brings two facts which seem detrimental to me and my everyday life understanding of the subject. First, it introduces the element of formless inhumanity. (The voice that eventually, after many clicks, replies to Carter's call is "deep; hollow; gelatinous;

remote; unearthly; inhuman; disembodied," 184.) Second, the result of its intervention is not more but less consciousness, as it evidently sends Carter down the path of madness. ("In answer [I] heard the thing which has brought this cloud over my mind," 184.) The Other now responds in a voice for which there is neither "accounting" nor "description," but as this language operates in the situation of medical examination or transference, its words are bound to appear (as replies to doctors' questions) but refuse to add up to one coherent description of the Other's voice. Each adjective forms a separate unit, but neither exhausts or completes a description (it is followed by a line of others) nor relates to other adjectives coming after it (it is separated from them not by a comma but by a semi-colon which locks a given feature in a strange half-way position between independence and subjection).

There are, then, two important aspects of the inarticulate. One uncovers the underpinnings of reason, unconceals and liberates the reason's Other where reason possesses a life both deeper and less conscious than its articulate logical life. The other positions subject in a precarious territory of transition between the conscious and unconscious; what we designated as the syncopated subject is precisely this construction of human identity which is always moving on the edge of the unconscious which does not have the Freudian meaning but which addresses the area of, so to speak, ontological unconsciousness. (We shall touch upon this important problematic in the next section.)

The inarticulate manifests itself through a distortion and parody of the articulate, and thus a syncopated subject becomes almost a circus-like performance of monstrosity displayed to the eyes of curious viewers. The loss of stability and solidity on the part of the syncopated subject is a transformation of the old practice of viewing the marginal as a sanitary measure confirming and delimiting my own normalcy. (Think of the madhouse, Bedlam, as an entertainment in eighteenth-century London and as a comment on the self-annihilating protocols of science which ultimately negates its own ambitions to translate the unknown into the discourse of the familiar and neighboring. The voice of the Other comes from a distance which defies measurement).

In Edgar Allan Poe's "The Facts in the Case of M. Valdemar," the mesmerized subject speaks from the depth of space ("the voice seemed to reach our ears . . . from a vast distance") and its subterranean quality ("from some deep cavern within the earth") is matched by a twisted and agonizing performance of the face.[8] A harrowing movement of articulating speech organs, first of all, demystifies a unity of the body by demonstrating centrifugal tendencies of the particular organs of the body ("The upper lip writhed itself away from the teeth") and then leads to a replacement of the solidity of the sign in the process of communication by a sudden opening of a chasm in which a sign falls as in the domain of death ("the lower jaw fell with an audible jerk, leaving the mouth widely extended, and disclosing in full view the swollen and blackened tongue"). The contorted theatrics of the Other's face, where the face becomes the image of the entrance to the domain of death, are paralleled by the quality of voice which, in a striking similarity to Lovecraft's description, is "gelatinous or glutinous."

The adjectives refer to a certain essential formlessness of the Other's voice, the formlessness of its essence which defies the very concept of essence and turns the Other into a being without essence. But "gelatinous" also implies a regression toward a more archaic form of existence ("gelatinous" refers to a substance of animal tissue rich in collagen and exposed to a long-term impact of water, e.g., fish gelatin). Thus, "gelatinous" voice is a more primeval utterance of a being which, like a fish, is supposedly bereft of the gift of speech. However, the implication which leads us through the word *gel* also revives the image of something that is transparent and, despite its amorphous characters, belongs to the paradigm of cold and detached things. Here the similarity between the French *gélatineux* and *gel* turns out to be helpful. Thus, "gelatinous" voice of the Other signifies a sound which is (1) amorphous, (2) separate and coming from a distance, (3) activated by a sudden regression toward the zoological past (a voice of devolution or decomposition), and (4) constituting a certain obstacle, a challenge to a routine and smooth flow of everyday reality. (In French we speak about *gel de crédits*; in Poe's story, "Mr. L——swooned," hearing the gelatinous voice of M. Valdemar.) Such a voice can only be a parody of the human vocal production, not so much as voice but as "voice" ("I have spoken both of 'sound' and of 'voice'"). There is no syncopation of the subject possible without this experience of the voice of the Other as "harsh, broken, and hollow," without the Other becoming a disharmony, a negation of the "mellow tenor," without a sudden and acoustic revelation of the always-present mechanical principle in humanity. Thus, a subject becomes dehumanized, displaced from its privileged human position defined in opposition to the mechanical and automatic; the syncopated subject is ahuman, detoned; that is, it recognizes the power of the mechanical as an indispensable element of humanity. The fact that death, which authenticates human existence, is an epiphany of the automatic, robotic (the sound of M. Valdemar is that of "syllabification": "Yes;—no;—I have been sleeping—and now—now—I am dead") only amplifies the significance of the Other as a necessary lesson of repetition and return. The Other reveals itself as a position of logical ("Yes—no") and grammatical (a hesitation between present simple and present perfect) undecidability.

Regional Intentionality

The notion of the 'inarticulate' helped us to introduce the concept of a 'syncopated subject'—a construction of human identity which, while operating in the sphere of the conscious, remains in vital relationship with the unconscious and paralogic. The domain of such a subject was referred to as the *ontological unconscious.*

Intentionality is one of the key terms in Heidegger's philosophy, where it receives an interpretative bias quite different from that which it enjoyed in Edmund Husserl. Whereas Husserl concentrates on intentionality as a relation between consciousness and an object intended, whose matching remains a true substance of the conscious act, Heidegger tries to conduct a more searching analysis which, ultimately, must bring intentionality to the threshold of the unconscious. Thus what is at stake in Heidegger's meditations is a reflection on what precedes intentionality and literally makes it possible. In other words, what is highlighted in this philosophy is the ontological foundation of intentionality. Such a change of perspective must, it seems, involve serious repercussions in the construction of the subject, which is now deprived of the privilege of consciousness as the only ground for its formation. Hence the subject after such a move has to be reinterpreted in two ways. First, it is no longer tenable to speak of its centralizing and unifying functions guarded so far by well-mapped mechanisms of consciousness described by Descartes and Husserl. The subject is not definable in terms of algebraic, mathematical, or logical operations, or—rather—these protocols are only a part of strategies that generate and construct subject. Thus, to the Cartesian ambition of presenting modes of perception as far reaching and thus familiarizing the world, Heidegger replies by formulating a thesis according to which it is precisely the "distance-senses" (*Fernsinne*) such as seeing and hearing that must be subjected to the process of estrangement at the end of which one will see that their action of "bringing the world close to us" is based on a certain illusion and misunderstanding of the term *proximity.* If Descartes writes *Optics*, then Heidegger in his analyses in *Sein und Zeit* indirectly composes a masterplan for a *counteroptics.*

Second, the subject now is not a steady, solid, continuous being, but with an encroachment on the monopoly of consciousness to define subject, we turn it into a discontinuous structure fractured by various fissures and openings. A syncopated subject is thus a falling being; it represents a human self which has plunged in the chasm opened, most recently, by Nietzsche in his numerous metaphors focusing on the abyss (*Abgrund*) as the only available foundation (*Grund*) of being. A falling-flying-syncopated subject is thus a changeable and moveable constellation of powers which includes various types of logic and unconscious undergoing a process of constant translation into the discourse of the logical and conscious, the only type of language where subject can articulate itself. However, it implies, then, that there is another, more original, discourse of subject which does not recognize the very notion of the 'subject', and which—although indispensable—must then be translated into the language where 'subject' moves about freely. The Cartesian concept of subject led to a conclusion that it is the notion which underlies all other phenomena, and therefore has to remain solid and resistant to changes and perforations. Heidegger brings about a deconstruction of such a subject by demonstrating that it is itself composed of several layers, and thus cannot pretend to any ultimate solidity upon which the edifice of reality could be founded. To extend the architectural metaphor, the Cartesian subject cannot respond to violent moves and radical, tectonic, philosophical changes because, by pretending to be solid, it cut itself off from the possibility of tolerating gaps and discontinuities.

Heidegger postulates a subject which can, through the inbuilt network of holes and fissures, set itself in harmony with all the radical transformations (like Nietzsche's verdict concerning the death of God) and look for its perseverance not due its solidity but—just the opposite—its ability to stand without foundation. In his *Introduction to Metaphysics* (1935) Heidegger suggests that intentionality ought to be placed against the ontological background which involves a serious restriction imposed upon consciousness as the unique subject forming power. According to the philosopher, "consciousness does not itself create the openness of beings, nor is it consciousness that makes it possible for man to stand open for beings. Whither and whence and in what free dimension could the intentionality of consciousness move, if instancy were not the essence of man in the first instance?"[9] It is impossible then to stabilize the subject around the notion of 'intentionality' because intentionality itself is conditioned by another power, and thus, although by definition synonymous with consciousness, it dwells in regions which can be described as unconscious. Hence, intentionality extends to where a mere presentative aspect of consciousness has to be replaced and completed by another element. In his definitive article "The Place of the Unconscious in Heidegger," William Richardson argues that Husserl's reading of the subject as thoroughly conscious forgets (a very Heideggerian notion itself) the ontological dimension of understanding being (as opposed to understanding beings) and concludes that "Dasein, as Heidegger conceives it, is a self, to be sure, but not a conscious subject. It is a presubjective, onto-conscious self."[10]

By turning toward a "self" rather than "subject," Richardson implies that it is consciousness that designates in the Western tradition the individual's integrity, and hence rethinking of Descartes must necessarily mean a meditation on the role of the unconscious. Our syncopated subject is then, paradoxically, a subject which includes "presubjective" elements, a preconscious subject. Jacques Maritain who introduces the term *preconscious* does so to distinguish what he calls "a spiritual unconscious" from "Freudian unconscious," namely "the unconscious of blood and flesh." Thus, a presubjective subject is located in the unconsciousness with a necessary proviso that "the word unconscious . . . does not necessarily mean a purely unconscious activity. It means most often an activity which is principally unconscious, but the point of which emerges into consciousness."[11] Thus, the subject becomes a dynamic constellation of forces in which *intentio intellecta* is only one of numerous possible intentions and therefore cannot usurp for itself a central place from which the structure of intentions will be made exact and controllable. Such a subject of partly uncontrolled, discontinuously and disharmoniously arranged (un)conscious intentions is what we refer to in this book as a "syncopated subject."

The question, however, remains: Is it possible to locate such a subject, to produce its topography and geography? Heidegger, despite his attack on a highly spatialized thought of Descartes, still maintains the significance of space through the notion of 'deseverance' and 'directionality', claiming that "Dasein is essentially de-severance, that is, it is spatial" (SZ, 108/143). Deseverance (*Entfernung*) is, at the same time, a recognition and overcoming of remoteness; in the act of deseverance remoteness is acknowledged as the space of a difference separating beings and guarding their independence, but also it is due to this recognition that beings are viewed circumspectively and hence are brought close to one another thus annihilating distance: "Desevering amounts to making the farness vanish" (SZ, 105/139). A syncopated subject operates on this principle: it sees itself as different from its own conscious version and then, recognizing the difference, makes the "farness disappear," thus living in what Maritain calls *"le rebord de l'inconscient"* (*Intuition*, 91). The spatial metaphor remains valid, but—a fundamental innovation it is no longer used to measure the precision of subject's construction; just the opposite—it can serve now as a directional hint, a pointer, towards the unconscious hiding places of what, to use Richardson's comment upon Heidegger, is certainly a self, but not yet a conscious subject. In short, now the spatiality of metaphor can only point a direction of coming (*wohin*) and going (*woher*), of where a subject appears and toward where it vanishes but refuses to determine exact location. The subject becomes a sign of the self, and as such it "takes over the giving of directions in a way which is explicit and easily manipulable" (SZ, 108/143). But, we have to note very carefully, it is the "giving of directions" which is explicit; it is the subject which remains vague and unspecified.

Such directions lead, then, not so much to the subject's location but only, very generally, can point toward a certain region, toward what makes space possible, what opens space for Dasein. A region designates this *where* toward which a subject (in)tends, where it stops "fleeing in the face of itself" (SZ, 185/230), where it "belongs" (SZ, 110/145). Regionality of the subject does not signify its marginality or mere locality; rather it brings us toward a reflection on the subject's transparency: the subject is regional because (1) it cannot be locked in any one position but fluctuates between many, and (2) because it cannot be described as being here, but is an errant structure which belongs exclusively to some there, to a region different from (no)where it is now. Such a construction of the subject turns it into a form of anxiety: it faces what seems to be nowhere, and what is therefore threatening. But, as Heidegger says in his analysis of anxiety, "'Nowhere,' however, does not signify nothing: this is where any region lies, and there too lies any disclosedness of the world for essentially spatial Being-in" (SZ, 186/231).

Our concept of 'regional intentionality' is based on

1. a revaluation of the role of consciousness in subject forming strategies;
2. decentering of the subject;
3. its discontinuity; and
4. unevenness of its role as a conscious unit of identity, or what we call "syncopation," for most of our activities contributing to the effect of identity remain hidden or unconscious despite the fact that the subject is normally considered to be precisely a stronghold of consciousness;
5. essential spatiality which, however, does not localize but disperses and directionalizes; and
6. rediscovery of the function of time which now, when one deals with a liquidified, formless subject without foundations, acquires a crucial role—it is only in time that a changing subject can be brought to the dimension of responsibility for its momentary decisions, only taking into account what is antisocial or asocial, distortions, rebelliousness, and displacement, that a subject can become a truly social being.

The subject of regional intentionality is always here now, but also always over there.

The concept of the 'speaking subject' is a way to claim a mode of intentionality, though not the circumscribed, hard-edged Cartesian or authorial mode. The concepts of 'tone of voice', 'textual voice', and 'detonation' are ways to keep a regional intentionality while remaining sensitive to the society and the history of the text. The wish has been to reduce terms to the minimum that can be defended.

Literary criticism needs stronger justification for doing what it has always done in presuming things about the social intentionality behind tone of voice. One underpinning for criticism and teaching is a strong and nuanced theory of the speaking subject. Such an account is already in existence, and this book includes and extends it; what is largely lacking in criticism to date, though, except in rare places, is an account of *tonelessness*. Here we will foreshadow our final chapters by confronting intentionality with its most powerful challenge, namely the detonation performed by textual voice. We present two case studies of texts that baffle any traditional reading for the kind of tone of voice that we used to describe with an adjective of social merit, such as *prattling, judicious, noble, scrappy, seductive,* and so on. Notions of 'volition', and 'agency', and 'subjecthood' need revision if they are to be brought near such texts, but such texts do exist, and indeed our two examples come from very likely the greatest writers of two different places and times.

In Edgar Allan Poe's "The Imp of the Perverse," a story of 1845, the protagonist is a master and monster of rationality.[12] The murder is an effect of a long and painstaking process of rethinking various possibilities: "For weeks, for months, I pondered upon the means of the murder." The operations and conscious goals of reason are, within the terms set up, perverse, and the process of reasoning is from the ethical point of view misdirected. The vehicle of death, a candle, is also a medium of knowledge—physical and mental illumination: "I knew my victim's habit of reading in bed" (1224). The perfection of perverse rationality in actualizing one's intentions is placed on a god-like level: "The coroner's verdict was—Death by visitation of God" (1224). However, there is another discourse coexisting in the story, the discourse of whatever is formless and horror making: "By slow degrees our sickness and dizziness and horror become merged in a cloud of unnameable feeling" (1222). Words in this latter discourse are doubly uncertain, for they are repeated while the speaking subject is not aware of repetition ("I arrested myself in the act of murmuring," 1225), and they exist in the shadowy region between silence and vocalization ("half-aloud"). This discourse of the formless intention announces itself through the hesitant grammatical mode of the subjunctive ("I am safe . . . if I be not fool enough to make open confession," 1224). Eventually, though, the disclosure cannot be contained, and "the long-imprisoned secret burst forth from my soul" (1224). The speaking, forced and vomitous, of this intention is a disarticulation of the subject, who now will be subjected to the severity of the law. So we may say of this formless intention, lethal to self, what Werner Hamacher says about language in Paul Celan's poetry—that its speaking is "self-disruptive, self-dispersive, and disseminating." The power of the formless intention, which we should also call a "regional intention," is the energy of the conditional; this brings about the unconcealment of the secret and its conscious or central intention, and eventually leads to the subject's dramatic displacement. "Today I wear these chains, and am HERE! Tomorrow I shall be fetterless—but WHERE?" (1224): the rational intention specifies *here*, the formless intention leaves us with the horrifying, interrogative *where*? The speaker, overwhelmed, can barely recount his own story.

One should listen with Nietzsche's "small ears" to Poe's dramatic question which not only raises one of his constant and characteristic dilemmas concerning death and post-mortem condition but, pertinently here, revives the issues of freedom, time, and space so important for the philosophy of the subject. In Poe's analysis the "here" and "now" ("today") are domains of restriction ("chains") but, at the same time, it is interesting to note that only such a positioning of the human turns him or her into a subject—an agent and object of the law. The human being's responsibility is thus linked with a certain oppressiveness which (unlike Hobbes and other social-contract theorists wished it to be) results from the human being's *involuntary decision*, one which is forced upon him or her not by *intentio intellecta*, but by a regional, (un)conscious, formless intention which, as we can clearly see, contributes to our subjecthood and our social accountability for our acts.

Conversely, Poe's concept of 'freedom' is relegated from now to the future ("tomorrow") (the subject is a being toward its future subjecthood which destroys its present status of a subject), and thus produces a reading of subjecthood which is (un)founded upon a belief that a subject is a subject to the extent to which its present being is unsatisfactory and limiting, and which must (in)tend toward its other, future, version. The limitation is to be understood both in terms of human subjugation ("now" is a restrictive space where the subject immobilizes itself, through a supposed possibility of excluding the unconscious from subjecthood), and the denial of freedom (the subject gets immobilized by the law, which can respond only to the subject as petrified and stopped in its becoming, to a subject which thus has ceased to be a subject) as well as spatial confinement. The latter is noticeable not only in the sense of physical imprisonment but, predominantly, in the ontological anxiety (as we have said, a syncopated subject of regional intentionality is an anxious subject whose subjecthood is [un]founded on anxiety) made manifest in the insistent question "Where?" Like Heidegger almost a century later, Poe knows that the issues of *wohin* and *woher* are places of crucial debates which bring the indefinite into the construction of one's subjecthood: "That in the face of which one is anxious is completely indefinite" (SZ, 186/231). Poe's "Where" spells the indefiniteness of the subject as a region of the freedom to come and thus of a subject as a region of fear which discloses human being as a being toward the (indefinite, thus monstrous) subjecthood ("world as world is disclosed first and foremost by anxiety, as a mode of state-of-mind. . . . Anxiety makes manifest in Dasein its Being towards its ownmost potentiality-for-Being" (SZ, 187/232, 188/232).

One possible answer to Poe's dramatic quest would be its repetition, a *where* subjected to the process of "eternal recurrence." A Heideggerian would answer to his where with nowhere, which does not specify a mere negation or the place of absence (such a reading of the word nowhere is characteristic for the existence possessed by curiosity and ambiguity and thus inauthentic), but which emphasizes the closeness and proximity of anxiety which has to remain nameless and placeless but which is always "there." It cannot be "here," as such a location would neutralize and domesticate it, and hence the there as a necessary and only residence of anxiety and the (impossible) seat of a solid subjecthood ("it is already there, and yet nowhere; it is so close that it is oppressive and stifles one's breath, and yet it is nowhere") (SZ, 186/231). The no of nowhere is not a mere contradiction and denial (a not of "not subsisting," SZ, 284/330), but it is constitutive of the very essential feature of subjecthood as moving away from the captivating and petrifying now toward the liberating, although always postponed, future. The subject is what is no-where, where no signifies a necessary ontological dimension of what has been normally considered a routine and unproblematic spatial description (where). In short, the subject is constituted by the ways in which it problematizes its own space.

The question of where returns again in our other example. Paul Celan's poetry seems to locate the answer to this question in the Other, in a You. As Emmanuel Levinas notices: "Le poème va vers l'autre. Il espère le rejoindre delivre et vacant. L'oeuvre solitaire du poète ciselant la matière précieuse des mots est l'acte *débusquer dialogue éperdu. . . . Rencontres, chemin d'une vers un toi vigilant.*"[13] But what looks like a completion of an I is, in fact, its double desubstantialization (*désubstantiation du Moi*, as Levinas refers to it) first, because it shifts the main impact toward the Other, thus suspending an I in a certain lacuna;

second, because the Other turns out to be a version of nonbeing, or *Nichts*. In an early poem Celan will say that a sense of individual identity is no more than a darkness which we see in the eye of the Other:

> You opened your eyes—I saw my darkness live.
> I see through it down to the bed:
> There too it is mine and lives.[14]

The subject is located in the process of transition which goes from an I toward a You. However, this activity is bereft of the ultimate destination and shown to be performed by a power totally beyond the control of either I or You. The subject now is no more than a depersonalized and transitory construct, similar to Maritain's placement of a subject on the edge of the unconscious. In short, a subject, a passage from an I to a You, is only a part of the larger and incomprehensible activity of It (*es*).

> O einer, o keiner, o niemand, o du:
> Wohin gings, da's nirgendhin ging?
> O du grabst und ich grab, und ich grab mich dir zu,
> und am Finger erwacht uns der Ring.
>
> [O one, o none, o no one, o you:
> Where did the way lead when it led nowhere?
> O you dig and I dig, and I dig towards you,
> and on our finger the ring awakes.]
> ("Es war Erde in ihnen," Hamburger trans., 152–53)

The process of subject forming is designated by the act of digging which refers to hollowing out a space or drilling a tunnel in the ground, but also, if we remember the German original, to excavating (like digging out coal) and carving (digging one's name or initials on a certain surface; Celan seems to combine all three readings in an opening line for another poem where he states that "That which was written grows hollow," *Das Geschriebene hohlt sich*, 251). Thus, digging toward the Other is a painstaking movement of struggling through darkness aiming at bringing up to the light of the surface the Other who constitutes my name. We must also remember that the excavation in question is also an act of a grave digging (and thus stands in the immediate proximity of exhumation and death) and wounding of the earth. The former reading is clear in the German word *Grab* (a grave), the latter in another related substantive *Graben* signifying a moat or a ditch.

But the act of digging, although definitely performed by individuals ("they dug and dug") is a part of a larger process which is depersonalized or, in the English translation, subsumed under the term *the way*. Digging marks the impossibility of a final formation of the subject but makes the subject a fragment of a depersonalized, anonymous way of the world which leads nowhere. Thus, an important Celanian insight is added to our theory of the subject: there is *no where* for the subject to take place. The subject is essentially homeless, which does not mean to say that it is spaceless. Just the opposite—it recognizes space as its element; however, the space of the subject is not a static container but a dynamic energy flow which centrifugally displaces and continuously dislodges the subject. The digging acquires yet another reading: it describes not only the action of individuals and of the anonymous *Es*, but the latter "digs" in the sense of removing solid foundations underneath one's feet (see a German proverb "wer anderen eine Grube grabt, fallt selbst"). Thus, the subject is thinkable only as forming and dissolving in a shrinking place: "But now shrinks the place where you stand" ("Nun aber schrumpft der Ort, wo du stehst"), concludes Celan in "Soviel Gestirne" (158). Thus, the subject is at the same time one and no one, an impossible you, a "multi-you" (*aber-du*) suspended, like a breath, "between there and not-there" (*dort und nicht-da*, in "Soviel Gestirne"), lost "on the ways there" (*wege dorthin*) which turns out to be hazy (*blubbernde*) (in "A la pointe acerée," 192). The Celanian formula, as put forward in "Radix, Matrix," presents the I as moving toward and encountering the You, but the You is no more than a construction of an I looking for its own identity. The encounter is not with *the* You but with *a* you, because the very you is also implicated in the search for its own integrity and, therefore, also denied determined characteristics and location. A you becomes "a sister to me" "from a chasm" (187) which is, ironically enough, the only available description of a home, and the scene of the encounter is that of double nothingness, a nothingness of the night and a nothingness of nothing—"you in the nothingness of a night" (187).

At this moment Celan's poem becomes a text of *Aber: du in der Aber-Nacht Be/gegnete, du/Aber-Du-* (which Michael Hamburger gives as "you in the multi-night en-/countered, you/multi-you"). A you dwells in the *Aber-Nacht*, and is itself an *Aber-Du*. *Aber* disseminates, rather than concentrates, the meaning of a you. It combines opposites (in the previous line night is constituted by nothingness)—thus defies unequivocality—and also warns us that previous qualifications have to be taken with caution (the night is *Aber* because it overcomes a previous restriction and thus shows its vanity and futility). But certainly *Aber* speaks also of recurrence as a mode of being of both night and you, of the return as the only possible manner of their presencing, the return which, however, is always marked with a difference, with a hyphen in which a newly returned you vanishes again. *Aber-Du* is the Celanian description of the subject caught in the movement between yous; an I is a mode in which a you always strives toward itself through an endless series of repetitions.

But this implies that *Aber-Du* making itself manifest in the *Aber-Nacht*, is also an obstacle for an I, a difficulty which an I has to overcome; a you is a scene where an I doubts of itself. The *Aber-Du* is what intervenes and makes subject formation impossible; it does not surprise us then that Celanian spelling specifies a you as a sister and, at the same time, an adversary (*gegnete of Aber-Nacht-Be/gegnete* is related to a preposition *gegen*—"against," and a noun *Gegner*—"rival"). One of the meanings of *Aber* in a nominalized form is exactly one signifying difficulty or obstacle. If we remember that a German term for a neighborhood or region is *Gegend*, then we can conclude that *Aber-Du* is also a region where a you ceases to be a mere partner of our everyday life and becomes a complicated network of relationships, a cluster of contradictory directions and involvements.

This impossibility of closing and rounding up the subject is rewritten in the text of *da* in the same poem, "Radix, Matrix" (186):

> Damals, da ich nicht da war,
> damals, da du
> den Acker abschrittst, allein:

The text of *da* is again a script of absence ("when I was not there"), but now the absence has doubled. It speaks, on the one hand, about Heideggerian grafting on an I unto "there" (*Dasein*), but also concludes that even such a "there" may be vacated, hollowed out, that *Sein* may be not only removed from a here but also from a there. Thus, *Dasein* evolves toward a double *Da* becoming a *Dadasein* with all the implications of absurdity and tragic playfulness of the term. *Da* is then another denomination of a you (*du*); it is a there where an I is not and a you "paces the ploughed field, alone."

The answer to "where?" seems to be on the hazy roads between "there and no-there" (one may wonder to what extent these paths are dramatic reworkings of Heidegger's *Holzwege*)—"in the eternalized Nowhere" (in "Das Geschriebene," 251). The shrinking of the place where the subject does not *take place* is also amplified by the blurring of vision, that is to say, the subject is always separated from its Other (i.e., from itself) by unrecognized obstacles. This lack of recognition and impossibility of seeing account for the uncertain status of the space occupied by the subject. The subject is where it cannot see where it is and where the name loses its definitive power. In "Engfuhrung" it is a recurring motive:

> Nowhere
>
> does anyone ask after you—
> The place where they lay, it has
> a name—it has
> none. They did not lie there. Something
> lay between them. They
> did not see through it. (137)

Nevertheless, at the end of this suggestion in Celan's thought, the annoying question comes back:

> in the eternalized Nowhere, here,
> in recollection of the too-
> loud bells in—but where?,
> ("Das Geschriebene hohlt sich," 250–251)

The question asks itself insistently, and the answer parodies Wordsworthian "emotion recollected in tranquility," which meant to be a response precisely to one specific place such as Tintern Abbey, reverberating with memories. The romantic self is formed by recollections and anamnesis; the Celanian subject is belittled by memories which do not perform an act of determining one's location (even if only in a purely nostalgic way). Memories instead speak of one's suppression by recollections bringing up a place which immediately begins to shrink, thus changing into an opening, a chasm. Also memory is hopelessly locked in a tension between being and nothingness: "The / marguerite, unbroken, passed / between home and chasm through / your memory" (171). "Where" is nothing else but a shrunk version of "Nowhere."

The Chasm of the Inarticulate

Articulation, that art of coherent and clear argumentation, that lucidity of logic unthinkable in the sphere where speech gives way to moos, clucks, and burbles, is the skill enabling a speaking subject to explore reality. The speaking subject is most exploratory when it shares with the reader or hearer the same structure of understanding, when the main message of the world is accompanied by a complicated and delicate system of allusions. Without these cultural allusions, the meaning may be trivial or propagandist. It may assume that the reader does not deserve the privilege of contesting for a common world but must be handed a ready-made world deprived of nuance. In the not-long-past reality of eastern Europe, one system was the guarantor of the main meaning, crude and coercive; it was the sphere of personal, underground counterdiscourse that was swarming with hints and allusions and, as one used to say, voices.

It would appear that both the main body of the Western cultural text, and its margins scribbled over with allusions and glosses, are possible due to the clarity of articulation, both phonetic (markedness functions intact) and logical (commonsense linkage and progression intact). Articulation means both spacing and connecting; things articulate themselves in distinction from other things. This paradox of articulation secures our rootedness in reality which defies the incursions of chaos, but also specifies a certain metaphysical criterion from which objects emerge from nonbeing and begin to exist within our horizon to the degree to which they obtain their own contour, to the extent to which they are drawn in both senses of pulling through and penciling. Articulation is, then, a sanction and a mechanism of elocutionary, metaphysical, political, and psychological sanity—a norm from which one can deviate only at the highest price. Thus it might appear that the alternative scenario, that of the inarticulate, opens itself, like a huge chasm, only in the extraordinary and rare moments of excitement or flight of spirit. But is the inarticulate closed to the ordinary person? Is it a region to be feared, condemned? We hope to show that the danger of the inarticulate constitutes a large part of our thinking, that the lining of inarticulate sounds hides beneath the smooth surfaces of elaborate language. For there is no articulation possible or meaningful without this sudden scandal of the minimal.

Let us start, as we usually do, with the opening of our eyes, with the moment of the first contour, when by waking ourselves, we wake the reality. What could be more spaced yet connected than the vision of early morning in Paris, for example, with its rigorous pattern of streets and boulevards, which were designed by Baron Haussmann to protect and guard the social articulation of classes and economic interests with wide streets where troops could more easily impose the dominant discourse upon the rebellious element of margins? (Paris is a city where even the gardens and parks, areas of recreation and rest, have been dominated by a corset of geometrical design.) Paris wakes, writes E. M. Cioran:

> On this November morning, it is still dark: on the Avenue de l'Observatoire, a bird—just one—tries out its song. All at once, growls and grunts in the vicinity. Impossible to know where they are coming from. Finally I catch a glimpse of two bums sleeping under a truck: one of them must be having a bad dream. The spell is broken. I clear out. In the Place Saint-Sulpice, in the urinal, I stumble over a half-naked little old woman. . . . I utter a shriek of horror and dash into a church where a hunchbacked, squint-eyed priest is explaining to a dozen of disinherited of all ages that the end of the world is at hand and that the punishment of the Last Judgment will be terrible.[15]

This scene of waking begins with a double ambition: it wants to be the articulation of a new day, a new beginning, but also it aims at providing this beginning already with a highly elaborate level of articulation; the day begins with a bird's song. The attempt is at the same time tentative (the bird "tries out its song") but also clear; only one bird, so no danger of cacophony. Human attention completes this paradigm of animal articulation which humans have traditionally charged with various aesthetic meanings; the human "stop[s] and listen[s]." It is precisely this act of attentive stasis that turns a sequence of natural sounds into a song which otherwise would have to remain just noise; the human being, in an attempt at turning reality into a sense-making world, must, through care and attention, transform what is inarticulate into a readable message.

John Clare, himself threatened by the language of psychological crises, noticed one hundred years before Cioran that general principle of congruence between natural sounds and the human drive which turns these sounds into signals linking natural cycles with appropriate symbolic representation. In "Birds: Why Are Ye Silent," a poem written in the Northampton Asylum, Clare is evidently troubled by the lack of congruity between nature (spring-like in February) and symbolic representation of nature (despite warm weather, birds are not singing):

> Why are ye silent
> Birds where do ye fly
> Winters not violent
> Wi such a spring sky
> The wheatlands are green snow and frost is away
> Birds why are ye silent on such a sweet day[16]

In Clare the threatening silence, matched by the other absences of irregular spelling and lack of punctuation, is an encroachment of the inarticulate, perhaps of madness. This silence in Clare is replaced in Cioran by a noise—a series of sounds which obviously border on the inhuman but is not neatly separated from the human sphere. In Cioran the inhuman opens right next to the human: growling and grunting comes from the "vicinity." Whereas the articulate, or rather the human effort at transforming a neutral sound into the articulate, is clearly positioned, the inarticulate is vague and its source and location detectable only after a search. The inarticulate is concealed in three senses: it is physically difficult to spot (the bums are "under a truck"); the noise comes from underneath the reality as a part of a dream; and it is a bum that is a producer of the noise, that is, a marginal human being pushed to the outskirts of orderly discourse. As we can see, the day opens with a revelation of the articulation already disturbed by the inarticulate, by the logic of consciousness and aesthetics frustrated by the nonlogic of dream and bodily reactions of dreaming and growling. The list of these disturbances is longer: a half-naked old woman in a men's toilet and a hunchbacked, squint-eyed priest. For the writer, if not perhaps the reader, these are plainly images of distortion, the loss of order. As Cioran with his example strives to demonstrate, the articulate reality opens spaces of a very different character, territories which do not belong to anyone, which provoke horror not only by the Other's inarticulacy but also by rousing speechless revulsion in the reader: the philosopher surprised by the sight in the urinal utters "a shriek of horror." There seems to be no escape from the encroachments of the inarticulate: neither the low (the urinal as the theatre of body's sincerity) nor the high (the church as the space of the spirit and salvation) can offer us shelter, can exempt us from facing the inarticulate. The inarticulate is a disturbing link between the subject and the Other; beneath the ornamented and officially signed bond of the socio-aesthetic there is another bond scribbled in, the bond of the inarticulate.

The articulate and inarticulate contracts take as their documents the human body, but whereas the former tries to mask the body under the concepts and cogitations, the latter reveals it perhaps not in its nakedness but, more daringly, in its problematic character. For the revelation of the inarticulate, the starting point is always a suspicion that the link between word and thing is dubious and uncertain, and thus what is considered a most coherent description and naming could be exposed as a profusion of noises some would call "meaningless." Nietzsche in an early fragment "On Music and Words" discusses this issue precisely in relation to voice—which, in his theory, becomes not so much a carrier of meaning but the changeable substance of human life. According to Nietzsche, voice is the realm of human presence, but this presence has all the features of the grammatological absence: it marks but a trace of man's "primal cause" and has a semiotic character. In Nietzsche's diagnosis the closest one can get to a revelation of the human subject is to study the phonic substance of its utterance, but even this will provide us not with the subject but rather with its manifestations in the discourse.

> All degrees of pleasure and displeasure [*Lust und Unlustgrade*]—expressions of one primal cause unfathomable to us—symbolise themselves in the tone of the speaker [*Tone des Sprechenden*]; whereas all other conceptions are indicated by the gesture-symbolism [*Geberdensymbolik*].[17]

Later on in the same text Nietzsche will formulate a law according to which the relationship between the tonal structure (which for us will represent the inarticulate) and the word is parallel to the most fundamental connection between "our corporeality" and the "original phenomenon," namely the "will." However, what we have decided to call the "inarticulate" is responsible not for production of meaning on any scale, but rather for making such a production possible at all. Before the word is formed, it is grounded in the inarticulate, and only on the strength of this grounding can it function in the discourse of the logical. Thus, Nietzsche refers to *"Tone des Sprechenden"* as the "tonal subsoil" (*Tonenuntergrund*), that is to say, what lies under the ground and what provides the soil with the force to produce. The ground of the articulate is conditioned by the "underground" (with all its religious, philosophical, cultural, and political connotations) (*Untergrund*) which, in turn, cannot be revealed as it has to remain hidden in order to perform its function. In this aspect of being "unfathomable," *Untergrund* becomes also the ground, or rather the groundless ground of being; thus acquiring the features of the abyss [*Abgrund*]. We could say then that the *Totenuntergrund* is also the *Tonenabgrund* of Nietzsche's anthropology. Further, since the inarticulate is the groundless ground, the hidden undersoil, of words it is not available itself but only through a representation, through a sign, or as Nietzsche calls it, a "symbol." Thus the inarticulate can never be what it promises to be: it can never reveal itself as inarticulate, that is, lacking a sign, but is always mediated by a sign. Accordingly and henceforth, it will be more accurate to speak of minimal articulation or minimal articulacy. Nietzsche knows that it is impossible to stand outside language, and even his definition of truth presents this most venerable notion of 'philosophy as an army of metaphors'. His thinking does not aim at the inarticulate but tries to locate itself in the field of transition between the articulate and the inarticulate. For him the philosopher is the one who thinks always against the background of the inarticulate. So philosophy and human speaking must remain a most arduous defense of the articulate, but such a defense is effective and convincing only when the scientific precision is threatened by the ghost of the inarticulate.

Cioran is aware of this situation which, for him but not for us, divides philosophy down the line between writing and speaking. What is admissible in writing, as the domain of articulation, is not possible in speaking (where the inarticulate lurks as *Tonenuntergrund*). Hence, one can write death, the inarticulate, but one cannot say it, because by saying it one confirms life and articulation. Cioran writes: "I spend my time advising suicide in what I write and advising against it in what I say. This is because the first case concerns a philosophical issue; the second, a being, a voice, a complaint" (118). Like Nietzsche's "tonal subsoil" Cioran's speaking does not allow the inarticulate otherwise than through a negation. The inarticulate manifests itself indirectly, as what I can promote only by criticizing it, compromising its values, annihilating it. Nietzsche's writing—nervous, inherently contradictory, prolific, and restless—is centered round the problem of how to teach what has not ever been taught, how to represent what goes beyond representation—to write down the thought which is based upon a semiotically scandalous revelation that a thing and a word do not coincide, and that the most sophisticated intellectual structure could be nothing else but a cacophony of sounds. (In this sense the Superman and the Eternal Return are the highest manifestations of the inarticulate. Young Nietzsche jots down in his diary in 1868 and 1869 a note where the *Tonenuntergrund* suddenly acquires another meaning; *Untergrund* is here the realm of the dead and horrifying, the domain of terror which must be revealed in all articulated utterances: "What I am afraid of is not the terrifying figure behind the chair, but its voice. No, not the words, but the horrifyingly inarticulate sound of that creature. If only it spoke in the manner of human beings."[18]

Erich Heller interprets this passage literally as an example of the "terror of the inarticulate" to which Nietzsche's "orgy of wordmaking" testifies.[19] Nietzsche's epiphany is in fact another reworking of his philosophy of *Tonenuntergrund*: he is not afraid of words but of the tone and manner of their delivery which is clearly nonhuman. The philosopher reacts with dread to the fact that words suddenly melt into a phonetic magma, as in a children's game in which one word repeated many times turns into a meaningless cacophony or turns into another word. Thus it is not the fear of the inarticulate that motivates Nietzsche, but the fear of an articulate which can collapse any moment and expose the pretense of knowledge. If the ghost spoke in the manner of human beings it would have nothing to reveal or announce. It would merely repeat well-known, socially acceptable phrases—it would cease to be a ghost. The inarticulate, or rather as we see in the Nietzsche passage, the minimally or nonhumanly articulate, is the ghost of revelation which must speak from under the subsoil of tone in order to break into petrified formulae of language. The ghost that young Nietzsche saw behind his chair in Leipzig is an apparition of error, of the erroneous and marginal element pushed out of thinking, which must make its comeback. It is this return which will later become the Eternal Return, the affirmation of the world where being is replaced by becoming (not *Sein* but *Wesen*). Thus Heller's interpretation of this doctrine as "the world's only chance to become wholly articulate" (184) seems to miss the point, as the Eternal Return is an attempt at philosophizing from within the minimally or nonhumanly articulate. If Nietzsche came to be praised as a master of style, it is only because of the experience of the inarticulate which enabled him, inevitably through fear and Angst, to contain in his writing the abysmal (*Unter-* and *Abgrundlich*) possibilities of the minimally articulate which humans discover in and through the body.

In a list of instructions given to Lou Salomé, Nietzsche will link the question of style with the awareness of one's body. One writes and speaks well when one has discovered the "pleasure and displeasure" of one's instinctual structure (*Triebe*) which are detectable in the domain of the minimally articulate (*Tonenuntergrund*): "[In writing] Beware of the pause. Only those people are entitled to it who draw a deep breath in speaking as well. For most the pause is an affectation."[20] Cioran too knows that contemplation of the minimally articulate must involve a step toward the abyss, counteracted by the nostalgia for the word which is another name for excellence of style: "One does not withdraw one's confidence from words, nor violate their security without setting one foot in the abyss."[21] The minimally articulate, then, leaves the domain of socially accepted utterances; or, if it uses these, it is only after a terrifying experience of hearing the voice from behind a chair. It is only outside social discourses that the abyss could be thought and expressed. If articulation is insertion of an utterance into a network of contexts, then the articulation of the inarticulate is such an insertion into a context which cannot be specified, an insertion into the territory which defies easy contextualization and begs for the association with the sublime or supernatural. If articulation normally means appropriation (by means of speaking, I own a part of the familiarized world) the minimally articulate delays the law of appropriation and leaves humans suspended in the nothingness. To achieve this purpose the minimally articulate must abandon, or at least look with an ironic glance on, the social elocutionary exchange. As Antonin Artaud, probably the greatest philosopher of the inarticulate, maintained (summary by Danielle André-Carraz): Social words, consecrated by usage and tradition, known for their public utility, cannot speak this fundamental state that, for Artaud, is unique, incomparable.[22] To render this "fundamental state," Nietzsche will spend his life writing works in which the sophisticatedly articulate shows its origin in the *Tonenuntergrund*, but when in despair he would immerse himself in the language of Cioran's *clochards* and Artaud's *parias de la Pensée*:

Buatschleli batscheli
bim bim bim
Buatschleli batscheli
bim![23]

Birdsong

The minimally articulate, we have said, is the sublime hidden in articulate discourse; *Tonenuntergrund* is the subliminal lining of the logic of voice. This is not a separate factor in phonetic production, an element which can be put aside and classified as a danger zone to be avoided. It is inextricably intertwined in the very texture of voice—not another voice but a modification of voice. Nietzsche is bothered precisely by this modification of the tone of words—not by a secret, new language that would be accessible only to the initiate.

Hence, two provisional conclusions concerning the minimally articulate. First, it is a fundamental modality of the articulate with which it constitutes one spectrum of linguistic production. The inarticulate is a dangerous mode of the articulate, and vice versa; for the articulate is domesticated inarticulateness. According to Edmund Burke, the great power of the sublime consists in the fact that it precedes our thinking and exerts a formative influence on it: "Hence arises the great power of the sublime, that far from being produced by them, it anticipates our reasonings, and hurries us on by an irresistible force."[24] Nietzsche reacts to this overwhelming force of the modified voice from behind a chair, to the minimally articulate quality of words which are recognizable as words, but alien as the tone. Second, as we have noticed, the inarticulate must betray itself by and in the act of (minimal) articulation. Thus not only is it marked by a certain lack of loyalty to itself but also by excess: it has to overflow, exceed, its own sphere to become known, signalled, indicated. By the excessive character of his writings, Nietzsche shows that the minimally articulate comes not only at the beginning of thinking but also at its critical closing down: a complicated mesh of crossreferences and contradictory statements is a profuse manifestation of the minimally articulate as a critique of thinking through its abundance, repetitiveness, and self-reference.

This minimal may be defined by analogues and negations. It is strictly related to the eighteenth-century sublime—overplus of reality renders us speechless. As Peter de Bolla puts it, "When we enquire into the status of the sublime itself, into its sense of self, we note that it lacks a narrative, a history, a form in which it can be cast unless it resorts to the mobilization of the concept of excess, the overplus."[25] Thus, "The road of excess leads to the palace of wisdom" and "Excess revealed itself as truth" would, respectively, be Blake's and Nietzsche's formulae for the minimally articulate.[26] We are interested in the sphere where language is troubled by an enigma which is its condition and solution. Levinas describes such a revelation of the enigmatic and necessary Other as "illeity" and carefully emphasizes that to deal with it means to leave aside traditional visual metaphor of cognition (understanding as "seeing") and turn toward "hearing": "We hear this way to signify—which does not consist in being unveiled nor in being veiled, absolutely foreign to the hide-and-seek characteristic of cognition, this way of leaving the alternatives of being—under the third person personal pronoun under the word *He* [il]. The enigma comes to us from ILLEITY."[27] Levinas states that there is some modification in speaking which is "absolutely foreign to the hide-and-seek characteristic of cognition" (71), and which grounds each phenomenon. If we remember that we described the articulate as the basic model of scientific cognition, then it would appear that this "enigmatic modification" in voice is just what we call the "minimally articulate." In his study of the sublime, Burke also uses the concept of 'modification'—the "modification of power" that produces the sensation of danger. As Peter de Bolla notices, the very concept of modification has traditionally been associated with vocal production. Our own point has been that the minimally articulate is what undermines the power of human voice as the chief sign by demonstrating its belonging to another sphere. Lévinas supports such a point of view by claiming that what makes the enigma transcend the game of cognition is not its rejection of human epistemology but its way of operating on a different time level. Nietzsche's otherworldly *Tonenuntergrund* now acquires still another value: as *Untergrund* it is located on another plane from the *Grund* with different laws, of which the most striking is the law which introduces a time gap between the enigma and human epistemology. The human present cannot grasp the enigma (although it is expressed in the human present, in the same way as the inarticulate is expressed thus becoming the minimally articulate), because the enigma "does not lend itself to the contemporaneousness that constitutes the force of time tied in the present"—"it is already too old for the game of cognition" (71).

With the aim of looking for the traces of these modifications of and in voice, which reveal the nonhuman, enigmatic, and *untergrundlich* character of the temporality of the minimally articulate, we turn toward representations of birds. Let us begin again in Paris. Cioran in one of his walks through the city arrives at a bird market which becomes for him a splendid, almost Dionysian manifestation of life; not because of people, those who buy and sell, but because of birds, those which are seemingly mere objects of transaction:

> What power, what determination in these tiny frantic bodies! Life resides in this bit of nothing which animates a tuft of matter, and which nonetheless emerges from matter itself and perishes with it. But the perplexity remains: impossible to explain this fever, this perpetual dance, this representation, this spectacle which life affords itself. What a theatre, breath![28]

The theatre of birds is "impossible to explain." Nevertheless, the very rhetoric does not let us proceed as if nothing happened. Cioran repeatedly talks about the spectacle, theatre, representation. What begins as a triumph of the body and life unobservedly but inevitably becomes a triumph of semiotics. On the one hand, we have the absurdity of life which is animated by a "bit of nothing"; on the other hand, there is the ostensive function of dance, spectacle, breath, sound. Birds are for Cioran the embodiment of the paradox of the inarticulate which to become known must start articulating itself: a smooth movement from "nothing" to "something," of emerging and disappearing, which defies human measures of time. (When a human being dwells in a specific temporal segment the dance is "perpetual.") The nonhuman can be revealed as nonhuman only to the human and by means of the human system of understanding and communication: through becoming a sign. No matter how hard Cioran, or Nietzsche, would try to present the inarticulate, they are bound to resort to the articulateness of signs, since as Levinas argues, "The significations of nature are but the result of a transfer of meaning from the anthropological to the natural" (69). The essential thing is to be "perplexed," to locate meaning in the difficulty to explain, in the enigma which, however, is not a cosmic character but which always underlies each sign. Cioran dramatically expresses the existential principle of the inarticulate when he contends that the secret must remain hidden even to the one to whom it belongs: "What is to understand? What we have really grasped cannot be expressed in any way at all, and cannot be transmitted to anyone else, not even to oneself, so that we die without knowing the exact nature of our own secret" (95). To come down to biology from this level of generality, it is well to report what birdsong is a sign of: territoriality, sexual display, assertion of power.

For John Clare, birds represent another aspect of the enigma. They embody the secret of dwelling (illustrated by a whole series of poems dedicated to birds' nests) and of voice. The two facets of the philosophy meet where birds become an emblem of the voice whose location (unlike human speech) must remain inaccessible. In "The Landrail" the voice of the bird is a constant feature of the landscape, calling out "from day to day," accompanying humans in their labor ("we hear it in the weeding time"). Nevertheless, its source evades our efforts and ridicules attempts at finding; even the boys who "know the note of many a bird" are far from succeeding:

> They look in every tuft of grass
> That in their rambles met
> They peep in every bush they pass
> And none the wiser get[29]

The bird represents the unlocatable force of saying, the force of the nonhuman which cannot be defined otherwise than in most ambiguous terms: "we know tis something," "it surely cant be under ground / Nor is it in the sky." Still this minimally articulate voice hovers in the vicinity (like the nonhuman sounds in Cioran's Paris morning) protecting its secret:

> We know tis something but it neer
> Will blab the secret out
> . . .
> A mystery still to man and boys
> Who know not where they lay

The secret of the inarticulate is, however, generally observable, and the world exists to the degree to which it is permeated by an enigma which, as Levinas carefully emphasizes, "does not come from afar to obscure a phenomenal manifestation" (69). Similarly, Clare stresses the fact that the enigmatic bird which is no more than "something" and which protects its secret is a most common phenomenon:

> And yet tis heard in every vale
> An undiscovered song
> And makes a pleasant wonder tale
> For all the summer long

The most striking characteristic of the bird is that its carefully guarded secret of dwelling turns out to be no secret at all, for the landrail "lays without a nest." The calling voice is then a nonhuman modification of voice, because this bird dwells without dwelling, and efforts at locating a nesting place are futile from the very beginning. This contrasts with the human voice, which is always located in the subject who, in turn, lives to the degree to which the subject *builds* a home (such, at any rate, is Heidegger's point). So the voice of the minimally articulate cannot be reduced to one speaking mouth: the identity of such a speaking is withheld not in a sense that it is nonexistent, but in a sense that it imposes, through a complete lack of features normally associated with the identity (such as dwelling, personal name, individual grain of voice), a certain forgetfulness or amnesia necessary for the inarticulate to be both heard and, at the same time, unidentified. When the eggs of the landrail are found, it is, first, not as a result of the conscious operation of cognition but by sheer chance ("Yet accident will often meet/The next with its way"; "And mowers on the meadow lea/Chance on their noisey guest"). And, second, the very moment the traces of the bird are found, the one who has found it asks a question as to the name of the bird:

> And mowers on the meadow lea
> Chance on their noisey guest
> And wonder what the bird can be
> That lays without a nest

For Clare the bird is a sign of "that superior power" which transcends the limitations of the human time. In another bird poem he confesses that when surrounded by the birds which come "unbid" to "give their music to my pleasures," he feels

> that rapture which the world hath not
> That joy like health that flushes in my face
> Amid the brambles of this ancient place
> Shut out from all but that superior power
> That guards and glads and cheers me every hour[30]

In "The Moorhens Nest," he speaks about "the ancientness of joy" (220), thus evidently associating birds and their "modification" of voice with what Levinas will, over 150 years later, describe as the power of the enigma to transcend human cognition through its defying the measures of merely human time. We will remember that when analyzing the enigma the philosopher presents it as "too old for the game of cognition."

In the works of a modern naturalist writer, Annie Dillard, we find another vivid instance of the minimally articulate: the enigma which does not come from afar, but whose location has to remain forever in doubt. The world of Annie Dillard is dramatically an acoustic one, where the sound marks (with all the semiotic overtones of this verb) the unseen presence of something which defies our attempts at grasping by means of sight. On an August night, writes Dillard, "sounds fell all about me; I vibrated like still water ruffed by wind."[31] A birdsong is an interpretative notation which makes the phenomena of the world noticeable: "Birdsong catches in the mountains' rim and pools in the valley; it threads through forests, it slides down creeks" (105). Sounds produced by birds and insects reveal the phenomenon, a mountain or forest, not as new but as something which, in its familiarity, opens suddenly a hollow emptiness. A birdsong, a manifestation of the minimally articulate, hollows out a phenomenon, presents it as empty. Interestingly enough, "long lyrics [which] fly in the air" are not only signs of the absence unexpectedly disclosed in the sound normally taken for granted as a mere vehicle of meaning, but they demonstrate that phenomena link with other phenomena, thus constituting the world as we know it, the world of meaningful connections, and all due to the resonating chamber of absence and nonidentity suddenly disclosed in their known status. As Levinas puts it, "The gaping open of emptiness is not only the sign of an absence. A mark traced on sand is not a part of a path, but the very emptiness of a passage ("Phenomenon and Enigma," 65). This is what Dillard notices about the objects of everyday life when these are subjected to the minimally articulate: they acquire a new dimension which can only be described as that of emptiness.

> The mockingbird that nests each year in the front-yard spruce strikes up his chants in high places, and one of those high places is my chimney. When he sings there, the hollow chimney acts as a sound-box, like the careful emptiness inside a cello or violin, and the notes of the song gather fullness and reverberate through the house. (105)

The minimally articulate discloses in the phenomenon the "careful emptiness" which disturbs the usual integrity and identity of the object (a chimney as a modification of a cello or violin). The mechanism of this disturbance is that of unlocatedness and semantic chaos. In the former the temporal displacement plays the essential role: the song of a bird refuses to be understood in terms of the human now, as it is a sign of something Levinas called "too old for the game of cognition." Dillard, listening to her mockingbird, visualizes it as a voice of the process of development and evolution where looking for a meaning is an extremely risky enterprise. Dillard imagines, by a reversal of evolution, the bird as a lizard:

> I see its scaled legs and that naked ring around a shiny eye; I shrink and deplume its feathers to lizard scales, unhorn its lipless mouth, and set it stalking dragon-flies, cool-eyed, under a palmetto. Then I reverse the process once again quickly; its forelegs unfurl, its scales hatch feathers and soften. It takes to the air seeking cool forests; it sings songs. This is what I have on my chimney. (105)

So the writer is justified to claim that the song of the bird is "a modified lizard's song"—"a wild, utterly foreign music" (106). The descriptions are significant: the minimally articulate is what comes to us from within the careful emptiness of the phenomenon (or word) bringing, as in Clare's philosophy of birdwatching, a disturbance within the sense of the familiar and domesticated. The birdsong bothers Dillard's sense of dwelling through its characteristics which defy any specific location (geographic, temporal: "the crickets have been calling their own tune . . . since the time of Pliny," 217; or musical: "the frogs added their unlocatable notes, . . ." 217). In other words, the inarticulate, as manifested in birdsong, fills the word with enigma, or as Dillard says, with "plaintive mysterious urgency" (217). This urgency implies that the force of the inarticulate cannot be easily evaded, at least not without a high price of the total humanization of the world.

Dillard's passage on spring inscribes the problematic of the birdsong in a wider scheme of translation. The lyric of a mockingbird, like the French word *oui*, signifies a foreignness which cannot be totally domesticated by a move toward another language. Such an automatic equivalent-finding process is not a genuine translation. The automatic process may be based on the principle that my language makes sense whereas all other discourses are mere "gibberish." A more capacious translation requires a cultural re-imagination of the other, an act of learning new senses which will have to remain never adaptable to the very end, which will always preserve the residue of the "wild, utterly forgotten music." So we read about Dillard's first approaches toward French: "I realized that I was going to have to learn speech all over again, word by word, one word at a time—and my dismay knew no bounds" (105). This is precisely the position of the inarticulate in language; it is this mysterious urgency which abolishes the systematic truth of language, the truth of wholes and units (like sentences), and returns us to the level of microunits which do not simply add up to form coherent clusters of meaning. The inarticulate operates on the plane of subversive elements which undermine the stability of the system (linguistic or political), like a particular sound or a syllable. It is interesting to note that the first and primal objection of writers unsympathetic to Nietzsche and to avant-garde literature, was the disintegration of complete sentences into fragments and syllabic crumbs.

Dillard, responding to the song of the mockingbird, actually believes that the power of dispersed crumbs of phonetic production has the ability to preserve meaning, meaning which "will never make sense in our language but only in its own" (107), thus once again reiterating the main significance of the inarticulate. This is what signals that the language is not ours, and that our functioning in the language is a never-ending, and sometimes not fully conscious, work of translating the "mysterious urgency" into the human sense which can remain human only when it discloses the acoustic sublime. One can provisionally identify the inarticulate with the articulate for the purposes of scholarly classification and identification of scientific phenomena; empirical students of birdsong do this. Our wish here is to understand the sense of the inarticulate which opens in a phenomenon the possibility of "careful emptiness." A good example of where the empirical and the philosophical come together is in one of the methods of identifying birds used by birdwatchers—where the sounds of a bird are turned into human words. The eastern towhee "says" (the verb *sing* is often replaced by the verb *say*) "Drink your tea," while a yellowthroat asks "Which is it? Which is it? Which is it?"[32] The ornithologist warns us not to believe that the bird actually says these things, indicating that the method could be used only as a classificatory vehicle; whereas the sense of the song seems to go beyond human semantics. Thus we are told that, although for some the chestnut-sided warbler says "Good morning to dear teacher," to others it is "I wish to see Miss Beecher," or even "I'm very pleased to meetcha!"; still the sense of what remains inarticulate, or rather what has been made minimally articulate, is not in words but in the length and rhythm of the typical chestnut-sided warbler's song. It is thus rhythm, the disturbing force of orality described in the philosophical analyses of Henri Meschonnic, which is to be found in a birdsong which "threads through forests."

Exclamations, Cries, and Other Transgressions

The inarticulate disturbs the coherence and unity of the system which is now seen not as a static structure but as a movement between the sense in my language and the sense which is reserved to the language of the Other. (At this point: no longer a monologue, not yet a dialogue.) We saw how a birdsong opened a possibility for the phenomenon to reconstruct its identity through "careful emptiness." We saw also that one human response to the challenge of the minimally articulate is to rethink the temporal in a constant movement between the proprietary moment of the now and the abysmal time gap which defies the human measure: Dillard reverses the process of evolution visualizing the bird as a lizard only speedily to bring it back to its form. It is this movement between the extremes that seems to be characteristic of the inarticulate which is never in the state of rest but which is the motor element of thinking. The inarticulate is not a nonsense but a countersense; if it operates on the level of units which do not "make" immediate "sense" it is only to make thinking possible by allowing language to slip into silence, by maintaining operations of the voice. As Meschonnic puts it, "Also the nature of language has a horror of the void. Also the phoneme, which modern structural science has deprived of sense, fills itself back up with sound."[33]

We might now claim, accordingly, that what has been minimally articulated has already been supplied with a sense, even though this sense defies our everyday understanding of the term. This power of voice to sustain itself vis-à-vis the dulling repetitiveness of sentences, the power of alertness and attentiveness, care and solicitude, is the sublime in language. Finishing the first division of the analytic, Immanuel Kant turns toward a birdsong to demonstrate that the regularity and artfulness of man-made music quickly exhaust themselves by producing, in effect, the sense of fatigue and boredom. A birdsong brings for the philosopher the unexpected, which is not lurking hidden in silence, but rather is articulated in a manner which defies the routine measures of human articulation. It is important that the birdsong is not illogical or chaotic, it simply actualizes a sound pattern difficult to subsume under the usual concept of (aesthetic or political) 'ordering'. So the vocal production of a bird must seem brutally trivialized when rendered in terms of the potential human-language equivalent. What constitutes the birdsong is its untranslatability into human articulation. Kant writes:

> Even birdsong, which we cannot bring under any rule of music, seems to contain more freedom and hence to offer more to taste than human song, even if this human song is performed according to all the rules of the art of music, because we tire much sooner of a human song if it is repeated often and for long periods.[34]

Kant associates the semantically "empty" song with freedom and gratification of taste, but he also extends its operation to the domain of the body—introducing another dimension to his concept of the 'beautiful'. The satisfaction described by the philosopher is not merely derived from the subject's feelings—"There can be no objective rule of taste [:] The basis determining it is the subject's feeling and not a concept of an object" (79)—but from its exchange with the Other which cannot be imitated or reproduced. Such a reproduction would inevitably annihilate the effect Kant is describing:

> And yet in this case [birdsong] we probably confuse our participation in the cheerfulness of a favorite little animal with the beauty of its song, for when bird song is imitated very precisely by a human being (as it is sometimes done with the nightingale's warble) it strikes our ear as quite tasteless. (94)

The sense of the minimally articulate is then doubly erroneous. First, it is produced by the subject's attunement to the Other (thus, turning sense making into a communal operation); second, it is "confused" as to its classification (it is not the song which is "beautiful" but our "participation in the cheerfulness"). Such a sense must necessarily go beyond the restricted version of the subject's sense-making activity: not only is the subject deprived of its central position in these operations, but also it is misled in its own estimate of its own reactions. The sense that the subject makes of itself is shown as fragile, restricted to certain models of reality. What makes sense in the articulate human song does not in the inarticulate birdsong.

Such an ambiguous positioning of sense is characteristic of the aesthetic category of the sublime, which Kant himself defines in the following way: "The sublime is what even to be able to think proves that the mind has a power surpassing any standard of sense" (106). So for Kant the sublime is that element of our thinking (Kant insists on ascribing it to the sphere of human reactions, and not to the characteristic of an object) which defies thinking itself. The sublime is the power to make sense despite the apparently raging nonsense. In our terminology the sublime would be another name for minimal articulation, or the pervasive and stubborn power of the voice to be heard not *in* but *despite* the words which seem totally to domesticate and encapsulate it (Kant also talks about birdsong as the domain of liberation).

Meschonnic, without recourse to the concept of 'sublime', also refuses to consider mere voice treated musically, the semantically empty voice, as the embodiment of the nonsensical or irrational. Such an assumption must result from acknowledging the possibility that there can be voice without language. We agree with Meschonnic. The minimally articulate assumes, through the very act of its articulation, a sense-making potential: voice without sense. "Is there voice without language?" Meschonnic asks.[35] His answer is decisively negative. Even in the experimental productions which tend to dissolve the semantic charge of voice (Meschonnic uses Schoenberg and Berio as examples; we could include Jackson MacLow and his activity in the field of experimental poetics) where the voice is reduced to "cry, babble, the chanting of grand opera" (275), the lack of sense is but another mode of making sense. This mode Meschonnic calls "allegorical":

> The want of sense is an allegory of sense in language. The want of sense still speaks of sense. This is an irony of language. It is quite as much a parable of the end of sense as it is of the beginning of sense. There are these margins of language, where voice is (or seems) at the verge of leaving language.[36]

In such a passage, Meschonnic approximates the sublime without naming it. For him it is rhythm and tonality which carry the signification of the speaking subject. The apparent nonsense of voiced babble, on the boundary that separates language from nonlanguage, is the equivalent of what Kant calls the "colossal," something "almost too large" (Kant): what defies articulation and can still be articulated is another description of the sublime. Meschonnic also ascribes to voice the attributes of a highly literary rhetoric: a shout is an "allegory" of sense, a "parabole" of the place where the end and the beginning of sense meet. It follows that in keeping with his views Meschonnic disclaims a treatment of the oral element as a mere negation or alternative to the written; the oral is an important overcoming of the dichotomy spoken-written: "The oral isn't any longer simply the spoken, and orality has a greater literary than linguistic value" (Meschonnic, *La rime*, 283). In keeping with Kant's analysis of the oral, the minimally articulate is what goes beyond the articulate in the same way as the sublime surpasses the beautiful. It is the allegory of sense, a representation of a certain confusion; where, according to Kant, "art is almost confused with nature" (180). Allegory is what permits us to present the unlikable by the likable, to combine the harmonious with the discordant.

In his version of the sublime, Uvedale Price makes much of this allegorical power to combine and confuse the two realms:

> The most beautiful and melodious of all sounds, that of the human voice in its highest perfection, appears to the greatest advantage when there is some degree of sharpness in the instrument which accompanies it; as in the harp, the violin, or the harpsichord: the flute, and even the organ have too much of the same quality of sound; they give no relief to the voice.[37]

This brings us to the singing voice. With the view of tracing the margins of language in cry and babble, we turn toward a domain of song as the intensified form of physical presence. We put stress on the term *form* in this definition because obviously in very many cases the sense of presence has nothing to do with a physical agent, a singer, being present at the moment when the song is enacted by means of recording and playback. The term *form* describes a way in which the song exerts its power upon the listener to reconstruct the fictitious presence of the singer. The singer marks a vitally important, but vacant, position in the sequence of sounds, the position in the musical discourse which must be filled. It is not the physical singer who marks a presence in the act of listening, but a singer-effect necessitated by and in the sounds. Whereas in the reception of a written text such a form of presence is more difficult to detect, partly due to the problems associated with authorship as well as intricacies of the problematic of intention, in a popular song such a presence is strongly motivated by what we may call the "blurring" of the word. Derrida commenting upon Artaud notices that when we want to abolish the domination of the written text, the way to do it is not by means of the annihilation of the letter, but by its subjugation to the illegible.[38] To read the letter into the illegible seems to be the Artaud-Derrida project, which seems not so much to get rid of presence but to remove and reshape it in another form. Such a project is at the heart of the popular song.

In John Lennon and Paul McCartney's "She Loves You," the sounds, "yeh, yeh, yeh" do not invite chaos, do not erase the articulated sounds but blur them, remove the sharp contour of precise phonetic and semantic senses. This is also true by a general rule of a stage performance where words, even if originally meant to be articulated, are usually thwarted and suppressed by amplification regressing toward the level of sounds.[39] In the Beatles song, the "yeh, yeh, yeh" functions as a parody of the articulate or full word "yesterday" rendered in such a way that it slowly disintegrates in the massive attack of sound: "Well I saw her yesterday-yi-yay." The quotation illustrates a general principle of the popular song according to which a word does not cease to exist but falls into the domain of forgetfulness: in a song, words do not disappear but become forgetful of themselves. The terminology is here overtly Nietzschean, but so is the diagnosed situation. In his early book on the birth of tragedy, Nietzsche constantly reiterates that the Dionysian principle of intoxication (*Rausch*) is only a metaphorical description of the process of desubjectivization, or the annihilation of the self presented by the philosopher as self-forgetfulness. These two mechanisms, blurring and forgetfulness of the word, foreground the minimally articulate as one element of song. It is produced on the basis of the regressing word, just as Artaud's theatre of cruelty is produced against the text-dominated theatre. Inevitably the concept of the 'body' must reappear in our discussion. The song, like Artaud's theatre, dwells on what is minimally articulate because it is constituted in the fissure between presence (of the body) and its absence (language, a record replacing a performer). The body represents presence in the world of the popular song, especially in live performance, but here this representation comes under a specific form, evoked by blurred words, whispers, shouts, screams. Popular song makes an extraordinary call for performance, audience, and response, precisely because here more than elsewhere in culture the word exceeds its status of sign and tends toward the body which is its source.

Through voice in popular song, a new form of presence is constituted, a presence which is to be created by the listener, without whom the song cannot exist and through which the listener makes a self into a speaking subject.[40] This is accompanied by the whole phenomenon of stardom where a fan imitates an idol in the way of dressing, manners, and speech, thus virtually transforming into a subject, the subject which is real through its unreality, present through the absence of the imitated singer. All these points converge in Meschonnic's theory of rhythm, according to which

> Traditionally, sense is what counts most in language. And the idea of sense, by its history and constitution, is the greatest obstacle to the theory of language. Empirically speaking, language never ceases overflowing sense, overflowing sign: by means of body, gesture, intonation, rhythm. . . . To speak of the music of poetry is to act as a ferryman moving outside of sense, unaware of this overflowing, which is an overflowing of signficance. . . . Because with language it is always a question of significance. Even and perhaps especially when sense escapes, or gets lost. What escapes is a force. This is the subject's force.[41]

When we are speaking about voice we speak about the figure not so much of presence, but of the power of transgression *(débordement)* which makes itself felt through an absence, not absolute emptiness, not even a trace, but forgetfulness, the feeling of something which has been lost. What has been lost is not here with us, but neither are its traces; what is lost exists in our effort aimed at finding it, and thus, through the absence, constituting our status as subjects. But as Meschonnic says, it is always a question of "*signifiance* as *débordement*" in which absence becomes a form of presence, and where voice brings us not to sense but to the body. We come back to the voice which says "yeh, yeh, yeh" or the voice which says "Aa!!" This repetition of the beginning ("A"), the impossible redoubling of the first move (if doubled then no longer first) forces us to begin anew.

Aa!!

In 1826 Adam Mickiewicz published a collection of poems which is an emotional travelogue of a trip to the south of Russia. The trip was not a totally private undertaking, as it occurred during Mickiewicz's exile from Vilnius and in itself was instigated by General de Witt, a Russian intelligence officer in whose custody Mickiewicz remained at that time. The acoustic rhetoric appears very early in this sequence of sonnets. Toward the end of the first sonnet, "The Akerman Steppes," the visual recedes before the aural:

> Stójmy!—Jak cicho!—Słyszę ciągnące żurawie,
> Których by nie dościgły źrenice sokoła;
> Słysze kiedy się motyl kołysa na trawie,
>
> Kędy wąż sliską piersią dotyka się zioła.[42] (11. 9–12)

> [Let's stop!—What silence!—I can hear cranes
> Flying high beyond the reach of falcon's eye,
> I hear where on a blade of grass a butterfly sways,
> Where, with a slippery breast, a snake touches herbs.]

What occurs in the lines is a specific, almost Heideggerian, validation of silence which does not mean absence of sounds but a resonance which informs us that we belong to a particular place; cranes, which cannot be seen but heard, relate to man from within their element, air. The lack of voice marks a situation of expulsion or exile and stigmatizes the place of such an absence as uncanny. We learn further on that the poet "strains his ear" (*ucho natężam ciekawie*) to hear a voice from his native Lithuania and, when nothing is heard, he desperately commands the party to continue their trip. Whereas animals can, in the Heidegerrian sense, "dwell" in the world producing sounds, the human being remains mute—forgetful of a dwelling; no voice from Lithuania reaches the poet's ear.

Julian Klaczko, an admirer of Mickiewicz writing later in the century, meditating on a passage from Alexander von Humboldt's *Cosmos* in which the philosopher claims that all human affection toward nature must inevitably evoke sadness, formulates his own judgment:

> When the human soul feels hurt in its most subtle attachments, where it sees the disintegration of the ideal which it lived, then a sudden desire to become subjugated to nature is awakened, and our spirit huddles to nature's bosom like a child huddles to its mother's when people have hurt it. A defeat in one's hearth: this is the reason of all emigration.[43]

The law of emigration which Klaczko prompts us to consider is very attractive for our meditation on voice. We become exiles when we have suffered a collapse of the sense of dwelling, when we can no longer speak from within our territory, our dwelling place. After we become exiles we may still speak and write, but this production will be voiceless, will be the effect of either ego games (the mid-century exile, Cyprian Norwid, called it "personalism") or social convention (Norwid's "assimilation"). As it appears from Mickiewicz's sonnet, an emigré is a person who cannot hear his dwelling's call and who, displaced, cannot call out himself (the home place is a resonating chamber of voice). How does a person, such as Mickiewicz with his Lithuania, go about finding a dwelling, that is, the possibility of a voice which is not owned in terms of appropriation but in terms of values shared with a topography and community?

The Crimean Sonnets proclaim the Hölderlinian truth that shelters are built near danger. In the fifteenth sonnet, called "A Path along the Czufut-Kale Abyss," the protagonist makes light of his guide's warning and looks into the bottomless chasm:

> Mirzo, a ja spojrzałem! Przez świata szczeliny
> Tam widziałem . . . Com widział, opowiem—po śmierci,
> Bo w żyjących języku nie ma na to głosu.
>
> [Mirzah! but I did look! Through the chinks of the world
> And I saw there . . . What I saw, I'll tell—after I die,
> Because in the mortals' speech there is not voice to match it.]

The world is seen no longer as a systemic, smooth, monolithic whole, but as a cracked, folded space, and the cracks and crevices allow for a knowledge which one may describe as peripheral or abysmal (in the next stanza the thought "drops . . . towards the depth of chaos"). The problem again builds itself up round the question of voice: the traveler does not claim that he *will* not relate what he has seen, or that he cannot do so; instead he makes us a promise that he will tell us what he has seen through the chinks of the world if he finds a proper voice. The voice in question is conscious of death: it cannot belong to the sphere of the living. To find one's voice must therefore mean to uncover death amidst one's life and amidst one's speech: a language that belongs exclusively to the living can never be mine. How are we supposed to understand these moments of death suddenly opening in the cracked surface of speech? It is not dead silence, neither is it the silence of death; the Pilgrim speaks, and he promises to speak more in the future. Death, in this context, is an inarticulate cry, when the utterance does not remain restrained to the level of the linguistic, does not form a part of a semantic and syntactic whole, but operates on the level of disclosure involving the speaking subject's body, gestures, and setting. A shout overflows the speaker's body but remains part of the body.

What Mickiewicz describes in these terms in sonnet 15 is tested in sonnet 5, "View of the Mountains from the Kozlov Steppes," in response to the mountain of Czatyr-Dah. The peak has made its appearance elsewhere in the cycle. In sonnet 13 Czatyr-Dah is presented as a political and religious superior: it is a "Padishah" of mountains whose oriental splendor of rich adornments, a turban "embroidered by lightnings," is not a mere show of brutal power, for the mountain is also an interpreter, a mediator between humans and gods. This mediation has the role of witnessing, an attentive and speechless listening. Czatyr-Dah remains forever "deaf" to human success or suffering; his concern is to "listen to what God says to his creation"—"*słuchasz tylko co mówi Bóg do przyrodzenia*" (l.14). It is this interplay of deafness and listening that interests us here. How is it possible to be deaf and an attentive listener at the same time? The very adjective *gluchy* (deaf) appears at least two times more in the sequence. In sonnet 12, Mickiewicz refers to a night which is "deaf" ("*w dolinach noc głucha*") which implies speechlessness and silence dominating the scene; and in 6, the adjective qualifies the abandoned walls of the Khan's palace slowly eaten up by greenery ("*głuche ściany i sklepienia*") with a prevailing element of desolation and loneliness. So *głuch*y combines the element of a physical defect (inability to hear) with a particularly sharp awareness of language. It is strikingly evident in sonnet 12, where in the "deaf night" the "air speaks to the heart in the voice secret to the ear" ("*mówi do serca głosem tajemnym dla ucha*"). The "air," the most immaterial of elements, does the speaking, and the voice addresses itself to the "heart," that is, in this romantic discourse, to the very essence of humanity.

Thus when Czatyr-Dah is described as "deaf" then what comes to the fore first of all is its readiness to hear not a mere speech, but the speech for which the mortals find no word, the inarticulate discourse of "what God says to his creation." What gets formulated in the sonnet is a certain philosophy of things according to which objects do not remain passively locked in their entities but spill over their contours in the act of attentiveness; they go beyond the restrictions of their identity and become mediators. How does a poet respond to the thing that has overflown, an object which no longer functions within the limits of meaning? Let us return to the sonnet where the mountain is again shown as the epitome of elevation, seat of thunders, eagles, winter, and rapid streams; where the response is hidden in the spillage, in the overflow of the poetic form, in what goes beyond the frame of genre. The Pilgrim responds to Mirzah's description of the glory and horror of the mountain with a prolonged "Aa!!":

Widok Gór Ze Stepów Kozłowa
Pielgrzym i Mirza

Pielgrzym

Tam? czy Allach postawił ścianą morze lodu?
Czy aniołom tron odlał z zamrożonej chmury?
Czy Diwy z ćwierci lądu dźwignęli te mury,
Aby gwiazd karawanę nie puszczać ze wschodu?

Na szczycie jaka łuna! pożar Carogrodu!
Czy Allah, gdy noc chylat rozciągneła bury,
Dla światów żeglujących po morzu natury,
Tę latarnię zawiesił śród niebios obwodu?

Mirza

Tam?—Byłem; zima siedzi, tam dzioby potoków
I gardła rzek widziałem pijące z jej gniazda;
Tchnąłem, z ust mych śnieg leciał; pomykałem kroków,

Gdzie orły dróg nie wiedzą, kończy się chmur jazda,
Minąłem grom drzemiący w kolebce z obłoków,
Aż tam gdzie nad mój turban była tylko gwiazda.
To Czatyrdah!

Pielgrzym

Aa!![44]

[View of the Mountains from the Kozlov Steppes
Pilgrim and Mirza

Pilgrim

There? Did Allah raise a wall of frozen foam?
Or for his angel hosts rear a throne of clouds?
Or did the gods lift half a hemisphere
To keep at home the caravan of stars?

The summit flames. Istanbul on fire!
When night spread out her cloak, did Allah
Hang up a lantern in the sky to steer
The worlds that roam through the sea of nature?

Mirza

There? I know that region.—Winter lives there?
And streams and rivers drink from its cold plain.
Where storm-steeds pause and curb their madness,
I've breathed the air which even the eagle fears,
And there with only stars above my head,
Where thunders sleep without their wild hurrah
This is Czatyr-Dah!

Pilgrim

Aa!!]

It is the nature of this exclamation that draws our attention here. We notice that the naming of the phenomenon that stuns the Pilgrim is withheld until the end of the poem. The list of questions asked by the wanderer is not, in fact, accompanied by answers but only by a series of personal recollections (the guide tells the Pilgrim that he actually visited the distant place but does not disclose its name). Czatyr-Dah cannot be simply named because it is the object overflown, a witness of the "voice of God" and thus a name which in everyday transactions is not employed. A name can only be an adjunct, an addition to the poem. The answer "This is Czatyr-Dah" is given when the poem has ended. It does not appear simply at the end of the poem, but after the poem, in the fifteenth line of the fourteenth line form. The Pilgrim's

"Aa!!" comes then as a spilling over of a spilling over: when the object has been revealed to us as it is (and merely as it is named) our response has to go beyond the articulated language of questions and answers. The "Aa!!" transgresses not only the form of the sonnet, but also leaves behind articulated language, coming not as a primeval unformed sound but at the other end of the spectrum; this is what follows the highly elaborate and painstakingly constructed aesthetic (a sonnet) and epistemological (questions aimed at achieving certain knowledge) cogitation. It is worth noticing that the exclamation is deprived of any phatic function; it is placed at the end of questions and answers and is an utterance where the harmony between the individual (modal) and social (communication, speech) is established. It is the moment where the individual goes beyond the limitations of its privacy without falling into a trap of becoming exclusively social. Like Meschonnic's rhythm, voice is in this case intimate but not private. It is also the territory where the public sphere remains clearly present (the poem is a conversation, after all); but it does not subject the individual to the discourse of truth usually arranged in the form of catechism (a question followed by a clear answer).

In "Aa!!" the subject positions itself in the world by means of two basic mechanisms: repetition (or echo) and rhythm. The doubling of "A" signifies that the ejaculation is not a mere incident but an extended production, a process. Let us add quickly, this is a process which does not begin (despite the "A" which is the first letter of the alphabet) as its very doubling makes the beginning impossible: nothing can have two beginnings. The repetition of the "A" locates us already in the middle; whereas collaborative comprehension (*comprehension commune* is the phrase in Meschonnic) can and must have a beginning and ending, minimal articulation can belong only to the domain of the middle. Rhythm is not a mere musicality (as Meschonnic has shown) but a play of margins: the "A" is a "first" letter of the series, but by this very fact it stands on its periphery. So does the exclamation mark, again doubled, but it closes the series. And still this double repetition and double rhythm (of the letter and the punctuation mark) signifies only to the extent to which it defies any specific meaning. We know from its positioning in the sonnet that it does have a sense, but in a way it subverts it at the same time, rejects a suggestion of being inscribed into the structure of sense. (It stands outside the form of the sonnet and outside the series of questions and answers.) As Derrida puts it on the margins of Lacoue-Labarthe's work, *"la rythmotopie ouvre la possibilité du sens intelligible, elle ne lui appartient pas."*[45] It is this not belonging to sense that characterizes minimal articulation, governed by the law of rhythm which is the law of the "peri-rationnel" (Meschonnic), of the peripheral and regional. Through the law of rhythm, the minimal of literary voice refuses to be subsumed in the centrality of the total.[46]

And yet the mechanism of the "Aa!!" goes beyond a mere repetition, or rather it plays on the written mimicry of letters to compromise it: the doubling of the "a" and "!" occurs only in print, on a piece of paper, whereas voice will melt the boundaries between the letters and sign replacing them with one prolonged utterance. The repetition of letters is a parody of what the uniqueness of the exclamation was to be: it was to mark the going beyond and over the name that can be repeated endlessly. Hence, if we are talking about the rhythmical aspect of "Aa!!" we must remember that, as Meschonnic points out, "repetition is not rhythm. . . . As the psychoanalysts wished it to be. Because repetition is one limit of rhythm. An illness of rhythm."[47] Minimal articulation plays, then, both on the written and on the spoken; it capitalizes on the potential for repetition and mimicry of the former and uses it as a background for its own subversive activity aimed at destroying the general, total, and centralized pulse of repetition and replacing it with the regional gestures of the body.

CHAPTER 3. Early Modern Speaking Subjects

Grammatical and Legal Position of the Speaker: John Donne and René Descartes

No longer is it possible to hold a strict parallel or synonymity between voice and the subject. The subject speaks, but this speaking is changed by the reverberation of other voices, which means that the first voice is not thoroughly or only its own. The power of the Other participates in the subject and locates the subject as actualizable only in exchanges with the Other. So there can be no theory of the subject without the theory of the Other. Levinas: "The relation with the other is not an idyllic or harmonious relation of communion, nor is it a sympathy by which we put ourselves in the other's place, rather it is external to us; the relation with the other is a relation with a Mystery."[1] The alterity of the Other is so difficult to admit, and to trace, that we may tend to swerve back to self-analysis or a minute focus on acts of thought separate from pronouns or speaking subjects. René Descartes was not immune to such avoidance of dialogue:

> [S]ince nature seemed to cause me to lean towards many things from which reason repelled me, I did not believe that I should trust much to the teachings of nature. And although the ideas which I receive by the senses do not depend on my will, I did not think that one should for that reason conclude that they proceed from things different from myself, since possibly some faculty might be discovered in me—though hitherto unknown to me—which produced them.[2]

Cartesian consciousness is here the only agent of purity, calling into question the possible false pretenses of nature, but this very consciousness is not a well-mapped territory. There may even be an entire faculty of outwardness hitherto unknown! The natural world and other selves might be Descartes after all.

One task of philosophy, particularly in the period since Descartes, is to produce a map of the self, or to use Charles Taylor's term, the *sources of the self.* One possible approach is to think in the categories of anatomy—to draw an anatomical chart of consciousness. Descartes says, "When reasonable soul shall be in this machine, it will have its principal seat in the brain" (101). The reasonable soul in the machine is like a cartographer who can assume placement external to the space to be drawn; maps of selves and worlds in this period increase the sense of the objectivity of knowledge. In this respect, Descartes' anatomical reflection is comparable to early collections of navigational charts like Lucas Waghenaer's *Mariner's Mirror,* first printed in 1584 at Leyden but quickly translated into many languages. A century after Waghenaer another Dutchman, Samuel van Hoogstraten in his treatise on art (1678) claims, "How wonderful a good map is in which one views the world as from another world thanks to the art of drawing."[3] All very well with souls and with harbors, but with social mapping involving speaking subjects, how legitimate may it be to assume placement external to the space to be drawn?

Though now in question, the cartographical image for seventeenth-century experience is not exhausted. Terra incognita is still at issue: just as a cartographer masters possible fear of the unknown by careful mapping, a writer may externalize frustrations and experiences by the gridwork of rhyme and poetic structure. John Donne in "The Triple Fool" imagines a parallel between the earth filtering water and poetic measure taming unruly life:

> Then as th'earths inward narrow crooked lanes
> Do purge sea waters fretfull salt away,
> I thought, if I could draw my paines,
> Through Rimes vexation, I should them allay,
> Grief brought to numbers cannot be so fierce,
> For he tames it, that fetters it in verse.[4]

Drawing, in its double sense of producing a picture and pulling through, is a filtering activity disciplining psychology (bringing it "to numbers") through the silent work of rules, scales, instruments of measuring. Such a work is, though, disturbed by the Other, by voice as the Other:

> But when I have done so,
> Some man, his art and voice to show,
> Doth Set and sing my paine,
> And, by delighting many, frees againe
> Griefe, which verse did restraine.

The intervention of voice is fundamental. The subject comes to awareness of itself only through this voice of the Other which removes the subject's emotions from underneath a protective and disfiguring layer of poetic form. Voice spells the movement against the restriction and enslavement of the subject in its own productions, but it is always the voice of the Other that can fulfill this task. In this way the Other becomes a necessary part of the subject, even as it frees the fierceness of the subject's experience to be re-experienced. Voice must, then, signify a fundamental danger or at least uneasiness for the vulnerable speaking subject. Voice in this role is the realm within the subject where the subject can be traced but not mapped, heard but not drawn, intuited but not rationalized.

Compare Descartes on the danger of voice. Descartes systematically blocks the external assaults on his senses, but he still must rely on a conversation with a voice from within:

> I shall now close my eyes, I shall stop my ears, I shall call away all my senses, I shall efface (*j'effacerai*) even from my thoughts all the images of corporeal things, or at least (for that is hardly possible) I shall esteem them as vain and false; and thus holding converse only with myself (*m'entretenant seulement moi-même*) and considering my own nature, I shall try little by little to reach a better knowledge of and a more familiar acquaintance with myself. (157)

Such conversing, which gives knowledge of self, must introduce a division into a seemingly coherent structure of the subject; this splitting, implemented by voice, turns all self-knowledge into a very tentative and uncertain undertaking (*peu à peu*). For Descartes, the subject is at this stage a temporary constellation subsumed under the first person singular but threatened by the Other represented as voice: one feels the threat when he asks, "I myself, am I not at least something?" The subject, that particular "thing which thinks" (*une chose qui pense*) is unconcealed by the mode of a double withdrawal—first the leaving of the world by blocking eyes and ears, second the leaving of "myself." A few pages later Descartes will recapitulate this second movement by saying that his is "not a subtle air . . ., a wind, a fire, a vapour, a breath," to conclude that "I only leave myself certain of the fact that I am somewhat." (These *somethings* and *somewhats* intensify the lack of positive description.) And yet "it cannot be that when I see or when I think I see, that I myself who think am naught" (156).[5] In the third meditation, Descartes approaches this question of the subject by stating that he may be "something more": perhaps the perfections he attributes to God "are in some way potentially in me, although they did not yet disclose themselves, or issue in action" (167). This not yet is what interests us here: the subject in Descartes' philosophy is the boundary between the I and the not-yet-I. Through the not-yet-I the subject opens the possibility of transcending itself and rejects tight closures of either grammatical or economic-legal character, those areas of organized knowledge and possession: "my self."

That the seventeenth century felt the plurality and ambiguity of the subject is evidenced by a sectarian experience of the Quakers and Ranters in England. Conceiving of the human self as a receptacle of Eternity, they hit upon an elaborate system of naming and renaming whose purpose was to show how difficult it is to capture the seat of an "I." If the Cartesian self is homeless, in the sense of being never fully disclosed, and also invaded by the not-yet-I, the Ranters' self is trapped in the plurality of names. To find a way out of this predicament Joseph Salmon, in his *Heights and Depths* (1651), suggested the need to introduce a roman "J" (to render the inner self) and an italic "I" (to express the physical aspect of the human being):

> To declare to all men what J am not, only in what "I" am not: if thou Reader are so wise as to discover my spirit by what I shall here declaim, thou wilt spare me the labour of making an after profession of my faith, which "I" confess "I" shall hardly be drawn to declare to any man.[6]

This subject must be made public, in order to link public and private knowledge, but this is possible only through denial of what is publicly available. The subject is thus a denial of the I, but a denial performed through the linguistic code that only the I has mastered. If we followed the logic of Salmon's argument, the subject—the inner self, the J—cannot be pinned down, since the very moment it is declared it ceases to be what it is. Salmon uses a strongly performative "declare," here, calling forth the J which appears only through what it is not, the I. *Declaim* follows *declare* and seems to reinforce it. It implies a loud voice and an audience, but the verb seems also to carry the undermining undersense of unclaim.

There is a similar uneasiness concerning the grammatical and legal position of the first-person pronoun in Donne's "The Legacie":

When I dyed last, and, Dear, I dye
    As often as from thee I goe,
Though it be but an houre agoe,

And Lovers hours be full eternity,
I can remember yet, that I
    Something did say, and something did bestow;
Though I be dead, which sent me, I should be
Mine own executor and Legacie.

I heard mee say, Tell her anon
    That my selfe, (that is you, not I)
    Did kill me, and when I felt mee dye,
I bid mee send my heart, when I was gone,
But I alas could there finde none,
    When I had ripp'd me, and search'd where hearts did lye;
It killd mee againe, that I who still was true,
In life, in my last Will should cozen you.

Yet I found something like a heart,
    But colours it, and concerns had,
    It was not good, it was not bad,
It was intire to none, and few had part.
As good as could be made by art
    It seem'd; and therefore for our losses sad,
I meant to send this heart in stead of mine
But oh, no man could hold it, for twas thine.[7]

The speaker's death has turned him into his own executor and legacy. He is equally agent and object of an action. He belongs to the past as a victim and to the present as an executor. He is also the legacy to be distributed. He is caught in the toils of the law as self-killer, victim to be dissected, legacy to be distributed in the name of society. So this I survives its own death only to become its own anatomist. A crucial turn occurs here, for the very heart of the victim is not there ("I could there find none") because it has already been taken over by the Other. At the heart of the I there is always the "Thou," and the subject is precisely this relationality located between the two pronouns. The subject is a transient event hovering on the threshold of consciousnesses. This I observes its own acts as the acts of another: "I heard mee say . . . my self . . . did kill me . . . I felt me . . . I bid me." We can see how this contrasts with the Cartesian stance. For the French philosopher the main purpose was to "converse with myself" to gain self-knowledge. The subject was a strategy in which the I was domesticating the Other—the Other who could not be anything more than a version of the original I. For Donne, by contrast, the fully dialogic, separable, external Other is paradoxically at the heart of the I. For Descartes no confusion of pronouns is thinkable. For Donne, a functional but disconcerting disarray within the grammatical sphere is essential: "my self, that is you, not I." The I does not have a heart, cannot live otherwise than through the thou; even the substitute heart is not a stronghold of the I: "I meant to send this heart in stead of mine, / But oh, no man could hold it, for twas thine." Donne's Other is a lover, that most intimate of dialogic partners; Descartes' Other is a theoretical construct. (Still, it defines Donne and his era that he is not able to imagine the woman's reply or point of view within the dialogue.)

Descartes' "first maxim was to obey the laws and customs of my country" (122) so his thinking subject is loyal to the law. Donne's speaking subject is more vexed in its legal standing because it cannot execute a legacy: the object to be donated to the heir is false, "something like a heart . . . made by art," and it is already owned by the person to whom it should be given ("twas thine"). This subject as lover, which we have already shown to be both victim and killer, is apparently nonessential with regard to the law—the law cannot deal with an uncentered subject. So Donne's speaking subject must function on the margins of the law even though it uses legal concepts (legacy, executor) and tries to meet the demands of the code. Despite the fact that the document signed by the subject sanctifies a fraud ("my last will should cozen you"), the whole procedure involved in executing the will leads to a new knowledge of the subject. What begins in the honesty of passion turns into a legal fraud to bring about more self-awareness. The subject actualizes itself through the margins of the law, loopholes of regulations and codes. It is the I that signs documents in full knowledge that no signature can bind the I to the Thou in minimal dialogue. The poem's little fiction, its hyperbole, is that lovers are so nearly one that documents, communications, even separate pronouns are unnecessary.

Thou is embedded in the very weave of I. So my voice, the epitome of my identity, is necessarily a voice of the Other. The figure of this strangely reverberating voice, in which words are barely not identical with themselves, is echo.[8] The essential feature of this figure is that it forms an acoustic palimpsest in which one pronouncement is not distinguishable from another and several meanings occur at once.

Such a mode of utterance does not have a decidable speaker; we deal with two or more speakers in a ceaseless dialogue or choral work of voices. The Other is at the end of "my" voice, whereas "my" voice is already penetrated by the voice of the other. One could say that communication is possible to the degree that I is effaced by Thou, which in turn constitutes the very center of the I. George Herbert used an echo in "Heaven" from *The Temple* (1633):

> Who will show me those delights on high?
> Echo. I.
> Thou Echo, thou are mortall, all men know.
> Echo. No.
> Wert thou not born among the trees and leaves?
> Echo. Leaves.
> And are there any leaves, that still abide?
> Echo. Bide.
> What leaves are they? impart the matter wholly.
> Echo. Holy.
> Are the holy leaves the Echo then of blisse?
> Echo. Yes.
> Then tell me, what is that supreme delight?
> Echo. Light.
> Light to the minde: what shall the will enjoy?
> Echo. Joy.
> But are there cares and business with the pleasure?
> Echo. Leisure.
> Light, joy, and leisure; but shall they persevere?
> Echo. Ever.[9]

Echo locates the Thou in a position of authority; it is the Other of my voice that knows the answers to my questions. This authority comes not entirely from the outside, but is contained within the questions asked by the interlocutor. The very identity of Thou is revealed already in I's utterances: "Who will show me these delights on high? / Echo. I." The identity of Thou is the result of the erasure and effacement of I's voice. Thus the figure of echo undermines the very concept of 'originary voice', subverts its meaning, and turns the discourse from a logical to a paralogical argument.

Paralogy is dissensus, a state of never-settled conflict, a litigation between voices that play different language games.[10] Here is yet another difference between the Cartesian and Donnean subjects. The Cartesian self, in its stress on translatibility of various discourses into one language of science, believes that discourses are replaceable and any harm can be repaired by increasing the precision of description. Donne's subject, and Herbert's with its echo voice, know that the rules of one discourse (this of the I) are not those of the other discourse (that of the Thou). The Donnean subject knows that the I has already been taken over by the Thou. For this reason, the damage is accompanied by the inability to prove the damage. It means endless litigation for the speaking subject in English Metaphysical poetry.

The issue of translatibility takes seventeenth-century conceptions of voice all the way from language theory to theology. Donne takes up the issue in his meditation "Upon the Translation of the Psalmes by Sir Philip Sidney, and the Countess of Pembroke His Sister." This poem opens with severe restrictions placed upon naming, the never-ending task of matching a signifier with a signified:

> Eternall God, (for whom who ever dare
> Seek new expressions, doe the Circle square,
> And thrust into strait corners of poore wit
> Thee, who are cornerlesse and infinite). (388)

The poem continues by raising the problem of the lack of identity between voices translated and translating: Donne's phrase *division of tongues* brings up associations with the Tower of Babel, that primal scene of the philosophy of translation viewed as an ontological practice. The division of tongues is, for Donne, inherent already in each individual subject and bears a metaphysical sanction; God inflicted the diaspora upon humanity, and yet, on the positive side, through such a mismatch of languages human creativity achieves its highest perfection. Poetry of the biblical Psalms, in Sidney, is a work of "a cloven tongue" but nonetheless puts "the highest matter in the noblest forme." If the speaking subject's voice is necessarily "cloven," then Donne cannot forget that it was two English people, a brother and sister, who produced an exquisite version of the Psalms. What, in the language of the Psalms, seems unified was actually produced by the ceaseless dividing force of linguistic production:

> As thy blessed Spirit fell upon
> These Psalmes first Author in a cloven tongue . . .
> So thou hast cleft that spirit, to performe
> That worke again, and she it, here, upon
> Two, by their bloods, and by the Spirit one.

The subject is here represented—as in the echo voice examined above—as dwelling in the back-and-forth process of translation in which the I attempts to render the Thou which speaks in the I's voice; and v(o)ice versa. In Donne's philosophy of the subject as translator, it is not only the linguistic element that is subjected to the law of translation, but also the ontological. God is a supertranslator whose task is to translate humans from nonbeing into being, and thus the subject is represented as a translated translator:

> So though some have, some may some Psalmes translate,
> We thy Sydneyan Psalmes shall celebrate,
> And, till we come th'Extemporall song to sing,
> (Learn'd the first hower, that we see the King,
> Who hath translated those translators) may
> These their sweet learned labours, all the way
> Be as our tuning; that, when hence we part,
> We may fill in with them, and sing our part.

The lack of fundamental unity and harmony constitutes the subject, but God's prowess as a translator may be an image of what speaking subjects may aspire to, once free from the exclusive rule of the I inherent in the limitations of grammar and law. Though infinitely lesser, literature and translation are other images of freedom from narrowly defined identities.

Scenes of Parting: Donne and the Metaphysical Poets

History begins with the scene of parting. The reflection on the past or future implies a rethinking of the now-problem-fraught present. The scenarios may involve a discovery that the present could be constructed on the basis of the past, as in Thomas Cole's early-nineteenth century paintings on the course of empire—warning Americans with ruins of European cities; or they may involve a discovery that the past itself is a construct of the present, that historical facts are imaginings. Jacques Derrida's claim that since *écriture* has been revealed as a mode (but by no means essence) of human being, the present can be looked upon only as a provisional construction of a semiotic character, adds new elements to scenarios of Nietzschean skepticism. Because each human being is already invaded by absence and death and distance, inevitably a historical mode of being accompanies each speaking subject. Nevertheless, such a critical history is mute, "a silent work of quotation marks and italics" (Derrida).

When we start to articulate history, even if this history is only minimally articulate like a sigh or tear accompanying a sentimental parting, we imply a certain awareness of distance, comparing now with then or later on. Because we cannot fully identify with now, now is precarious. Thus we are always in a scene of parting. Such a philosophy which begins as travel compulsion (we depart even before arriving) must privilege wandering as its trope. It is banal to remember that Nietzsche was a traveling philosopher who advises us in *Ecce Homo* not to trust any thought that occurred to us while sitting and who believes that sedentary life is a sin against the Holy Spirit. Even Descartes' *Discourse* is a travel diary: "All that time I was in Germany" (116); "As I expected to be able to achieve this [ridding oneself of one's opinions] more readily by talking to other men than by staying shut up in the stove-heated room where I had had all these thoughts, I set out on my travels again" (125); "Exactly eight years ago this desire (not to be taken for what I was not) made me resolve to move away . . . to this country [Holland]" (126). In Descartes the motivation of incessant trips is that they promote a better knowledge of one's self, the illusion of lived history which despite obsessive chronological precision ("exactly eight years ago," "nine years past by") must remain a fable-history for and in a self always separated from itself by the Other.

The self of seventeenth-century poetry in Donne, Crashaw, Herbert, and Marvell approaches history through the analysis of weeping which crowns the scene of parting, the scene of valediction. The context of love poetry in which the parting is inscribed implies breaking, or at least problematizing, that unity which "make[s] that, which was nothing, All" ("A Valediction: Of Weeping"). But such a parting is inevitable since the subject incessantly relives the presence of the Other within, shuttles, travels between the I and Thou to the degree that there is no other option but to identify oneself with the Other ("Our two soules therefore, which are one," as Donne puts it in "A Valediction Forbidding Mourning"). Nevertheless, to speak of such an identity presupposes a distinction between I and Other; thus parting, with constant journeying, belongs to the very structure of the self. The self is what passes between the I and Thou, courser and cursor retracing its own steps and writing down scripts of parting.

Such a situation where the subject is thrown and formed (deformed, reformed) in the subtle space between the identification with the Other and its constant negation, where the Other is formative and deformative, in- and misinformative of the subject, puts history itself in a difficult position. If this presence is shown to be of a very special type which suspends its arrival and is thinkable only as a "coming" which is always on its way, a delayed signified which never arrives, then the very notions of the 'subject' and 'event' must be redefined or put under erasure.

> Come [*Viens*] beyond being, it, engaging perhaps in the place in which *Ereignis* (no longer can this be translated by 'event') and *Enteignis* unfold the movement of propriation, comes from beyond being and calls beyond being. . . . "Come" cannot come from a voice or at least not from a tone signifying "I" or "self." . . . "Come" does not address itself to an identity determinable in advance. It is a drift [*une dérive*] underivable from the identity of a determination.[11]

History is formed by what we say in the scene of parting which confronts us with a necessary and inevitable departure and arrival, but no proper determination—"addresses without messages and without destination," Derrida says of such scenes. But there must be a way of telling this parting which forms human history; there must be a way to notate the oscillating movement.

Such a vision of the compression of history is found in John Donne's "The Annunciation and Passion": on 25 March, 1608, Lady Day coincided with the Crucifixion, so life occurred simultaneously with death, "fast" with "feast," "coming" with "going." The history of a day is made by the fact that it has been invaded by death. As L. Elaine Hoover has written, Donne and Quevedo are master historians of this invasion:

> As major representatives of their time, Donne and Quevedo articulate the basic Baroque obsession with death's invasion of all aspects of life. In the Baroque, we also find that the metaphorical association of death with parting, physical separation . . . reflects an acute sense of loss, and awareness and consequent fear of its unavoidable absoluteness. . . . Baroque poetry of absence in love often emphasizes the logical corollary of absence in life.[12]

What consequence does this have for human time, which remains measurable? Impossible to deny the precision of that date: 25 March, 1608. The date cannot be questioned, and yet as Donne says, it is "doubtful." This doubtfulness has nothing to do with Cartesian methodological doubt: it is not the I that doubts. The I is a part of this "doubtfulness" because it is the ambiguity, the dazzling brightness and darkness, of the compressed history as the only possible history of the subject, that makes the subject's telling of a personal story possible.

Later on we learn that God "hath made" creation "one period" with the last judgment (11. 36–38). If life is doubtful then the subject must fall victim to the same anxiety. In the same way as the subject was the "airy nothing" between the I and Thou, now his life is shown as suspended between ("all betweene") "coming" and "going." Let us not simplify: what is at stake is not a crude metaphor for life's restriction points of birth and death. What concerns us here is human time and history. The history of the subject is a multiplication of absences and partings. The invasion of death is a repetition of nothingness folding upon itself.

The day is doubtful not because it cannot be chronologically catalogued, but precisely because it can, and then the question must arise "What has actually happened?" Let us listen to Donne's answer:

> this doubtful day
> Of feast or fast, Christ came, and went away;
> She sees him nothing twice at once, who's all;
> She sees a cedar plant it selfe, and fall,
> Her Maker put to making, and the head
> Of life, at once, not yet alive, and dead (11. 5–10)

The historical event is what is seen despite the fact that it cannot be seen ("she sees him nothing"). What is more (or perhaps shall we say, less), this nothing which should not be seen even once is evidently (what could be less evident?) seen twice. Neither is the event unique (as a linear, chronological version of history believes). Instead, the event takes place (but obviously, to use Rilke's phrase, "without taking place"—as it is nothing) "twice" and "at once" which belies even the cyclical theory of history where events do repeat but never "at once." The present tense of Donne's intellections is not incidental: Our Lady "sees" (not "saw"), because what constitutes the subject matter of the text is the analysis of being, the analysis that reveals being as proliferation of absences, a growing density of parting, a palimpsest where one "nothing" is graffitied onto another absence.

The event thus takes place eventually; it does occur, but we can never pin it down. The event happens "all betweene" "coming" and "going," in the same way as the subject is actualized "all betweene" the I and Thou. History is then a description of the nothing which announces something, and that nothing which comes when the something is dead. History is the story of the life of what has not been born and died, of what in Donne's profound phrase is rendered as "not yet alive, and dead." Hence we do not know what actually happened; we can only know what happened eventually. We can know what was initiated *as voice* (the Annunciation), what was heralded and dictated by the voice (the Annunciation is a paradigmatic situation where future events are viewed as bound to happen under the dictate of the voice; the Jonah story is equally powerful in this respect), what was foreseen as a future, but what we can see only as a past. "He shall come, he is gone" (1.39) is Donne's formula for this model of history.

The final couplet suggests also an economic interpretation of this reading of history: the event is "not yet alive, and dead," "to come" but "gone," a double absence or nothingness, yet it is this nothingness that provides the subject with a stock of commodities (wholesale market; "gross") to be reached for and distributed in particular occasions (retail market):

> The treasure then, in gross, my Soul uplay,
> And in my life retaile it every day.

The event is absent but has the power to regulate individual lives in the same way as the economy of the invisible, removed and stocked goods regulates the consumer's life. Within this event, within this double nothingness, moves about the individual who, by making his own decisions, participates in what has already happened (economy, God's plan for salvation), helping to actualize it, even if the individual choices may be dictated by one's reluctant attitude toward the event. (In case of economy, I may object to this or that product, but still I will buy something which, even though it seemingly disrupts the chain of consumerism, eventually strengthens and restores it. The detours of my reluctance may thus help to introduce modifications, but will not cancel the event of the market economy. The Jonah story is a religious master pattern of such a situation: Jonah evades God's command, travels in the direction opposite to that required by Voice but nevertheless, eventually, helps to actualize the original plan for the event).

But then a stubborn question returns: Things happen to us, but who is us? Here the answer remains in keeping with the reading of history as "nothing" seen "twice at once." The subject to whom events happen, but who is also in a strange manner active in this process, can only be described in terms of "all betweene." It refuses to be permanently located or positioned in one place not because, like the Cartesian ego cogito, it wants to know the thinking I by encountering the Other, but because it is the Other and yet can define itself only by reliving the gap which separates it from the Other. In this sense Donne's "Abridgement of Christ's Story" is still of another valour: it deprives man of history (I am the Other, thus nothing comes between the I and Thou and there is no space where history could appear; the archaic use of "abridgement" links it precisely with deprivation, as in Abraham Lincoln's phrase about the "abridgement of human liberties"), but it also insinuates the inevitability of the rift, a fissure between the I and Thou where history is exactly the mode in which the I tries to recapture the thou.

Here we should note that the word *bridge* constitutes the central part of *abridgement* which allows us to interpret this concept as 'a-bridge-ment'—the process (the prefix *a-* conveys the meaning of an ongoing activity) of constructing bridge(s) which activity is a mode of human being (the a- also attributes to the word that follows the quality of a manner, as in saying something *aloud*). At the same time, this activity is fundamental (a- is a clear beginning marker) and, ideally, ought to lead to its cancellation: when the unity is achieved no bridge is needed (the a- also conveys a negative determination as, for instance, in the words *a-historical* and *a-chromatic*).

The subject who listens to the Voice announcing the event is thus locatable only in between positions which she (Virgin Mary) cannot take, not because she rejects them, but because they are accepted without the exclusive identification with either of them. Richard Crashaw in "The Weeper" says,

the virgin mother stay
Reclus'd at home, Publique at Golgotha.
Sad and rejoyc'd shee's seen at once, and seen
At almost fiftie, and at scarce fifteen.[13]

What Crashaw sees as human madness in rejecting God can also be considered the maddening situation of the impossibility of locating the subject whose being is unquestionable.

O, madness! the savage miracles of human madness!
There is no place for him without whom there is no place.

Such a subject, whom we must describe as active in a strange manner (the subject who is pregnant with the public meaning and yet closed in her virginal separateness) is a part of the general event structure. The subject is a receiver (buyer) of a commodity but also, in turn, becomes a commodity itself: "Gabriel gives Christ to her, He her to John" (l. 16). In a word, the subject is not full, Donne writes, "Not fully a mother."

Another way to put it would be if the subject's being is this dramatic multiplication of nothingness, and the formula for its being is "not yet alive, and dead" (the I lives by the promise of the Thou which is, as we have seen, the I's heart, and yet the very separation spells death to the announced, heralded subject), then we also deal with a perpetuation of death and the subject must be the scene of mourning.

The theatrics of weeping are extended over the whole of human being and cover the erotic (in Donne's "Valediction: Of Weeping") and the religious (in Crashaw's "The Weeper"), the economic (again "Valediction: Of Weeping" where tears are coins), and philosophical (in Andrew Marvell's "On a Drop of Dew" where a tear gets a strong neoplatonic underpinning). To mourn is to actualize the self bereft of the Other who remains encrypted in the I as its originator and destination point. The encryptment is a funeral terminology, but death does not stop the process of exchanges, of restless shifts of ownership and production. Since authentification by the face of the Other requires the making external of the Other, parting and mourning must be inherently present already when the joy of identifying seems to be complete and overwhelming. Hence Donne weeps not in the absence of the woman but in her presence:

> Let me powre fort
>
> My teares before thy face, whil'st I stay here
> For thy face coines them, and thy stamp they beare,
> And by this Mintage they are something worth.
> ("A Valediction: Of Weeping")

Even when "forbidding mourning" Donne does it not to propagate the sense of presence, but of absence (l. 15) which invades even moments of sexual union: "So let us melt, and make no noise" ("A Valediction: Forbidding Mourning").

It introduces departure:

> As virtuous men pass mildly away
> And whisper to their soules, to goe.
> ("A Valediction: Forbidding Mourning")

However, as Patricia Garland Pinka reminds:

> To "goe" [is] a phrase that can mean "to experience a sexual climax." Further, the man describes the couple's disintegration at parting with the word "melt," a common term for "to experience orgasm."[14]

The tear is, philosophically, the representation of being as parting and, geographically, the representation of the world as the scene of parting.

> On a round ball
>
> A workman that hath copies by, can lay
> An Europe, Afrique, and an Asia,
> And quickly make that, which was nothing, *All;*
> So does each teare
> Which thee doth wear
> A globe, yea world by that impression grow,
> Till thy teares mixt with mine doe overflow
> This world, by waters sent from thee, my heaven dissolved so.
> (ll. 10–18)

The encryptment is of diverse character. It is not only entombment but also pregnancy ("each teare Thee . . . weare, . . . pregnant of thee"), not only interment but also impression; in the latter we should hear not only the overtones of coin minting and fascination, but also of "vague ideas, imprecise observations," as in "I have an impression that," or even forcefully levied service, as in "the navy impressed people to man its ships." Nowhere is this overarching quality of mourning more visible than in Donne's phrase "Weepe me not dead" ("A Valediction: Forbidding Mourning"). On the other hand, it draws upon the geographical metaphor where the tear is a figure of the disaster of flooding ("overflow"), the dangerous excess ("over-") which threatens the order of reality. On the other hand, if the subject wishes to remain alive, to survive the scene of parting (in this sense being is inevitably surviving, and a profusion of disaster literature in the seventeenth century especially in countries exposed to natural cataclysms, such as Holland, is a telling testimony of this fact), he must be wept, as it is only to the extent to which his face is preserved in the tears of the Other that he is entitled to being.

This mode of being, under impression and in the impression, is another version of being "not yet alive and dead"—of belief that "Death and conception in mankinde is One" ("The Annunciation and Passion"). This postmortem reality which Donne ascribes to the subject is the state of being "not dead" rather than simply "alive" (Donne's instruction, in this case, reads: weep because only through mourning you can bring back this nothing which I was by the separation from the thou; weep, as it is only mourning which can keep me "not dead").

It comes to us as no surprise that Marvell refers to weeping as to a distinctive feature of humanity ("For others too can see; / But only human Eyes can weep [from "Eyes and Tears"]), and endows tears with values exceeding those of economy (sea trade), sexuality (pregnancy), and beauty. From "Eyes and Tears":

> Not full sailes hastening loaden home,
> Nor the chaste Ladies pregnant Womb,
> Nor Cynthia Teeming shows so fair
> As two Eyes swoln with weeping are.[15]

Mourning is, through a persistent association with encryptment, doubly ambiguous. It is involved in parting as dying, and the "impression" that mourning undertakes to carve is an inscription on a tombstone. Also it belongs to that other aspect of parting which marks a new beginning, or another beginning represented by commercial and imperial conquests of the new world and the adventure of human sexuality. The attractivity of new contents and the female body meet in the fascination with cartography and eroticism.

We saw how in Donne's "Valediction: Of Weeping" the act of inscribing or impressing a "round ball" with continents changed it into a globe, a mini-world, approximated the shape of the well-rounded belly of a pregnant woman. In "The Good-Morrow" love "makes one little room an everywhere" in the same way as a cartographer, through his operation, "quickly make[s] that, which was nothing, All." Vermeer's painting provides a masterful formula for this facet of mourning: an apparently pregnant woman reads a letter (already a significant sign of absence) in front of a big map of Europe. The woman and the map are two prominent figures of mourning which orchestrates its sad music round the nothing at the center of both of them: whiteness of paper and dark emptiness of the womb.

But, as we have said, such a mourning marks another beginning. The stress on pregnancy is not only an expression of the interest in eroticism but tries to render the position of the subject in the world where things cannot be methodically organized; indeed, things chaotically reflect one another, produce and reproduce their own likeness. If humans have been created by God as his image (and thus separated from the divinity), then human tears are the image or "offspring" of humanity, but this image, in turn, is pregnant with the reflected likeness of the Other (the face reflected in a tear). This series of pregnancies must inevitably question the absolute finality of one of them. Even God does not seem to be a closing point of this circulation of images as the weeping, the product of the "pregnancy" of human eyes "coined" by the Other's face, returns to God as if reflecting divinity itself. Compare the famous Baroque trope of tears flowing upwards, most strikingly elaborated by Richard Crashaw in "The Weeper" but also appearing in Marvell's "Mourning."

Weeping is then consolatory and ecstatic, funereal and erotic, natural and sophisticatedly artificial. (Images of "pearls" and "jewels" recurring in the context of tear poems emphasize this double intention: a pearl is a "natural" product of a shell but, at the same time, a highly elaborate ornamentation when it comes as part of a necklace.) To find a general formula for this kind of mourning, Marvell wrote

> What in the world most fair appears
> Yea even laughter, turns to Tears.
> ("Eyes and Tears")

Mourning is apparently a highly ambiguous operation, with the abundance of meaning, which will take over especially those activities which seem most distant from it. Weeping is what eventually must appropriate our individual histories because it is the master event of human history as the self, the object and agent of history, of the subject which is "all betweene" the I and Thou.

In "The Annunciation and Passion" Donne pointed at navigation (itself a child of geography and cartography) as a model activity where the position of the subject can be determined only by the adherence to a changeable star, not to the "selfe-fix'd Pole":

> As by the selfe-fix'd Pole wee never do
> Direct our course, but the next starre thereto
> Which shows where th' other is (ll. 25–27)

In "Mourning" Marvell finds yet another trope for this activity: mourning is an act of the woman, belongs to the sphere of the feminine, and thus the truth of weeping is a woman. Marvell sees mourning as a cleansing operation ("whatsoever does but seem / Like Grief, is from her Windows thrown"), a consolatory act ("those precious Tears / Would strow the ground where Strephon lay"), an amorous stratagem or subterfuge ("pretending Art . . . only to soften near her Heart"), and a self-centered act of autoeroticism ("she courts her self in am'rous Rain"). Similarly, Charles Cotton sees woman's weeping as a potential trick: tears accompany "Sweet sorrow dressed in such a look / as love would trick to catch desire."[16] Mourning is evidently closed to hermeneutic efforts. It is a succession of interpretative interactions, none of which can lay claim to finality. The dream of determining the ultimate and unique sense of mourning must remain a dream as such a meaning could be established only at the expense of a total unification of the I with the Thou—which is untenable because it is the difference between the two that constitutes the subject and thus puts an end to mourning as well (has not Marvell decided that "only human Eyes can weep"?). What would be left in such a situation is nothing but a mourning of a mourning, a weeping over weeping, a tear reflected in a tear.

CHAPTER 4. Bardic Voice: Vestiges of the Oral and the National

Every Polish schoolchild absorbs without instruction the national anthem with its negative syntax, "Poland Is Not Yet Lost," and every Polish schoolchild is made to memorize the opening, "O Lithuania!" of the national epic, *Pan Tadeusz* (1834), where Adam Mickiewicz addresses the lost ancient heartland of the nation. Every American schoolchild learns to pledge the flag, to sing "My Country 'Tis of Thee" and also "The Star-Spangled Banner," with its strangulating pitch changes. Some few go on to college where they read and enjoy other national texts like Allen Ginsberg's "America, I'm putting my queer shoulder to the wheel" and his laments for the loss of America in "Howl" and "Wichita Vortex Sutra." The difference between the Polish children and the American children has until recently been heartbreaking, for with the exception of the period from 1921 to 1939, for the last two hundred years there was no independent Polish nation. A nation with a proud language and literature and a tradition of passionate idealism has had to make up for the lack of autonomy with representations of the nation in *Pan Tadeusz*. Americans have never had to suffer a daily national life where to such an extent the impalpable literature—made up for, supplemented, and atoned a deficiency of the palpable. However, in the age of multinational corporations and the global movement of capital, when Poland is ready to give up some of its infrastructure to foreign companies and America is erecting barriers to keep out German, Japanese, and other industrial giants and purchasers of real estate, there is at least the possibility that decentered Poland and centered America will become more alike—as bases for multinational capital accumulation, sources of labor and consumption. Liberal economist Robert B. Reich, stumping the U.S. for his ideas, repeats his war cry for the abandonment of national presumption, "We no longer know what the pronoun 'we' means or who is 'us.'"[1]

Earlier chapters in this book, developing a minimal philosophy of voice, have focused on the perplexities of the solitary self, as voice gets past various resistances to dialogue with at least one lover or neighbor. The present chapter traces, across several historical instances, a national presumption in literature, one that still has some claims to life and currency in a world where nationhood is in new ways emergent (Lithuania, Soviet Georgia, Poland), in new ways residual (Myanmar, Angola, Nicaragua, the Russian Republic, post-colonial U.S., and England). This is the maximal end of the philosophy of voice. Our name for this national presumption, and the rhetoric it brings with it in the literary sphere, is *bardic voice*. The literary bardic operates in a more deluxe and mediated way than pledges and anthems, of course; but, reduced and drained since the time of Thomas Gray and Adam Mickiewicz, the bardic continues to operate in a bourgeois public sphere as defined and periodized by Jürgen Habermas and others.[2]

From our stereoscopic view from both sides of a dissolving geopolitical line or curtain, the topic of nationalism is dangerously fraught, and it may be well to admit here that even its most glorious and stirring cultural products have for us an ugly underside. Nation is at least as much a negative as a positive notion. What was a magnificent gain for Russia in 1831 was the loss of Poland; that one example of a terrible price paid may stand for European and American nationalisms of all sorts and their disastrous results for humanity. The bardic, as a mode of representation, is a myth of national memory. We study it here in its difficulty and decline not to approve the romantic nationalism it carries, but to show forth the foundations and history of a kind of writing that brings voice into the public sphere—a genre directly political and historical, in a hopeful if pitiable relation to existing power. New Critical and other more recent scholarship of poetry has tended to focus on interiorized lyric to the neglect of these more directly historical works of art, and that indeed is also part of the difficulty of the bardic: scholarship's withdrawal from any idea of the nation in an era when nations are mass murderers. To examine this not-yet-dead literary ideal and the national ideal behind it, which is also by no means abolished but in fact insurgent and in some places rampant, is not in all instances to approve what is being studied.

The first difficulty of the bardic is its literariness, a written-down and secondary mode of existence that is fully recognized by all the writers we consider—from anonymous temple scribes at Delphi to Allen Ginsberg putting his queer shoulder to the wheel to help America. This difficulty, where things become for us worthy of analysis, may be phrased as follows: How does this secondary mode legitimately claim some attributes of primary communication—speech genres, speech acts, at work within the citadel of writing? The next difficulty is historical and derives from the movement further over time from the origins of nationhood. Selectively we show some episodes of turning points in this historical process. Unconnected to the history of nations, yet pertinent here, is the attenuation over time of the relation of speaking to writing. When taken together historically, these two declinations have made thoroughly suspect earlier claims for the power of poetry, to the point where by the end of our century bardic voice is one of the possible historical options least speakable, and thus a seeming dead end, absolutely noncanonical. How did we come to a moment in literary history where the kinds of power that used to be transacted between poet and audience—oracular, Orphean, or bardic energies hanging in the air over a nation at a moment of danger—are impermissible modes of illegitimate presence?

Since *Of Grammatology* a generation ago, philosophers and literary scholars have doubted the orality of oral speech and the metaphysics of oral presence that was assumed by all previous generations, which privileged speaking over writing. Abandonment of that myth of presence was correct and long overdue. Nonetheless, it remains on the agenda of theory to study how and why voice as presence in the former sense endured so long, and to rethink the problematic of the human voice as a metaphor or guise of self and of nation, in the very same text. What is there in that long history of text making and speculation that can still be defended as logical, possible, productive? One of the most direct ways to confront this issue is by examining the voice that seems archaic and original in ancient writing. Archaic voice in Greece and the Semitic lands is so old it claims to be transmitting from the real presence of divinity. The word of Apollo and of Yahweh is inscribed on the stone or the page, and we face profound questions of scholarship in determining how it got there.

In his monograph "On Divine Places," Jean-Luc Nancy has shown how inescapable are ideas of divinity in the philosophy of an era of professed unbelief.[3] We would not wish to escape such ideas, since their relevance to questions of voice must be the starting point of this chapter's survey. Here we will re-examine real presence in religious and national texts, in order to question whether it was always understood as enabling myth. Below in our case study of *Pan Tadeusz* we will test whether it is possible to employ theology-soaked terms from Heidegger but without the attribution of Being, except insofar as Mickiewicz himself was almost frankly, almost convincingly, creating a metaphysical myth of the absent nation.

The Voice of the Living God in the Delphic Oracle and the Book of Jonah

Delphic: enigmatic. Stories of a dragon-slaying Apollo, a cleft in the earth producing vapors and strange foreknowledge, ecstatic possession of women by the real presence of God, and dark riddling predictions that changed the course of empire have gathered about the national-religious oracle at Delphi.

Oracular: Godspoken. Until the work of Joseph Fontenrose, accounts have been reluctant to sort out myths from what can be known historically, or to sort out one purported mantic speaker from another. Fontenrose's *The Delphic Oracle: Its Responses and Operations with a Catalogue of Responses* (1978) divides the oracle's recorded responses into those that are historical, quasihistorical, legendary, and fictional—with the first two of these categories judged, after investigation, to be genuine or not genuine.[4] Within the historical and quasihistorical questions to the oracle are many from states like Athens, asking about imperial wars and monarchial succession, but there are just as many from private parties asking about religious or everyday matters. Reading the responses, we sense the historical life of a great religious institution, adapting to change across centuries: affairs of states, affairs of family.

Here is a late historical response to a question by Kleitosthenes of Trales, on the occasion of some affliction on the land. The question concerned the salvation of the city; the reply was direct and in verse:

> Response: Having expiated the thousand-year wrath of Zeus, sacrifice to Poseidon wreathing his altar, in a grove, offering wheat and fruits. Call him Asphalios, Temenuchos, Apotropos, Hippios, Arges; and praise Seisichthon and Zeus with hymns and dance. (194)

Fontenrose calls these late historical oracles "uniformly bad" because their poets had only a vague sense of their models, did not know "the conventions, structures, formulae, and diction of oracular verse" and "lacked competence and skill." This particular oracle "barely manages to show an ACE structure in which the salutation and an admonition to heed the god's words are almost casually inserted."

An early legendary response, from testimony but not in verse, to King Aletes of Corinth concerning the coming of Melas and Dorians to Corinth wanting to settle there follows:

> Response: In ambiguous language Apollo appeared to forbid Aletes to receive Melas, but Aletes mistook the god's meaning.

The content of this response is lost. "Melas," says Fontenrose in comment, "apparently persuaded Aletes that he had misinterpreted the oracle, and finally with reluctance Aletes accepted him as *synoikos*" (356). These examples are typical of all the others that have come down to us: the petitioner receives a response from the Pythia, and her voice will influence a coming choice. The oracle gives commands; this is performative speaking, perlocutionary language.

The practice of oracular speaking starts all our themes in this book. The word of Apollo is riddling, skewed, sometimes darkly metaphorical, and it has literary status through troping and verseform (most of the responses in verse were from the first century A.D. and afterward; before that the responses were unversified.) The Pythia as vehicle of the god's voice is relatively transparent, though in the myths about her ecstasies there are descriptions of wounded voice, writhing pain, even the death of the priestess; but the Pythia does not resist the prophecy, and this provides a dramatic contrast to Jonah of the Bible. Woman, either a virgin or past childbearing, is the vehicle for prophecy, but in addition there is a male priesthood including exegetes and, apparently, later in the history of the oracle, poets. The oracle is thus subject to interpretation, and it is possible to mistake its meaning and to take action without knowing wider context: kingdoms could be lost by misreading reported words. Even here, then, in such archaic language, the god manifests at a distance and through human form, language and speech, and the speech when written down (very little was written) survived the moment of its uttering. One does not go to the oracle for evidence of presence, because the oracle is "always already" an institution of secondariness. From our backward perspective of the era at the interminable end of the bardic, one goes to consult the oracle for the memory, the aura, of presence. And for an example of how, at the very beginnings of the Western tradition, womens' voice was purloined from women by a male priesthood.

Now to pass from Hellene to Israelite cosmology, we move to a biblical narrative where the voice of the Lord is quoted in Yahweh's own apparent words, where Yahweh has dialogues with his prophet and the prophet with others, and where a storyteller provides or, as we shall argue, elides some narrative linkages. The question of presence is not dodged: indeed it is foregrounded in the very opening of the text, in 1.3, where the word presence is, in one periodic sentence, twice used in the phrase *the presence of the Lord*; the original has a preposition, "before the Lord," in place of the noun, *presence*, but the sense is the same: Jonah flees from the face of Yahweh. The opening line of the story (in 1.1) has the following: "Now the word of the Lord came unto Jonah"; it came, it arrived, but the means of transmission is left unspoken, the time of transmission unrecorded; the word of Yahweh is there without vehicle or elapse of time, and that indeed is the point of the system of causality in the story itself and its phrasing.[5]

In a preliminary listing of voice events in the story, we count sixteen usages of the word *say* as in "he/they said," "saying." "The word of the Lord" occurs twice at major structural articulations of the text (1.1 and 3.1) where Yahweh gives marching orders to Jonah. The word *cry* as an intensification of *saying* occurs seven times, and the words *beseech* or *call upon* for *asking* occurs four times. There are other highly explicit usages of perlocutionary verbs: make vows, "I bid thee," *proclaim*, "caused it to be proclaimed and published through Nineveh by a decree," *repent, pray, discern*. The word *voice* occurs twice in chapter 2 during Jonah's strange prayer from the belly of the whale:

> And said, I cried by reason of mine affliction unto the Lord, and he heard me; out of the belly of [*sheol*] cried I, and thou heardest my voice. (2.2)
>
> But I will sacrifice unto thee with the voice of thanksgiving; I will pay that I have vowed. Salvation is of the Lord. (2.9)

So crying need not imply actually being heard; there is a voice specifically employed for the act of giving thanks. The discriminations among uses of voice would appear to be very fine indeed, and they drive down into the etymology of the Hebrew language; the discriminations raise basic differences in the routes to salvation, involving repentance, conversion, contention, choice making, and so on. Yahweh himself is one speaker among many.

However, we shall now argue that his speech is different from the others because his saying is also doing. No one else possesses that simultaneity, that ability at commanding multiple perspectives—except perhaps the anonymous storyteller whose interest is in showing Yahweh's transcendence. In the process of showing this, the teller gains some of the attributes of the aura of real presence.

Pursuing further an innocent but crucial phrasing already quoted from Jonah, chapter 2, "I will pay that I have vowed," we may say that there is a slippage between vow saying and actually performing: the space and time of human decision making, the voice choice that conjoins saying with doing. Chapter 3 has a passage of four verses that gives an epitome of the whole process, and of the range of differences between human and divine saying:

> 7 And he [either the king of Nineveh or Yahweh, for the pronouns could be read either way] caused it to be proclaimed and published through Nineveh by the decree of the king and his nobles, saying, Let neither man nor beast, herd nor flock, taste anything; let them not feed, nor drink water.
>
> 8 But let man and beast be covered with sackcloth, and cry mightily unto God; yea, let them turn every one from his evil way, and from the violence that is in their hands.
>
> 9 Who can tell if God will turn and repent, and turn away from his fierce anger, that we perish not?
>
> 10 And God saw their works, that they turned from their evil way; and God repented of the evil that he had said that he do unto them, and he did it not.

Yahweh repented! It is an amazing passage. Yahweh sent Jonah to preach. Jonah was effective, and Yahweh then saw the change among the Ninevites (not Israelites, not followers of Yahweh) and spared them. He changed his mind and his earlier speech. And Jonah was furious with Yahweh for being merciful, for relenting, for changing when the Ninevites changed, and for playing around with Jonah's prophecy. This passage is amazing because it shows that Yahweh's saying is reversible, flexibly moving about according to human decisions. Jonah wants a rigid God and cannot abide a malleable one; for a lenient God does not necessarily keep his word. Jonah cannot adjust himself to Yahweh's greater plan; he would foreclose on the plan and would wish to define the plan according to his own skills, preferences, and career.

The four verses just quoted may stand as a minor example of the grand myth of Yahweh's voice and how it actualizes itself in the Bible. Presence needs a free, rebellious will and an actual voice compellingly to speak out in human language. Yahweh, who is too intelligent to ventriloquize through a wooden dummy, builds into his system of communication the possibility of that slippage which is human free will. In these four verses the king must not only proclaim but must also publish his words. The king must say; then he must write or cause to be written, cause to be sent about the city far from the monarchial presence. Yahweh acts by a saying-doing, with the elision of the deed, so Yahweh is different from a King. Usually saying is doing in Yahweh's language, but, as we have seen, not always, for he can take back a saying and arrange a new doing. Verse 9, "Who can tell," has the generalized mind of the Ninevites, fearfully asking about Yahweh's ability to change his decree. This is the highest point of the Ninevites' intelligence, in biblical terms, because the city of Nineveh acts to reform culture even in the midst of doubts about whether Yahweh will understand. This is a leap of faith. Jonah cannot act according to his vocation with the kind of single-mindedness the Ninevites have found. Jonah is an authoritarian personality; he has the rhetorical force and the canniness that make him into a prophet but that also make him an imperfect prophet, unwilling to accept all of Yahweh's project by acting on faith.

The escape from Joppa (1) and the skeptical watching of the City of Nineveh in (4) are rhyming elements of the story. Jonah has not learned obedience even by the end of the story, and Yahweh is still giving him direction by question and deed up to the last sentence of the book. The gourd Yahweh grows over Jonah as a gift is worthless except as a vegetable symbol of sparing: Yahweh can grow as well as kill that plant, and Yahweh can do the same with persons who repent and even, oddly enough, with cattle that cannot ("sixscore thousand persons that cannot discern between their right hand and their left hand; and also much cattle"). Yahweh debates with his reluctant prophet, using arguments to convince Jonah.

Like the rest of the Old Testament, the Book of Jonah heavily uses a very particular causal rhetoric. Often a deed is announced, and then immediately, or much later on, an explanation is given of what has happened or the reason it has happened. For example, in 3 in the passage quoted, we hear only much later that at the start of these events God had said he would "do evil" to the Ninevites. Let us advance the hypothesis that with Yahweh saying-doing is the rule, perfectly normal for the all-knowing, but for the writer of the Book of Jonah there will sometimes be doing before saying, sometimes saying that brings doing, sometimes saying in the form of vows, cries, or beseeches that is detached from action. In the human world, saying and doing are detachable, and that goes for the world of the writer of this book of the Bible. But Jonah wants to say and have what he has said turn into deeds, namely the destruction of the city of Nineveh. He is wrong to aspire to that kind of rigid one-for-one saying-doing equivalence, because he is not Yahweh and never will be.

The gap between human voice and Yahweh's is shown in the Book of Jonah. It is an infinite irony. Jonah is still, even as a chosen one, infinitely distant from Yahweh's elision of the deed. There is in the Bible a desperate problem with language, if Yahweh has to adjust his message to Jonah and embody his meaning to humans. It is not Yahweh's problem, but ours. Yahweh is able to make a diversion, a deflection into the Israelite nation's language and history. He must manifest himself so humans may understand his voice. It is not Yahweh's fault but ours that language is a phenomenon of imprecision, slippage, approximation. The Book of Jonah has been called a "satire." The oddity of the details, the discontinuity of levels between the chapter 2 poetry in the whale's stomach and the prose elsewhere, and above all the scathing treatment of the reluctant prophet and of all human communication make this a credible reading of tone and intent.[6] So anonymity of authorship and quotation from divinity need not, indeed never do, guarantee a writing of presence. In the heart of the Hellene and Israelite eras of voice as presence there is already writing, interpretation, irony, and literature.

Vestiges of the Oral and the National: Eighteenth-Century Origins of the Bardic in England

Oracular and *Orphean*, *bard* and *muse* have turned into silly words, but there is abundant evidence to show that these terms are shadows of a very great art which we have lost beyond recall. Voice must be expressed by word manipulation and print alone, in the cultural moment of movable type, so that reading texts from before Gutenberg we have the surprised sensation of watching the birth of our own literacy in the passage from orality to writing. Requiring the imagination of a time when there was only memorizing and performing of a poetry totally oral, we even tend to forget that Orpheus, first among singers, was himself not a figure of origins but self-divided, a victim of the violent collision between the Dionysian principle, represented by the frenzied Maenads and the Apollonian ideal which he, as a poet, venerated. It is charming to think of the bards' ability to keep themselves for nine days in a trance, to prophesy, to perform their poetry orally, and to use venomous satires to bring out black blotches on an enemy's face and turn his bowels to water. But we also know that among the Celts, poets were a caste of learned men, with seven grades of poets in Ireland, each with certain meters allotted to its use, and with an unparalleled intricacy in their systems of versification. The very idea of the bard comprises the contradiction of solitary singers and public priest, personal voice, and voice of society. Doubtless such easy oppositions are as inapplicable to the earlier era of bards as they are to the poetry of today, so what we really need to inquire into is when and why we began to invent such myths of opposition to cheer or depress ourselves.

What we have called "the bardic" is one modern myth of opposition, a longing, a version, a vestige, a method. The bardic is print culture's nostalgia for oral culture. It is one of several subtle primitivisms which strike their roots in the European Enlightenment or a little earlier, come to magnificent if tortured growth in romanticism, and then get into difficulties in the moment of the modern and the postmodern. Fascination with the figure and achievement of the bard is the public, scholarly, and sociological side of the myth; on this side, and notably in the case of a genuine, representative, long poem like *Pan Tadeusz*, whatever is personal in the rhythms and tones of voice is to an extent lost in whatever is national and memorizable. Inwardly and aurally, the poetics of the bardic may be defined as a longing for personal voice and the will to simulate the illusion of personal voice.

As we understand this configuration in the history of ideas, the greatest difficulty of the bardic is the threat that the bardic is designed to counteract, namely, (1) the increasing need to keep national memory as the nation grows away from its origins in an increasingly competitive geopolitical economy of goods and forces; and (2) the increasing erasure of the self from poetry. Voice is the literary name for what in philosophy is called the "philosophical subject," and the speeded-up dispersion of empirical self, literary voice, and philosophical subject must (ultimately though not here) be related as effect to cause to a change in the historical series. Novel ideas of voice and the bardic, which emerge toward the end of the eighteenth century, are not just symptoms of the shift in the composition of society and the role of the poet; these ideas are also attempts in the realm of writing to overcome that shift. It is a mistake to overpsychologize ancient bards and treat them as romantic poets, but we are drawn into this error partly because the romantic poets, interested in the national prophecy and private personality of the bardic voice, saw their own ideal selves in the figure of the bard.

It happens that we can date exactly the moment when the bards became bardic. Thomas Gray's pindaric ode of 1757, "The Bard," gathers a good deal of arcane scholarship to tell of the tradition, now discredited, that Edward I, after capturing Wales in 1283, ordered all bards put to death. Lyre in hand, the last of the bards prophesied the end of Edward's line from a craggy vantage high above the Conway River. Sandy, Thomas Jones, Blake, Fuseli, and John Martin all painted the scene which Gray describes:

On a rock, whose haughty brow
Frowns o'er old Conway's foaming flood,
Robed in the sable garb of woe,
With haggard eyes the Poet stood;
(Loose his beard, and hoary hair
Stream'd, like a meteor to the troubled air)
And with a Master's hand, and Prophet's fire,
Struck the deep sorrows of his lyre.[7]

After predicting a new dynastic line for England, and a revival of poetry, Gray's bard leaps to his death. Gray said later, "I felt myself the bard." For Gray and the painters of this scene, it was an illicit excitement to imagine oneself away from the most civilized of all centuries, plunging back down the years to when inspired poetry, politics, and religion were all one in a unified sensibility. For that, Gray was willing, during the length of his poem, to abandon Englishness for an imaginary national identity. Like others who come later (Bishop Percy, Walter Scott), Gray does not escape the dangers of romanticizing early cultures along with early poets: the role of the old bards was defined collectively and religiously in a highly authoritarian culture, a culture whose passing can, at least now, be understood quite otherwise—namely as a liberation of persons and of poetry.

At the same late-century moment, and for the same reason as Gray, Percy and Scott collected old ballads, Chatterton and Macpherson pretended to be bards and hoaxed some of the public by inventing modern ancient poetry, heaping on plausible archaisms, because the genuine article was required and could not be found. In "To the Muses," written before he was twenty in a grand dismissal of all his century's poetry, William Blake curses the "Fair Nine" for abandoning their duties:

How have you left the antient love
    That bards of old enjoy'd in you!
The languid strings do scarcely move!
    The sound is forced, the notes are few![8]

In *Songs of Experience*, there are two further poems on bards, and of course the whole of Blake's career (like Walt Whitman's, Vachel Lindsay's, and Allen Ginsberg's after him) may be taken as a conscious project of writing with the themes and techniques of a modern bard.

There is a vast collection of lyrics since Blake's time which sets out to move the strings and multiply the notes, a poetry (at least in intent) of unforced sound, foregrounded sound, as in Poe's "The Bells," in Tennyson and Hopkins and Dylan Thomas. As a new laureate, Tennyson would read aloud from his Wellington ode with his broad Lincolnshire dialect, "Mouthing out his hollow oes and aes":

Bury the Greaaat Duke
    With an empire's lamentaaaation,
Let us bury the Greaaat Duke
    To the nooise of the moourning of a mighty Naaation.[9]

Among nineteenth-century writers, Wordsworth seems to have been most eager to discover an account of a voice which breaks when an identity breaks. But Wordsworth, after struggling with such thoughts in the *Prelude* of 1805, turned almost immediately to a lesser idea in the frame fiction of a conventional lyre-strumming bard in his dismal long poem, "The White Doe of Rylstone." Wordsworth could not make an English national epic and had to settle for a purely personal one in *The Prelude,* yet in countries outside the European center, Poland and Argentina, it was still possible to give what approached an adequate account of the society—possible because there the full encounter of an oral traditional culture and a written, rational-legal culture was reserved for a comparatively late culmination in the nineteenth century. Both Adam Mickiewicz's *Pan Tadeusz* (1834) and José Hernandez's *Martín Fierro* (1872) exaggeratedly speak of themselves as sung poems, but that is an engaging transparent allusion of the written to the oral. Such epics are the final arias of threatened classes and use the images and conventions of residual orality as one literary means to reaffirm values that are imperilled. Rather like national anthems, these become national epics by celebrating a certain purity which has largely vanished by the time of writing. In the case of Mickiewicz, there are these historical, but also biographical and textual, reasons for speaking of a mode of utterance hitherto undefined: exiled voice.

The Exiled Voice in Adam Mickiewicz's *Pan Tadeusz*

Pan Tadeusz, written in Paris (1832–34), emerges from a political and cultural situation wound through with paradoxes. It is a long epic poem in twelve books dealing with various aspects of the social life of the landed gentry, in Lithuania, closing with the arrival of the Polish legions in the service of Napoleon and their departure for the ill-starred Moscow adventure of 1812. Although the beginning of the plot can be located with some precision in the autumn of 1811, it is important to realize that as a national epic its initial stimulus returns to the life of a culture and can hardly be confined to the temporal scheme as revealed by the main characters. There are constant allusions to the continuity of the Polish culture of the landed gentry, a class of which the Lithuanian nobility was considered a part at least since the growth of a Lithuanian-Polish alliance during the fifteenth and sixteenth centuries. Another abiding theme of the epic is the stubborn juxtaposition, over centuries, of the civilization of western Europe and the sealed-off cohesive culture of Poland.

The poem is one of the primary examples in world literature of cultural nostalgia. Historical realities had terminated the myth of the happy Poland long before Mickiewicz wrote his poem. Three partitions of the Polish lands between Russia, Prussia, and Austria put an end first to the territorial unity of the country (first partition in 1772, second in 1793) and finally extinguished the political unity of the state (third partition in 1795). Thus when Mickiewicz celebrates the ancient Polish culture in 1834, even a brief period of Napoleon-sponsored and dominated reinstatement of Poland in the form of the grand duchy of Warsaw (1807–13) had long been past. The Congress of Vienna effectively, though not immediately, spelled the elimination of Poland as a political entity. This is so even though, in the short run, the Congress established the Polish kingdom with its large autonomy, liberal constitution, and political and legal system. The gains for the Polish cause were significant, so much so that their loss was for the Mickiewicz generation a greater catastrophe for the nation than the partition of 1795.

The failure of the November Insurrection of 1830 and 1831, where Polish patriots tried to throw off Russian domination, had spectacular results. It emphasized the historical law which dooms romantic revolutions to being unsuccessful blood-baths unless (as in very few cases) they are supported by a favorable arrangement of political powers outside a country. Political dissent was crushed inside Poland, and there was a massive emigration of Polish citizens mainly to France. As the years wore on and the situation did not budge, these exiles became desperate and embittered. "None of us," wrote one of the exiles, "had he been able to foresee that our road was . . . leading to long and inglorious exile . . . but would have let himself be beaten to the last drop of blood, but would rather have died, than to have doomed himself voluntarily to the fate which lay in store for us."[10] But also this drama of banishment and displacement, prolonged by another unsuccessful insurrection and indeed extending to the present day, had a political consequence with literary pertinence. It created a spiritual model of the ideal Poland. The Polish idea of fatherland does not evolve from eighteenth-century mercantile, legal, or constitutional thinking, but is a full-fledged manifestation of nineteenth-century idealism of the state. It is from this perspective of absence that *Pan Tadeusz* will be read in this study as a spiritualized vision of culture—a vision is aptly described by Jan Lechoń, another tragic emigre of Polish poetry, as "the awakening of an almost musical sense of Polishness contained in the solemn rhythms of a polonaise and our nostalgia for an ideal order both musical and social."[11] Since the history of the poem's structure is intimately related to the structure of Polish history, we proceed by capping a phenomenology with a sociology of the exiled voice.

Phenomenology of Exile and Voice

What is the nature of exile, and what is the nature of voice? One variety of modern criticism seems especially well suited to address these questions, namely the kind of phenomenology practiced by Heidegger and those who have followed in his line.

To begin by addressing exile with the terms and methods of Heideggerian discourse, it is first necessary to specify the spatial conditions of the emigration; there can be no exile without a *from* and a *to*. The philosophy of exile is always based on the interchange of thoughts between the place we have left and the place where we are now. In the text of exile, presence enters a dialogue with absence, but it has also a temporal facet; it is the present communicating with the past. If we address literary voice with the same terms and methods, we have to know whether it is the logos, the eternal sound of the Ever Present which Jacques Derrida believes to be a sad consequence of two thousand years of Western metaphysics, or a physical voice that speaks in and through the text. Is this a voice that comes to us from before or from behind a word, and only carries the word on its wave; or is it a voice which originates and ends, is born and dies simultaneously with a word? To restate this be means of grammatical definitions of active or passive voice, we might ask: Is it the word that *speaks* or is the word *spoken*?

The situation of exile is a tragedy of un-desired loci. The hypophon between "un" and "desired" describes the space of a thwarted desire which remains in a clandestine operation. It is a desire which is not lost and which is very different from an objective statement about undesirability of a given event or person. If I un-desire something, I suspend my own desire but do not cancel it; I open a process of a slow fading of the desire which eventually may become absorbed by the new reality of another place. The un-desiring is hesitant and painful and has little to do with whether or not I prefer the new place to which I have come. Still, in a typical drama of exile, these two different meanings of undesirable meet like the end of one word and the beginning of another in a discourse; we have to learn how to un-desire the place we consider ours while the desire to be there is incessantly active, and simultaneously to learn how to live in another place which is alien, threatening, and therefore undesired. Even if I escape from a physical threat hovering above me in my home place, to live somewhere else where I feel relatively safe may evoke in me a feeling of the uncanniness of not being at home. Hence, the insane logical space of the institution of political asylum, which on one hand provides one with a home, where we are safe but not *at* home, and on the other, results from one's giving up one's home. Thus, eventually instead of home we are provided with an asylum which is to be understood in at least three ways, all of which distort the sense of being at home: as a refuge, as an orphanage or sanitarium, or (finally) as a mental institution.

Hence exile produces the dilemma of a suspended, bracketed desire and a lack of desire, blank desire, between un-desire and un-desire, between a temporary absence of life as we knew it and nothingness which we had not experienced before. Exile is the illness of a locational desire.[12]

The relation between un-desire and desire is like that situation which Heidegger calls "conspicuousness" and describes in *Being and Time* as one of the possible modes of "unreadiness-to-hand."[13] The conspicuous thing, seemingly familiar and nearly internalized, loses its immediate usefulness and becomes an estranged object totally external. However, the usable referentiality of the thing to man "has not completely vanished from the [thing's] constitution; its concrete existential relationship to Dasein has only been radically subdued." Similarly, the fatherland has to be un-desired, subjected to a process of radical suspension but not cancellation. And yet un-desire is also similar as a notion to Heidegger's "obtrusiveness," which occurs when the object expected and longed for is not where it ought to be, and thus creates a hole, an absence which attracts our attention. Fatherland as absent to us from our exile becomes a gap which forces us to focus upon itself. Exile as a text of life is, then, an incessant reverberation of the past in the present (in the sense of a gift, and an openness) which nonetheless echoes in the void of denial (rejection, a being closed). So the style of exile is a style of antiphony.

Exile for Mickiewicz is not only a geographical migration from Poland to France, but primarily an ontological and existential expatriation. Like other members of the mid-nineteenth-century Polish intelligentsia, he remains deprived of his own desires or possibility of their gratification. Accordingly, we understand *exile* as a term referring not so much to particular elements of human experience of reality, a matter of simple geographical location, but rather as a style of thinking and philosophizing, as a style of epistemology which at the same time is epistemology as style. This style of epistemology brings back the importance of the interplay between the present and the past, between 1832 and 1811, because the un-desire which we saw to be the crucial element of exile seems to stand in a direct proportion to the liveliness of memory: the stronger un-desire becomes, the more it activates memory.[15]

Voice, if we are to deal with it phenomenologically, may be understood by means of the same dialectical discourse we have used for un-desire and the undesirable.[16] Speech has its character as a constant and implacable deferring. If exile is a spatial phenomenon, speech as voice reclaims its domain from time. To take the extreme case as a beginning convenience, we could say that voice as human speech is a measure of difference between human beings and their God; that is the way Milton considered it when he wrote in *Paradise Lost* (7, 176–179):

> Immediate are the Acts of God, more swift
> Than time or motion, but to human ears
> Cannot without process of speech be told,
> So told as earthly notion can receive.

Immediacy is juxtaposed to both time and motion and finally finds its utmost adversary in the concept of a 'process'; thus a real contrast between Acts (capitalized to introduce a further differential) and speech. The conflict between Acts and speech was, in the epoch of romanticism, viewed as the abiding tension between external nature and our own man-made reality of language, and one romantic task seems to be the attempt to bring the two types of thought—the immediate and the sequential, the original and the copy—into parity. In the process human actions would be elevated to the level of the immediate intervention of God or nature. From within this epoch, Mickiewicz's romantic voice speaks from within the awareness of the difference between divine Acts and human actions and tries to put the equation between them.

Romantic and post-romantic practice provides examples of writers who, to secure their loyalty to their vocation, decided to abandon voice and find the ultimate unity of Acts and actions only in a tell-tale silence. Aside from Mickiewicz, we have Matthew Arnold, Arthur Rimbaud, and Ezra Pound in his final years. Young, and dramatically premature, deaths of Keats, Shelley, and Byron are a silencing of voice that was already intuited, perhaps, in their works, but coincided with the silencing of the body. In the case of Mickiewicz, but less definitively than in the later instance of Rimbaud, we have a silencing of voice not as the fate but as the choice; a mute poet liberates his life, uncovers it from the layers of voice, reclaims the fundamental gesture of existence, what is conceived to be the true ontological language. (Some time after finishing the poem, Mickiewicz said of *Pan Tadeusz* amazingly, "I shall no longer use my pen for trifles.") Mickiewicz and Rimbaud give up gesticulation in order to recover gesture.[17]

Pan Tadeusz is one of the supreme nineteenth-century examples of the truism of recent criticism, that there can be literary works which in their craftsmanship, in the extreme moments of their literariness, tend to divorce themselves from literature and commit what may be called the act of "mutilation/munity and self-emaciation/emasculation." A letter can say good-bye to a letter only by means of another letter; voice has to sound if it wants not to sound anymore. A text is a terminus of another text, but the most interesting texts are those which try to reverse the relation between themselves and a prior experience. As Geoffrey Hartman notices in his comments on Wordsworth, a contemporary of Mickiewicz, "The poet's words are always antiphonal to the phoné of a prior experience . . . By phoné I mean voice or sound before a local shape or human source can be ascribed."[18] In the case of *Pan Tadeusz,* what the words listen to is plainly an anterior experience, but also a later, posterior experience. If the text was the antiphone to the phoné of reality, now it becomes the phoné the reality listens to and replies to through the text of the antiphone of *the poet's life.* A change from the status of antiphone to phoné is the borderline of literature. In the present essay, we will show this change beginning to occur in the relationship between the text itself and the epilogue. The voice, as understood here, describes the phenomenon of human speech which exists at the frontier of its own sound, a moment before it lapses into the silence of the voice. This is the moment when literature is closest to the world, although this has to be qualified by "almost": the process of signification is founded upon a difference, a lack of identity. In these early pages of the inquiry, we hope to take in the voice of the text in the moment it is aspiring toward becoming voice. This entails a phase of illegibility or inarticulateness. Before a voice is silenced and seemingly disappears, it has to go through a period of screaming and mumbling. The voice is exiled not only to silence, but also to inarticulateness.

Bardic Voice and the Exiled Epilogue

The literary public of Paris saw the first edition of *Pan Tadeusz* in August 1834. It was a handsome two-volume production from which Mickiewicz banished the epilogue. The manuscript of the epilogue, far from textual clarity, was found in Mickiewicz's papers after his death and published only in 1860 in the Klaczko-Januszewski edition of the poet's works, and then mistakenly placed ahead of the poem as a prologue to *Pan Tadeusz.* (Would not Jacques Derrida relish this strange interchange of monologues and prologues as the two out-texts?) Whether or not Kazimierz Wyka is right in assuming that Mickiewicz's decision to exclude the epilogue was dictated either by his reluctance to indulge in the debates of the Polish emigration circles in Paris, or by his plan to compose a continuation of the poem, we are faced by the document which has its being outside the final full stop of the work, a concluding couplet which imitates the formula ending of a Polish fairy tale. So the poem proper ends:

I ja tam z gośćmi byłem, miód i wino piłem,
A com widział i słyszał,w księgi umieściłem.
(12, 862–63)

[And I was with them drinking wine and mead,
And what I saw and heard all men may read.]
(Mack. tr., 282)

It also has its being outside the book itself, not printed in the original edition, and outside the outline of the poet's life.[19] As interpreters we may regard the Epilogue as a letter sent to the text from exile. Unlike the voice of the main body of the poem, which we will call "bardic," the voice of the Epilogue speaks from without its native element; it is a displaced voice which speaks from among threatening street sounds:

O tym-że dumać na paryskim bruku,
Przynosząc z miasta uszy pełne stuku
(Epilogue, 1–2)

[To think of such things in a Paris street,
Where on my ears the city's noises beat.]
(Mack. tr., 283)

The noise is certainly that of a big city, the same city where the poem itself was written: yet now it is shown a few lines below as "Europe's road," the clatter of an alien world endangering the clarity of the speaking voice. The voice of the Epilogue is displaced not only because it has to sound and communicate amidst the din of Parisian traffic, but mainly because it speaks from a wrong place, the place where the process of un-desiring has been initiated and acknowledged. While *Pan Tadeusz*, also written in Paris, is pretended to be sung from within the culture that accommodates the voice of the bard and supports it by the coherence of custom and tradition, the Epilogue is spoken when the bard is deprived of his listeners. To apply Heidegger's terminology, the bardic voice of the poem, by its deep rootedness, diminishes the gap between saying and speaking, while the epilogue expands the gap.[20]

Speaking of the conditions of possibility of epic, Hegel referred to an "all-embracing condition of human society," a "simplicity of primitive life," terms accurate enough for Mickiewicz's presentation of the district around Soplicowo, the imaginary country house and its estate. The rhetoric of Hegel is not so distant from Mickiewicz's own. In a vision of the poet, Mickiewicz strenuously emphasizes his belonging to a larger, more comprehensive, ideological and aesthetic, formation: "The first task of the poet is to paint things sensuously without indulging in scientific cogitations. Hence, the most enlightened poets seem to be ignoramuses copying common opinions."[21] But this nineteenth-century bard is not naive, and the form and pressure of Europe's roar manifest themselves even in the quiet Lithuanian village: Napoleon's golden eagles stand without, ready to rescue the silver eagles of Poland.

Takie były zabawy spory w one lata
Sród cichej wsi litewskiej; kiedy reszta świata
We łzach i krwi tonęła gdy ów mąż bóg wojny,
Otoczon chumurą pułków tysiącem dział zbrojny,
Wprzągłszy w swój rydwan orły złote obok srebrnych,
Od puszcz Libijskich latał do Alpów podniebnych,
Ciskając grom po gromie,w Piramidy, w Tabor,
W Marengo,Ulm, Austerlitz . . .
. . . Sława czynów tylu
Brzemienna imionami rycerzy,od Nilu
Szła hucząc ku północy,aż u Niemna brzegów
Odbiła się,jak od skał,od Moskwy szeregów,
Które broniły Litwę murami żelaza
Przed wieścią,dla Rosyi straszną jak zaraza.
(1,892–905)

[Such were the pleasures and the petty strife
Of peaceful Lithuanian country life,
When all the world in blood and tears was drowned
And that man-god of war, his troops around
Him like a cloud and armed with guns untold,
Who yoked the silver eagles with the gold,
From Libyan desert to the Alps was winging,
His bolts on Pyramid and Tabor flinging,
Ulm, Austerlitz, Marengo . . .
. . . .
The fame of deeds so rich in heroes' worth
Went roaring from the Nile far to the North,

Till it was thrown back on the Niemen's banks
As by a rock before the Russian Ranks,
which shielded Lithuanian with a fence
Against the news they feared like pestilence.]
(Mack. tr., 26)

This bard, knowing the geography of the external world, always speaks from within a limited and strictly determined territory, and, as we have seen, claims to have been there drinking wine and mead with Tadeusz and Zosia, characters who never existed. Similarly, when the chamberlain wants to remind the gentry of the old Polish courtesies, his language opposes inner and outer, and this time the French are not valued so highly:

Ach,ja pamiętam czasy,kiedy do Ojczyzny
Pierwszy raz zawitała moda francuzczyzny!
Gdy raptem paniczyki młode z cudzych krajów
Wtargnęli do nas hordą gorszą od Nogajów,
Prześladując w Ojczyźnie Boga,przodków wiarę,
Prawa i obyczaje, nawet suknie stare.
(1,415–20)

[I can remember well those early days,
When it became the mode to ape French ways,
And suddenly a swarm of petty lords
Descended on us like the Tartar hordes.
And God and our forefathers' faith abused,
Our laws and customs, e'en the clothes we used.]
(Mack. tr., 13)

Here as in all the conscious idealizations of the folk in European writing, the bardic voice arises from the acute awareness of the distinction between two radically different spheres of reality, but the bard does not speak from the gap, from the rupture between the two but always from inside the sphere which he considers home. Hence the bardic voice cannot be exiled, for what constitutes it is not only topographical links with a given realm but the awareness of the condition of the world which was (or might be) the fatherland. The bardic as a literary method is the final articulation of the concept of 'fatherland': for the Chamberlain, Poland is the universal area where the institutional has not yet been cut off from the personal.[22]

In *Pan Tadeusz*, the bardic manifests itself in a repertory of oracular styles through rehearsed Polish history and through present-tense fiction in the lives of the main characters. Also, in part, it relies on the dispersion of fatherland into a scheme of substitutions and representations whereby a material, geographical Poland is transmuted into signs, traces—the coffee ritual, the mushroom hunt, the telling of lists of old Polish family names. The customs specified by the Chamberlain guarantee both immediate actions and historical traditions, regulating the rhythms of everyday life and of overarching social pressure, rather like the noontime bell which invites guests to dinner toward the end of book 3, a custom preserved by the Judge because it unifies the days with the centuries. It is true that Chamberlain in his speech places "customs" next to "laws," but the laws alluded to are precisely those traditional unwritten instructions which operate parallel with, or overtly against, the written law. For the full triumph of the customary over the codified, which takes place in book 8 ("The Foray") and book 9 ("The Battle"), we are being prepared already at the beginning of the tale when the Apparitor, commenting on his presumption to move the tables from the house to the old castle, explains:

> Cóż złego,żc przeniosłem stoły do zamczyska
> Nikt na tym nie stracił,a Pan może zyska,
> Bo przecież o ten zamek dziś toczy się sprawa.
> My od dzisiaj do zamku nabyliśmy prawa,
> I mimo całą strony przeciwnej zajadłość
> Dowiodę,że zamczysko wzięliśmy w posiadłość.
> Wszakże,kto gości prosi w zamek na wieczerzę,
> Dowodzi,że posiadłość tam ma albo bierze.
> (1, 858–65)

> [I moved the tables to the castle–why?
> None lost, any you perchance may gain, thereby.
> The castle is the cause of this dispute.
> And by this action we make good our suit.
> For let the other side rage as they may,
> I'll prove we took possession of it today.
> For he who asks his guests thereto to feast
> Proves that he holds or takes possession at least.]
> (Mack. tr., 25)

The most dramatic example is to be found in book 5, where the warden encourages his master the count to disregard the codified law:

> "Zamek,wołał Klucznik,wieś i ziemie
> zabieraj Pan!" To mówiąc zwrócił się do Hrabi;

"Jeśli Pan chce mieć spokój,niech wszystko zagrabi.
Po co proces,Mopanku!sprawa jak dzień czysta
Zamek w ręku Horeszków był przez lat czterysta;
Część gruntów oderwano w czasie Targowicy
I jak Pan wie,oddano władaniu Soplicy.
Nie tylko tę część,wszystko zabrać im należy,
Za koszta procesowe,za karę grabieży.
Mówiłem Panu zawsze: procesów zaniechać,
Mówiłem Panu zawsze: najechać,zajechać;
. . . .
Co się tyczy dawniejszych z Soplicami sprzeczek
Jest na to od procesu lepszy Scyzoryczek . . .
(5. 811–21. 824–25)

["Seize castle, land and village, mark my word.
If you want peace, you must take it all, my lord.
No need for lawsuit—clear as day it is.
The castle has been ours for centuries.
Some land was taken after Targowica
And, as you know, was given to Soplica.
You should take all of it not part alone,
As costs and for their plunder to atone.
I say to you as I have always said:
Don't go to law but make a raid instead . . . .
. . . .
And when it comes to settling our dispute,
My little penknife's better than a suit."]
(Mack. tr., 124–25)

The Warden's penknife is his enormous sword; the raid is the foray after which the poem is subtitled ("The Last Foray in Lithuania"), an attack to retrieve one's property, not exactly legal, but nonetheless allowed. The Warden's speech shows how the internalization of fatherland, and fatherland's dispersion into signs and practices which manifest value, is accompanied by the internalization of law.[23] As in the Hegelian description of the social conditions for epic, the moral habit of the bardic world is protected against anarchy by the idea of order, the patterned mode of living which is not imposed but appears to be an outcome of the bond between humans and their world. It is not only a bardic composition that is free from the restrictions of the written medium, but also a society that conditions the bardic utterance by the "familiarity of [Dasein's] relationships" with the communal body.[24] It is not the order that embraces people, but the people who emanate the order. So the voice of the bard is possible only when the organization of the world is in a sense simultaneous with the moment of the tale. "In a sense," because plainly the voice is as much a fiction as the polity for which it speaks.

The bardic is a measure of human unity with the world. If the narration is broken by the horizontal sweep of description, or by a list of Lithuanian names, that is only to bring in another beloved context and naturalize it in the tale. If the Seneschal in book 12 describes the magnificent state centerpiece at length, he is interrupted by the Chamberlain who asks him to postpone the stories until later. "For we are hungry: bid them serve the feast," and thus the basic usability of the thing is reinstated. The bardic seems to be an alteration between the high usability of things, which makes them disappear in the chain of intentionality, and a sudden bringing forth of things which makes them obtrusive, blocking out the rest of the world. The people inhabiting such a world do not live in it, as within a spatial container, but remain in relation with it. They can relate each item of the world to a system of assignments, to an image of the whole world where all relations "are bound up with one another as a primordial totality."[25] Heidegger calls this situation the being of the ready-to-hand. Using an analogy from grammar, we could explain the pertinence of this by means of verb tenses: the world of the epic voice originates from the situation in which the voice as an *as if*, with a necessary lack of immediacy, becomes aware that its impossible desire for *it is* can be feasible only as *it has been*, the perfect aspect of this final verb-tense showing both open-endedness and all the former involvements of the process.

The following is an example from a privileged moment in book 1. The whole company has come back to the farm, falling into ranks with an unpremeditated sense of hierarchy:

> Właśnie z lasu wracało towarzystwo całe,
> Wesoło,lecz w porządku;naprzód dzieci małe
> Z dozorcą, potem Sędzia szedł z Podkomorzyną,
> Obok pan Podkomorzy otoczon rodziną;
> . . . .
> . . . . nikt tam nie rozprawiał
> O porzadku nikt mężczyzn i dam nie ustawiał,
> A każdy mimowolnie porzadku pilnował.
> Bo Sedzia w domu dawne obyczaje chował
> I nigdy nie dozwalał,by chybiano względu
> Dla wieku,urodzenia,rozumu,urzędu
> . . . .

Więc do porządku wykli domowi i słudzy;
I przyjezdny gość,krewny albo człowiek cudzy,
Gdy Sędziego nawiedził,skoro pobył mało,
Przejmował zwyczaj,którym wszystko oddychało.
(1. 210–13, 216–21, 224–27)

[And now the company are turning home,
Gay but in order: first the children come
Accompanied by their tutor; in their train
The Judge himself with Mistress Chamberlain,
And at their side the Chamberlain is found,
The rest of all their family around . . . .
. . . .
This marching order no one had commanded,
Each kept his proper place of his own will.
The Judge observed the ancient customs still,
Nor suffered disrespect or negligence
For age or birth, rank or intelligence. . . .
. . . .
The household grew accustomed to that style,
And, kin or stranger, he that stayed awhile
Within the Judge's house quickly acquired
The customs that the very place inspired.]
(Mack. tr., 8)

The order is kept without conscious thought, inspired by the place itself. (The Polish original says that the order is breathed by all the surrounding objects and persons.) People in this small cavalcade are literally assigned to their places. When coming into the world of *Pan Tadeusz,* if we enter it as readers identifying with these characters, we can participate only when we see ourselves entangled in assignments older than ourselves, antecedent to our conscious thought, and which we view not as an obstacle to our understanding of the world but as an inevitable necessity. Outside this scheme of involvements, says the Judge, houses and nations go to ruin. In lines omitted from the passage quoted, Kenneth Mackenzie translates: "Such order,'" says the Judge, "makes nations great/And families, and without it they abate.'" The bardic in this way speaks always from within the structure of commitments where the individual is not isolated, but emerges from the past ("ancient customs") reaching out toward the future ("Such order . . . makes nations great'"). In Heidegger's words, the individual character within the bardic world, created by the bardic voice, "stands out" (*ent-steht*) but not for himself, not toward himself, but "toward the things in the world and the world itself."[26]

Words, too, are in this bardic world rooted in the antecedent structure of involvements. The meaning of the bardic voice is not in the deed of the word, as it might be, say, in Mallarmé or Milosz, but in the condition of the world it discloses.[27] What then are the strata which condition the bardic voice and make it possible? We have already shown how the voice overcomes an inside-outside opposition by a radical identification with a system of local involvements (and these, constituting the world, become universal). We may now add that this voice also speaks from beyond another difference, disclosing the common world shared by human nature and outer nature. The bardic voice is relational in at least two more aspects, for it assigns a very special place to links between man and nature, and it frequently refers to historical events as to a family story, a tale of relatives and those who are not relatives, outsiders—the familiar and the familial. The world is domesticated, becomes the object of appropriate husbandry. Hence a most famous description of a sunset, also at the very outset of the tale in book 1:

Słońce ostatnich kresów nieba dochodziło,
Mniej silnie,ale szerzej niż we dnie świeciło,
Całe zaczerwienione,jak zdrowe oblicze
Gospodarza,gdy prace skończywszy rolnicze
Na spoczynek powraca. . . .
. . . .
. . . I wnet sierpy,gromadnie dzwoniące
We zbożach,i grabliska suwane po łące
Ucichły i stanęły:tak pan Sędzia każe,
U niego ze dniem kończą pracę gospodarze.
"Pan świata wie,jak długo pracować potrzeba;
Słońce,Jego robotnik,kiedy znidzie z nieba,
Czas i ziemianinowi ustępować z pola."
(1, 186–90, 198–204)

[The sun was near the boundary of the sky,
Less strong but reaching further than when high,
All ruddy like a healthy farmer's face.
Returning from the fields to his own place,
The day's work done . . . .
. . . .
. . . And suddenly all around
The ringing scythes and rakes drawn o'er the ground
Are still and silent. For the Judge decrees,
That on his farm at evening work should cease.

"The Lord of earth knows when our toil should end,
And when the sun, his workman, doth descend
'Tis time the husbandman should quit the land."]
(Mack. tr., 7)

In a parallel description of a belated sunrise in the opening lines of book 6, the sun becomes an example for village activities: "All earth upon the heavens seemed to wait;/The cattle to the pasture started late" (Mack. tr., 130). It is this coextension between the cosmic and the earthy which establishes the conditions of the bardic world: unity or near unity of earth and sky, human and divine. The singer from within the network of relationships; or rather the writing, cast in the thirteen-syllable line of the classical Polish couplet, pretends to bring about this delicate approximation of human and outer nature through song:

Po wieczerzy i Sędzia, i goście ze dworu
Wychodzą na dziedziniec używać wieczoru;
Zasiadają na przyzbach wysłanych murawą;
Całe grono z posępną i cichą postawą
Pogląda w niebo,które zdawało się zniżać,
Ścieśniać i coraz bardziej ku ziemi przybliżać,
Aż oboje, skrywszy się pod zasłoną, ciemną
Jak kochankowie,wszczęli rozmowę tajemną,
Tłumacząc swe uczucia w westchnieniach tłumionych,
Szeptach,szmerach i słowach na wpół wymówionych,
Z których składa się dziwna muzyka wieczoru.
(8, 9–19)

[The supper done, the Judge and people there
Went to the yard to enjoy the evening air,
And sat on benches built against the wall,
A mood of quiet gloom lay on them all:
They gazed up at the sky, which seemed to droop
And shrink and closer to the earth to stoop,
Until both, hidden by a dusky veil
Like lovers, they began a secret tale,
And all their love in stifled sighs confessed
And whispered words and murmurs half-suppressed,
Making an evening music marvelous.]
(Mack. tr. 164)

Earth and sky are intimate, like lovers: but this superb passage also draws our attention to the acoustic aspect of the union, a primordial language, a half-articulated speech which is the outer sign of the disclosed relation between man and world, anterior to any divisions into subject and object, body and soul, future and past. Mickiewicz's "half-uttered words" are Heidegger's Talk *(Rede),* which precedes spoken words and reveals being in the world. And this union of sky and earth, hemispheres that together condition the bardic voice, resembles Heidegger's fourfold *(Geviert)* which in *Holzwege* is characterized as follows: "Earth and sky, divinities and mortals . . . belong together by way of the simpleness of the united fourfold. Each of the four mirrors in its own way the presence of the others . . . . This mirror does not portray a likeness. The mirroring appropriates their own presencing into simple belonging to one another."[29] Divine becomes familiar, but the process is reversible, too, as in the elevation of the everyday in the striking passage, also in book 8, on the Seneschal's astronomy. The celestial is engaged in earthly activities, with God as first and model husbandman, but also the heavenly is the soil from which man grows. The human order mirrors the celestial pattern and thus towers over any exclusively human order which might be imposed without having grown from the unity of the earth and the sky.

It is interesting to note that the amalgamation of the earthly and the divine filtered through the natural has been previously seen by Mickiewicz as a vital element of the aesthetics of the epic poem where nature replaces mythology which, formative as it was for the Greeks, was absent from the Slavonic tribes. "The Greek poetry is of man. He acts there out of his own reasons . . . although locked . . . between the gods of heaven and those of hell. Slavonic tribes lack altogether these supernatural elements . . . . All images are taken from nature."[30] As Kazimierz Wyka puts it: "The Slavonic epic expresses the miraculous in its active attitude towards nature."[31] Hence, one more type of exile has been unconcealed by Mickiewicz himself: a text (already an outcast from the plenitude of voice) becomes a territory of gods who, banished from heaven, must domesticate nature. The epic is an asylum of gods.

Silencing of Voice

The bardic is bardic only insofar as it cannot be a subject to banishment; it remains within the meaningfulness of the fatherland as a sign of value. *Pan Tadeusz,* the poem, is written from Paris and is literally a voice from exile, and yet it is not an exiled voice in the terms of this essay—though there may be moments when it hints or implies another, more desperate way of speaking. The exiled voice belongs to the discourse of the Epilogue. We would emphatically agree, then, with Kazimierz Wyka, who has said that the Epilogue is "a return to the reality of emigration," and that is has the strength of a document which from outside the poem speaks against the poem itself.[32]

The Epilogue was exiled from the book's first editions, but first of all, in its writing, was banished from the being at home of the bardic consciousness:

> Dziś dla nas,w świecie nieproszonych gości,
> W całej przeszłości i w całej przyszłości
> Jedna już tylko jest kraina taka,
> W której jest trochę szczęścia dla Polaka
> Kraj lat dziecinnych!
> (Epilogue, 64–68)

> [For us unbidden guests in every clime
> From the beginning to the end of time
> There is but one place in this planet whole
> Where happiness may be for every Pole-
> The land of childhood!]
> (Mack. tr., 285)

The crucial statement about being unbidden guests of the world is accompanied by a specific disarrangement in the time structure, wherein the perfective becomes the mere past, and this pastness relates to the present in a way diametrically opposite to the action of "gathering." For gathering, *Versammlung* in the Heideggerian definition we would apply to this poem, is a moment or flash which appropriates the present from all events of the past, thus grounding the present in the continuity of what has been. The past acquires the urgency of the present. The unbiddenness of the Epilogue, in the lines above, reverses this relation for the Epilogue it is the present that becomes a distant, detached past. Whereas the bardic voice speaks the world of the totality of involvements, the exiled voice of the Epilogue discourses about this world which is long gone and past. This world that is spoken about is the ideal, hypothetical world of unchangeable ideas and images. The Polishness of Poland is immobilized and put at a distance:

> Kraj lat dziecinnych! On zawsze zostanie
> Swięty i czysty,jak pierwsze kochanie,
> Nie zaburzony błędów przypomnieniem,
> Nie podkopany nadziei złudzeniem,
> Ani zmieniony wypadków strumieniem

. . . .
Ten kraj szczęśliwy,ubogi i ciasny!
Jak świat jest boży,tak on był nasz własny!
(Epilogue, 68–72, 79–80)

[The land of childhood! that shall aye endure
As holy as a first love and as pure,
Unshattered by the memory of mistake
That no deceitful hopes can ever shake.
Nor can the changing tide of life unmake . . . .
. . . .
That happy country, happy, poor, and small!
The world is God's but that was ours—ours all.]
(Mack. tr., 285)

Ownership under the bardic meant participating, an owning for others and with others, but here it means partitioning, an unauthentic mode of being. Mickiewicz was acutely aware of the dialectics of appropriation. In his remarks upon Slavic literature we read: "Man always begins to exercise despotic power from fellow man. . . . Slavery has been known for a long time; but a thought of the unlimited authority over animals, trees, the earth, the whole nature, the thought that a man is the center and god of nature, an uncontrolled despot, is a product of recent times. It is the latest cry of the philosophical pride, the danger brought about by ownership."[33] The polarity of appropriation develops into the list of juxtapositions which follow—"that land where servants more for masters care/Than wives do for their husbands otherwhere," and so on. Hence too the shift of deixis from the "this" of the poem to the "that" of the Epilogue. The bardic voice always speaks from *here*, but the *here* of the Epilogue is the *there* so frequently alluded to and disparaged in the main body of the text.

To the objection that such was a situation throughout *Pan Tadeusz*, as a poem written in exile describing scenes long past, we would point out a fundamental difference. In the poem proper, the voice generally does not recognize the situation of estrangement, understands itself still from within the community it is a part of, and so it reflects upon itself as if from its own point of view. The poem has a voice that has not turned away from itself, that has not yet differentiated between itself and the world and thus speaks as if in unison with it. These are the features that make the voice bardic. In the Epilogue, however, the voice perceives its estrangement, acknowledges the fact that its absorption in the world is disturbed. The voice loses the internal perspective upon itself, and replaces this with social evaluation or, as Heidegger would say, with "public disclosedness."

The situation of Mickiewicz and his fellow exiles, as "unbidden guests," gives them an unfriendly environment: "Where on our ears the city's noises beat" (Mack. tr., 283). The only sound which the Epilogue listens to back in Poland is the voice of death: "every moment fresh news strikes a blow,/Sounding from Poland like a funeral bell" (Mack. tr., 283). In book 3 of the poem, a scene of mushroom gathering finishes with the bell, which for a romantically minded Count is a pretext for his fantasy: he hears it as a metaphor of death; "Thus fate ends all things with a clapper stroke" (Mack. tr., 70). Nevertheless, the signified here is far from eschatological, but relates to the locale of the has been, which is the territory of unending continuity, incessant unfolding:

> Odgłos nie smutny wcale ani pogrzebowy,
> Jak się Hrabiemu zdało,owszem,obiadowy.
> Dzwon ten,w każde południe krzyczący z poddasza,
> Gości i czeladź domu na obiad zaprasza:
> Tak było w dawnych licznych dworach we zwyczaju
> I zostało się w domu Sędziego.
> (3, 686–91)

> [By no means mournful or funereal,
> As to the Count it seemed, but prandial.
> Each mid-day from the roof that bell would call
> Servants and guests to dinner in the hall.
> For thus on old estates 'twas always done,
> As on the Judge's.]
> (Mack. tr., 71)

Thus the bell which interrupts one activity only to foreground it, and then unfold from it another event, is in the Epilogue replaced by a funeral bell which silences the voice and opens the way to death.

The Epilogue is a gradual silencing of voice. The tendency of the speaker to avoid the regions of storm and thunder is marked at the very beginning of the Epilogue, at line 21: "Beyond the thunder [*grzmot*] and the stormy zone"; and again below, "Our thought dared not to wing its passage there,/Where e'en the birds of thunder fear to fare" (Mack. tr., 283-84). The Epilogue speaks from between the sounds of festive bells and the wailing of the generations black with mourning. The transition is marked by death of silence; before the vesper bell becomes the funeral peal, death must intervene. The exiled voice of the Epilogue is distorted with noise, becomes mute amidst the uproar.

We hear the voice more faintly through the formless din of Paris streets, of lies and curses, but afterward we realize that the crisis is deeper, reaching into the ultimate problems of signification. On the one hand, it is a futile search of the signified for a signifier, of the thought for the word: "Whose lips would dare/To boast that they will find that word so rare/That it shall melt marmoreal despair?" (Mack. tr., 284). The futility of the effort is bound to lead into silence. On the other hand, stammering of the signified deprived of its signifier is matched by a lack of means on the part of the audience to receive the signifier, even if it could be found: "the world will not regard their woe" (Mack. tr., 283). The voice wants to speak but cannot find words, while the world wants not to listen and radically cuts off the very possibility of listening. The voice does not have a mouth; the world does not have ears. Paraphrasing Wordsworth's 1850 *Prelude,* we could claim that in the Epilogue "sad incompetence of human speech" (6, 593) is matched by a sad incompetence of human ear. The voice of the Epilogue stammers on the margin of communication.

Apparently the voice must journey into the noise, work its way through it toward a new voice of the recovered bardic. Voice must lose its lucidity through silencing or death in order to gain fresh authenticity.

This silence, which is the doom of the voice in the Epilogue, seems inevitable because of the incompatibility of the word and the world. The word the Epilogue voice longs for is expected to perform actions of utmost physical intensity: it must "lift the gravestone from the hearts of men,/And unlock eyes that brim with tears again" (Mack. tr., 284). The voice on the other side of the Parisian noise will be the voice transformed into action, will signify a return to the bardic tradition of the voice as a gesture, a stepping-out of the limits of the word. Friedrich Schlegel, in his *Literary Aphorisms,* speaks of the hoped-for situation of the exiled voice: "The life and vigor of poetry consists in the fact that it steps out of itself, tears out a section of religion, and then again withdraws into itself by assimilating this part. This also takes place in philosophy."[34] The new voice will have its immediacy by annexing sections of life and transmuting them into utterance; silence is the space assigned to the voice as it gets ready for its work. If this movement toward silence indeed describes the innermost meaning of Mickiewicz's career, the only continuation of writing possible in this case was to refrain from the poetic voice. Though he lectured and was active in Polish-exile politics, in fact he did not write any major poems after *Pan Tadeusz;* he wrote only a few short poems known as the Lausanne lyrics, which were published after his death. The Epilogue is the vesper bell which leads him, so far as major literature is concerned, to silence, in the evening of the unspoken, so that through silence he could transfigure the poetry of words into the poetry of gesture. Slow silencing of the voice in the unfinished, unpublished Epilogue is but a faint echo of last steps fading in darkness, steps initiating wandering toward a new light, toward the sphere where a voice possesses the immediacy of life, the sphere where it becomes my voice, my *own* voice, neither echoing nor borrowed. Thus exists one way out from the position of the exiled voice, which is but a quotation from childhood memories or a reverberation of other voices.

So the exiled voice exists on the verge of two collapses. One is a fall into inarticulateness, the stammering of a mouthless speaker in the direction of an earless listener. The other is a voice of the past, a voice cited, thus doubly deprived of originality, as not only would it be impossible for it to reach the immediacy of godlike gestures, but it would be a mere echo, an imitation of other, forgotten voices.

Sociology of the Polish Fatherland

Before the Epilogue ends, it turns upward briefly in a more positive direction with a nostalgic-utopian view of the poet's role and the possible future of his poem. The last twenty-two lines foreshadow a uture time ("Would I might live to see the happy day. . . .") when his book will be known to Lithuanian country girls:

Gdyby też wzięły na koniec do ręki
Te Księgi, proste jako ich piosenki!
(Epilogue, 115–16)

[Would that some happy chance to them might bring
These books as simple as the songs they sing.]
(Mack. tr., 286)

Then the final lines dart back into the past of the speaker, to the time when poetry is (or is claimed to be) interpreted by the "steward or landlord" to the young listeners; thus the Epilogue ends:

Tak za dni moich,przy wiejskiej zabawie,
Czytano nieraz pod lipą na trawie
Pieśń o Justynie,powieść o Wiesławie.
. . . .
I zazdrościła młodzież wieszczów sławie,
Która tam dotąd brzmi w lasach i w polu,
I którym droższy niż laur Kapitolu

Wianek,rękami wieśniaczki osnuty,
Z modrych bławatków i zielonej ruty.
(Epilogue, 117–19, 125–29)

[So at their country pleasures in my time
They sometimes read aloud beneath the lime
Justina's ballad or Wieslaw's fable . . . .
. . . .
And young men envied then the singer's fame,
Which echoes in their woods and forests still,
To whom the laurel crown on Jove's high hill
Is less dear than the wreaths of cornflower blue,
Twined by the hands of village girls with rue.]
(Mack. tr., 286)

Without being spoken in the bardic voice this is a statement of the theory of the bardic voice, of a writing which is (or is like) singing. The society of the bardic utterance is a group of listeners in the countryside, preferably village girls. The *wieszcz* is not celebrated with the laurel crown of ancient epic but with wreaths wound with rue and Polish cornflowers. *Pan Tadeusz* is as simple as a popular contemporary ballad. So expressed, this myth of the early and the oral has the quality of aspiration, and yet we trust we have shown how the poem itself gives over something very like what the Epilogue asserts.

It is important to mention that the poems of Justina and Wieslaw were popular lyrics of the recent past. Mickiewicz assimilates his classical epic to the sentimental and near-modern lyric and is ironic toward both modes. The *wieszcz* is not really, despite the English translation used here, a "singer," and was never in historical fact celebrated by wreaths of rue and cornflowers. Mickiewicz's little fiction is gently skeptical toward his own aspirations, which nonetheless remain symptomatically bardic in tendency and in detail.

Czeslaw Milosz has said of *Pan Tadeusz* that "its core is metaphysical not social," a contention fully supported by this essay's exposition of the bardic voice.[35] The epic poem conveys the myth of a nation when no nation existed. However, a phenomenological reading of the bardic and the exiled voices is compatible with a social reading which would show the constraints upon this poem's metaphysics (a metaphysics of harmonious fusion between characters and their world). For Mickiewicz is responding, through a profoundly comprehensive work of art, to changes in Polish and literary history by imagining an ideal traditional universe. The poem is a resolution in thought and in literary form of a perplexity which cannot be resolved in actions, given the powerlessness of the Polish exiles after the disasters of 1831. By careful contrivance to exclude perspectives and historical facts which are inconvenient, the poem shapes its values. Any reading of the poem which seeks completeness will show the poem's nostalgic and utopian urge, its performance of the bardic voice, and how this ideology is shaped into great art. We need, then, to demonstrate how the poem manifests the contradictions of its Polish provenance and its moment of romantic realism.

Mickeiwicz in 1833 spoke about his "poem on the *szlachta*." In the event he wrote about the *szlachta* as the nation, a fable not far from the facts so far as political power was distributed in Poland—with a fragmented aristocracy, lack of an effective central power, a legislature incapable of governing due to procedures that made for stalemate; and, from below, the serfs had no influence whatever up to and indeed after the time they were freed in the duchy of Warsaw and in Prussian Poland in 1807 (freed in Austrian Poland in 1848, and in the Russian Empire territories in 1861). Insofar as the tale itself concerns the eventual union of the gentry and the magnates and aristocracy in a symbolic marriage, it is an allegory of the bringing-together of the warring factions of Poland's ruling class.

Mickiewicz weaves three threads into the plot of his epic of Poland. The first is the story of a dashing young man with long moustaches, a perfect shot, Jacek Soplica, who kills the local magnate, Pantler Horeszko, and later returns in the guise of a Bernardine monk, Father Robak. The second is the story of twenty-year-old Tadeusz Soplica, Robak's son, whose relation to fourteen-year-old Zosia is complicated by family disagreements and by Tadeusz's being involved at first (an affair only hinted at in the text) with a woman of the world, Telimena. When Jacek-Robak's son, Tadeusz, is engaged to Horeszko's granddaughter, Zosia, the feud between the two families comes to an end. What lies in contest between the warring families is the castle. Soplicowo, which Robak received from the Russians apparently as a reward for helping in its capture. Robak has given the castle to his brother the judge, whereupon Gerwazy, known as the warden, and the count as the last of the Horeszko line connive to get the castle back. The third and last thread is the foray itself, an attempt by the count and Gerwazy to take the castle by force–a brave, all-but-illegal action to do vigilante justice in a country which lacks almost all central authority, but the kind of action which was increasingly less likely in the conditions of rational-legal modernity: hence the subtitle of *Pan Tadeusz, The Last Foray in Lithuania.* In fact, lateness is a primary value in the poem, which cherishes the ceremonies and even the gallant violence of the old Poland, and does so with the same intent and tone W. B. Yeats uses in "A Prayer for My Daughter," that shorter poem of a century later which regrets the loss of the social values of a country-house society.

Though not named in the title, Robak-Jacek is the story's motivating force. As a young man he kills the father of his beloved Ewa, because Pantler Horeszko has forbidden her to marry a man without land; the situation generally represents the division between the landed and the landless *szlachta*. The motives for the quarrel run deep: violation of blood, violation of property. Jacek's atonement must therefore be long and total through his years as a monk and as a secret agent for Napoleon in Poland. In his attempts to redeem himself, he inserts his influence secretly into the action and engineers events, up to the time of his death at the end of book 10. He saves both Tadeusz and the Count, a Soplica and a Horeszko, by killing a menacing bear with a single deadly shot (book 4) and in battle puts himself into the line of fire, taking the bullets which were meant for Gerwazy and the Count (book 9). He pays with his life for a crime committed in a moment of passion, but he has helped to achieve the union of the families and the building of a Polish force to march with Napoleon against the Muscovites. Mickiewicz's aims appear similar to Sir Walter Scott's, in the use of a major figure who operates behind the scenes, arranging the lives of the more ordinary characters.[36] The title character is the markedly ordinary Tadeusz, neither a splendid student nor speaker nor lover but loyal, honest, and a good fighter, a prime candidate for the Polish legions. By this device of the title, Jacek is subordinated to the whole as represented by his son, and the old Polish *szlachta* become the primary moral agents of the epic. The collective hero is the traditional society with its vanished way of life, the beauty and rich ordinariness of customary existence.

Mickiewicz introduces into the epic the immensity of homely detail, as if all the values of the epic and of Polishness were in those details. The poem represents a union of the methods and length of ancient epic with those of the modern novel after Scott. Some of Mickiewicz's enemies complained about these very details, speaking of "piggishness" *(wieprzowatość)* and we know that the author himself, referring to these things, said "I will never again use my pen for trifles." But of course much of the merit of the poem has to do with these very trifles and piggishness, the "little paper pods" which Zosia wears to curl her hair, Telimena's dismay when her temple of meditation turns out to be an anthill, the chasing of flies, the delightful mushroom-hunt, or the making of coffee in the old Polish way:

Tu roznoszono tace z całą służbą kawy,
Tace ogromne,w kwiaty ślicznie malowane,

Na nich kurzące wonnie imbryki blaszane
I z porcelany saskiej złote filiżanki,
Przy każdej garnuszeczek mały do śmietanki.
Takiej kawy jak w Polszcze nie ma w żadnym kraju
W Polszcze,w domu porządnym,z dawnego zwyczaju,
Jest do robienia kawy osobna niewiasta,
Nazywa się kawiarka, ta sprowadza z miasta
Lub z wicin bierze ziarna w najlepszym gatunku. . . .
(2, 493–501)

[Here the servants bear
Huge coffee trays that painted flowers adorn.
Upon which smoking pewter pots are borne,
And golden cups of Dresden china gleam,
And with each cup a tiny jug of cream.
There is no coffee like the Polish kind;
In all well-ordered households you will find
A special coffee-maker—'tis her charge
To purchase from the river-trader's barge
Or from the city store the finest beans.]
(Mack. tr., 42)

Books 1 through 5 are especially notable for their evocations of the idyllic restfulness and solitude of the country retreat of Soplicowo. There are comparisons, playful or serious, between the natural and the human world, often through epic similes that relate the story's doings to ordinary things—as when the Count mistakes a goosegirl for a woodnymph, a romantic illusion the author compares to a boy who blows at a dandelion puffball and discovers nothing there "but the naked shaft of a green stem" (book 3).[37] Dawns and sunsets, clouds and climate are all in sympathy with the human events in the tale itself. This moral vision of nature is a significant element of Mickiewicz's theory of epic as a form of Christian poetry: "A Christian poet is not satisfied by drawing an image, describing a dawn of evening, but tries to penetrate into nature. He attempts to grasp the moral sense of each natural phenomenon."[38] No place does this sympathy show more openly than at the end of book 10, when the beams of dawn make a halo around the face of Robak, symbolizing that at the moment of death his atonement is complete. This is the light that never was on sea or land; the imagination of a harmony between the characters and the world they live in is projected back upon 1811, the moment of the fathers and the grandfathers. The poem grew under the author's hand, in stages, as Wiktor Weintraub diagnoses it: "The poem developed in the process of writing, almost spontaneously, and the poet himself was surprised at the growth of his work."[39] The final two books move from dawn to dusk on a single day of 1812 just before the troops are to march on Russia, and they form an elaborate, delaying coda to the work. The more Mickiewicz wrote, the closer he came to the failure of Napoleon and the Polish troops at Moscow, and to his own exile in ignominy, the ignominy of Poland. He added materials at the end of the poem, including remarks about the Russians and Tadeusz's freeing of the serfs on the estate, which overtly express a revolutionary love of freedom. So the poem, as it progresses, extends from a country idyll toward political pronouncement; but at no point do these two intents become separated in the narrative.

As they knit the threads of the narrative, the last two books intend a persuasive harmonizing. A sixth of the poem is an elaborate closure which repeats images of unity in the natural and the social spheres. Book 11, "The Year 1812," with its many references to omens, emphasizes the unbroken skein between past events and the present moment of opportunity. This penultimate book contains a mass in a country chapel on a day in early spring, the news of Jacek's rehabilitation, the resolution of the running dispute between the owners of Bobtail and Falcon as to which of the two dogs is more capable (a mirroring minor subplot to the Soplica-Horeszko feud). Book 12, "Let Us Love One Another!" has a last banquet in the Polish style with a great table centerpiece from the old days, brings in Polish generals who actually existed to celebrate with the fictional characters, tells of Telimena's marriage with the notary, has Tadeusz asking Zosia to let him pardon the serfs that belong to her, and concludes with the playing of the dulcimer by the Jew, Jankiel, with the Polonaise—an elaborate national dance by all assembled—and with a rosy twilight that comes to bathe the whole party.

In the image of the coming dynastic marriage between the Soplicas and the Horeszkos, the disparate factions of the nation's upper class are brought together: Tadeusz and the Count are united against a common enemy—the ordinary man and the dreamer make up, together, a whole Polish gentleman. With the marriage, too, another Slavic nationality is brought into the Polish unity, since *Horeszko* is a Ukranian name and the Pantlers' heritage will be subsumed into the Soplicas, a Lithuanian-Nowogrodek line. With the freeing of the serfs, Tadeusz the title-character brings under the Polish law the vast majority of the population:

Bezpieczniej zrobię,kiedy władzy się wyrzekę
I oddam los włościanów pod prawa opiekę.

Sami wolni,uczyńmy i włościan wolnemi.
Oddajmy im w dziedzictwo posiadanie ziemi,
Na której się zrodzili,którą krwawą pracą
Zdobyli,z której wszystkich żywią i bogacą.
(12, 500-5)

[Twere safer if my sovereignty should cease,
And they enjoyed the law's security.
Being free ourselves, let's make them also free,
Let them possess the land which gave them birth,
Which by their bloody toil they've won, the earth
Which yields us food and riches by their hands.]
(Mack. tr., 272)

These splendid lines are within the poem somewhat undercut by the illiberal old Polish view of Gerwazy, who says, "Freedom's for gentlemen, not everyman!" (Mack. tr., 273), and who then gives Tadeusz and Zosia knowledge of a cache of treasure which will make up for what they've lost by throwing away their serfs. The freeing of the serfs has thus an ambiguous role in the final book, for even after the following interchange the reader is left wondering if (the book title) "Let Us Love One Another!" really includes persons outside the gentry. The serfs are given but a collective voice:

Zaledwie usłyszeli nowinę poddani,
Skoczyli do panicza,padli do nóg pani.
"Zdrowie Państwu naszemu!" ze łzami krzyknęli;
Tadeusz krzyknął:"Zdrowie Spółobywateli,
Wolnych,równych,Polaków!"—"Wznoszę Ludu zdrowie!"
Rzekł Dąbrowski;lud krzyknął;"Niech żyją Wodzowie,
Wiwat Wojsko,wiwat Lud,wiwat wszystkie Stany!"
Tysiącem głosów zdrowia grzmiały na przemiany.
(12, 604–11)

[Scarce have the peasants heard the news, when all
Before their new young lord and lady fall,
"Health to our fellow citizens!" he replies,
"Free Poles and equals!" and Dabrowski calls,
"The People!"; they reply, "The Generals!"
"Long live the Army, People and Estates!"
The thunder of their voices alternates.]
(Mack. tr., 275)

Jankiel, playing an uncanny and rousing folksong on his dulcimer, is another crucial element in the poem's closure, standing as he does for the roughly one-eighth of the population which was at that time Jewish. There are antisemitic references in the poem, spoken in the words of minor characters, but never in the narrator's voice; these seem to have their resolution, if not refutation, in Jankiel's triumphant music and his patriotism.[40]

The poem ends with the whole company of fictional and real characters toasting each other, and all their friends, "And all the dead of hallowed memory." Mickiewicz has brought present and past, fictional and actual, master and serf and minority into the imagined fatherland that existed in the no-place of Soplicowo on this marvellous day of 1812. It is as if he were thinking of all the divisions in Polish life that needed to be turned into unities before the nation would be worthy of existing once again. He concludes the poem with a couplet imitating the conventional ending of a Polish fairy tale.

I ja tam z gośćmi byłem,miód i wino piłem.
A com widział i słyszał,w księgi umieściłem.
(12, 862–63)

[And I was with them drinking wine and mead,
And what I saw and heard all men may read.]
(Mack. tr., 282)

This framing of the text is significant from at least three points of view. It definitely demarcates the text as within the sphere of a certain literary convention, the fairy tale. It comes to terms with the absence of the miraculous which worried Mickiewicz: the miraculous, traditionally provided by mythology, is here replaced by the fairy tale. And fairy tale, although a full-fledged literary form in itself, nevertheless hinges on a close proximity to the popular, oral forms current among simple people. The last suggestion is a particularly significant ornament on the frame of the *oeuvre,* as the allusion to oral genres not only closes, cuts off the main text of *Pan Tadeusz,* but also opens the text of the Epilogue—where the reader that Wyka calls the "folk reader" (*czytelnik ludowy*) is constituted and addressed very differently from the implied readers of books 1 through 12.[41] It is a transparent literary lie whose very obviousness is part of the shock it gives the reader. This pretended presence allows Mickiewicz to mingle with the fictional families and events so that he too becomes fictional, bearing out to the very end the fable of the bardic voice. He would not willingly leave himself outside the imagined unity of the fatherland.

Vachel Lindsay and American Bardic

Though the role of the bard is more difficult to sustain in a mass society—in a society with sophisticated communications, technology, international hookups, and travel—there are probably few poets who would abandon it entirely. (In the last chapter we consider a few of those, among the Language School writers, who make calculated massive reduction of the rhetoric of I-self-narrative-voice, as if that rhetoric is no longer capable of carrying the imaginative force of literature, but also as if most of literature's former boundaries have dissolved; certainly as if a national presumption in broad bardic gestures is strictly impossible.) Even Donald Davie, a poet of argumentation who despises the large gesture, ends his 1969 book of Essex poems with a vulnerable admission:

> The metaphysicality
> Of poetry, how I need it!
> And yet it was for years
> What I refused to credit.[42]

That metaphysicality is more persistently credited by Robert Graves and Robert Bly, writers who have spoken of poetry as invocation of maenads, muses, the White Goddess, the Great Mother. For them power summoning always and only occurs when a feminine principle is accurately portrayed, though Bly in recent years has been exploring images of the power of fathers and brothers, and thus has modified his earlier themes. Graves writes that "the reason why the hairs stand on end, the eyes water, the throat is constricted, the skin crawls and a shiver runs down the spine when one writes or reads a true poem is that a true poem is necessarily an invocation of the White Goddess, or Muse, the Mother of All Living, the ancient power of fright and lust—the female spider or the queen-bee whose embrace is death."[43] Reading Graves on the White Goddess and Bly on the Teeth-Mother, we often encounter a species of audience-taunting leg pulling, as in this passage, where we hear the writer in the process of trying to convince himself that a certain body of symbols will help him to write poetry. That bullying yet self-suspicious tone is itself one evidence of the difficulty of the bardic. Another evidence is the resonance, unwelcome but undeniable, of Graves's position with that of the Delphic priests taken up earlier in this chapter. We find in Graves's high modernist statement the same archaic, hierarchic principle that places female muse in the role of vehicle for the male writer, thus ruling out women as writers themselves.

This modernist mode of the bardic, narrower than the mode we encountered in Mickiewicz or Gray, builds up its own restrictive canon. The bardic itself as a type of writing has a specific relation to the canon in the twentieth century: bardic as a type is what the canon excludes. Turning now to American poetry of our century, the poetic canon is (or was until recently) a genteel canon. It associates heavily marked predictable rhythms and repeated lines with defects of learning and ear, defects of thinking. Our example is Vachel Lindsay in the moment of his flourishing—and after. The reasons, rhythmic and ideological, why Lindsay is now excluded are the same reasons why this hebraist, mystic, and profound Jeffersonian Democrat could burst with such success into a literary scene whose representatives are Moody, Markham, Stoddard, Aldrich, and Stedman. Bardic was needed as a defamiliarizing, antigenteel gesture in 1910, but in 1995 it is not.

Lindsay's grand gestures were intended to open all the doors and windows of literature, to let the winds of history blow through. In "Yankee Doodle," he imagines the American flag dividing the clouds and Washington riding across the sky; in the first line of "Above the Battle's Front," he addresses as friends St. Francis, Buddha, Tolstoi, and St. John.[44] Lindsay writes ambitious, broad-brush poems on historical change in Japan, on the opening of the Panama Pacific Exposition, on the heroes of world history, on the African-American race, on the last song of Lucifer, on the ghost of the buffaloes, and on the work of Johnny Appleseed; but also, perhaps fatally the opposite of such bravado, he has many poems of trivial humor such as "The Dangerous Little Boy Fairies" and "The Mouse That Gnawed the Oak Tree Down." Lindsay had a great and easy trade in chanting American names of heroes and places. Here is hortatory rhetoric in "Litany of the Heroes":

> Would I might rouse the Lincoln in you all,
> That which is gendered in the wilderness
> From lonely prairies and God's tenderness. (192)

It was even easier to chant about a place he knew not at all, "The Congo":

> Beat an empty barrel with the handle of a broom,
> Hard as they were able,
> Boom, boom, BOOM,
> With a silk umbrella and the handle of a broom,
> Boomlay, boomlay, boomlay, BOOM.
> THEN I had religion, THEN I had a vision.
> I could not turn from their revel in derision.

THEN I SAW THE CONGO, CREEPING THROUGH THE BLACK,
CUTTING THROUGH THE FOREST WITH A GOLDEN TRACK.
Then along that riverbank
A thousand miles
Tatooed cannibals danced in files;
Then I head the boom of the blood-lust song
And a thigh-bone beating on a tin-pan gong. (178–79)

Rhythmic regularity forces the reader to reproduce a violent fantasy on the vocal cords; typographical changes exert more control; and to further determine our response and extort a performance, Lindsay adds italicized instructions in the margins of these lines, to show how they must sound: *Solemnly chanted, A rapidly piling climax of speed and racket.* The sound effects are rather gorgeous, but it is with guilty pleasure that we indulge their racial stereotypes on our inner or outer speech.

In 1913, the strutting and flailing, barking and whispering of Lindsay's self-styled higher Vaudeville were emergent and unincorporated, and to some extent his bardic virtues still challenge the exclusions of the American canon. But around 1922, the year that Eliot (one of Harriet Monroe's newer protégés who had publicly called Lindsay "impossible") published *The Waste Land*, the higher Vaudeville had been eclipsed through the achievements of fierce high modernism. Like William Carlos Williams, Lindsay must have felt Eliot's poem to be a "bullet" to his own hopes for an American poetry, but he had none of Williams's resources to regenerate his own career. Unquestionably he understood what was happening. Lindsay's announcement before he died by suicide, "They tried to get me; I got them first," is to be read, with pity and respect, as his reply to the exclusions of the canon.

Looking back, we judge poems to be failures with the help of the canon acting as selective tradition. However, the canon may also be observed, to some extent, from the prospective point of view of the writer. Lindsay was so tangled in his family romance, a warring with the Campbellite religious and moral influences of his own mother and father, that he could not conduct a satisfactory struggle with the mighty literary dead even within his own bardic line. As a consequence, it was not his fault that he undervalued the role of educational ideals in producing canons of authority. No doubt Williams, Eliot, and Wallace Stevens were deformed as well as formed at their eastern universities, but all three learned some things a writer needs to know from and about a literary canon. Poetry, Stevens said, is the scholar's art. Every innovative or canon-changing poet was first a canonically informed reader.

This is not to say Lindsay should have gone to Harvard, but rather that his limitation derives from not being able to validate his own selective tradition. How that validation happens, as for instance with Eliot and his Donne, Dryden, and Laforgue, is not our brief to describe. The fact is that Lindsay does not validate his chosen, mainly nonliterary precursor figures. His Johnny Appleseed, William Jennings Bryant, and John P. Altgeld are genial and uncontradictory. In some other treatment perhaps they could be made to yield more heroism. The same is true of the verbal sources Lindsay lifts into literature: the anecdote, the fairytale, the sermon, the hymn, the college yell and jazz lyric—all promising for a poetry from and about the American people. Lindsay wanted a great poem about the common man which would also be read by the common man: that is why the higher Vaudeville stays close to speech and popular song in its flagrant attempt to be antiliterary, and that is why Lindsay wanted audiences to bring their books and follow along with his oral performances. The reading tours themselves, gospel by Pullman, were his way of bringing poetry back to the people from whom it came. It did seem to work for a while, until the inadequacy of the prosodic, literary, imaginative, and historical basis became evident even to Lindsay himself.

Lindsay's permanent value travels some distance beyond what he actually achieved as a poet. He is what the canon excludes; his American bardic is an indictment of the canon. It is an act of contestation to bring him forward. He is thus a reminder of certain other exclusions which can only be mentioned: Blacks and Chicanos, native Americans and Asian-Americans; women and homosexuals; American writers in other languages than English; writers in other genres than fiction and poetry; writers extreme in brevity or gigantism or difficulty.

If there is such a thing as American bardic, an overtly moral, declaratory, expansive writing, the line of transmission runs through Lindsay. He was oversold in the thirties, and the reaction that set in against him between 1940 and 1960 was devastating; then with the rise of Ginsberg and Olson in the sixties the bardic-epic mode was more permissible, and Lindsay returned in a small way as a subject of scholarly investigation. He went out of fashion and out of mind in the seventies, when the epic gesture came once again to seem an absurdity and the pricking of bardic balloons became a canonical method in poets like John Ashbery. We are now in the moment of his and American bardic's near-total obliteration, and this has occurred in strict adherence to Ernst Curtius's axiom of literary systematics: "The selection of authors presupposes a classification of genres." The hierarchy of genres, however constituted, wants to suppress American bardic from its pantheons and pléiades and must continuously find that this is an unkillable genre.

CHAPTER 5. De-tonation: Another Mode of the Minimal

De-Tonation in Nineteenth-Century Theory: Friedrich Nietzsche

In our second chapter, because the rudimentary voice that edges just beyond sound and phatic communication has not had sufficient development by phenomenological methods, we examined the question of minimal articulation: "yeh, yeh, yeh." The ensuing chapters, though with continuous reference ahead and sometimes behind, have followed a historical curve. In seventeenth-century poetry, the voice of parting played a crucial role in the conceptualization of the subject, through the metaphysical and legal consequences of the scene of dying. In bardic poetry from Gray through Mickiewicz to Lindsay, a much wider public sphere and a more comprehensive account of history expands the voice to fill the space and time of the nation (even and especially when the speaker is marginalized or in exile).

Derrida, with his philosophy of antiphonocentrism, draws certain consequences for a revaluation of the self that—by the end of the twentieth century—introduces increasingly radical forms of absence into the very structure of the human subject. For Derrida, speaking is always already writing, always citation—so speaking has no special privilege or priority of reality. For him reality is volatile, always accompanied by its undoing; the actual body of philosophy is the fragment in the form of notes, prefaces, accidental jottings, postcards en route. In death, in silence, the speaking subject is in perfect tune, never makes a mistake! The act of finding a proper tone is necessarily also an act of ruination, abandonment, de-montage, de-tonation. Derrida got to this point through study of Heidegger, and beyond Heidegger to

Nietzsche. We also are working back to Nietzsche and the nineteenth century, having worked forward already by a different route than Derrida, through the historical march of the topics and texts of chapters 3 and 4.

Voice, our leading concept, cherishes the myth and message of the general; a subset of voice is tone, which by long usage in the phrase "tone of voice" loves and produces whatever is selved, inimitable. But we know individual intention in language only differentially. Tone requires a rich sense of social context. We experience literary vertigo when we cannot pin down the social register of speech tones. Certain writers wish to drop us into this vertigo and see if we survive. Poe, in "Shadow. A Parable," exploits this need in us to identify the voice. In the absence of tone is terror: the spectre "was the shadow neither of man nor of God, nor of any familiar thing," and it comes before us as unstable veering tone, disintegrating syllables as messages from the human dead:

> And then did we, the seven, start from our seats in horror, and stand trembling, and shuddering, and aghast: for the tones in the voice of the shadow were not the tones of any one being, but of a multitude of beings, and, varying in their cadences from syllable to syllable fell duskily upon our ears in the well remembered and familiar accents of many thousand departed friends.[1]

The acoustic horror of the shadow comes from the many cadences, pitches, and intonations of the one voice, which turns into a choir of many subjects, none of which is fully articulated. Each voice of a dead subject loses its articulacy, its ability to live as sentence or word, but still will not melt or perish entirely. The tonal scandal is spectral also in a purely phonetic sense, for the subject is a subject now only in the distorted manner of its utterance—still barely enough for Poe's narrator to distinguish dead souls. In this passage from Poe, as in the postmodern philosophy of écriture, the subject's voice—traditionally considered to be the stronghold of self—is instead haunted by a spectral apparition of tone. The subject loses the coherence of social articulation, complete sentences, and becomes a collection of fragmentary units; this does not invalidate the notion of a 'subject', at least in Poe, but rather, for literary pleasure and terror, shifts it radically to a new position.

If the philosophy of voice has a logical end term, this is in tonal realization as the ever-ambiguous territory of the human subject. To be explored is the premise that full articulation frequently belies the subject through repetition of socially used and abused phrases and that, accordingly, the subject becomes traceable in the marginal and incomplete ruins of discourse. This terminology is, of course, soaked in romanticism and its cult of fragments and chorographic descriptions of ruins. But nineteenth-century terminology, and our examples from Poe, Norwid, and Nietzsche, will give us some basis for a non-naive faith that the ruined subject still shelters the ability to function as a subject.

The subject is ruined in this positive, aesthetic sense by a shift from full and coherent articulation to what we described earlier as minimal articulation. Experimentally we move down the level of generality, from semantic meaning to tonality itself, where the sense is to be painstakingly constructed by linking contexts and situations. The subject resists the tendency to disappear; it produces a network of relationships between its own subject modality and particular utterances. The resulting changeable constellations of sense escape any temptation to make up a totality or plenitude. The subject is de-toned—exploded—but also deprived of one general tone and given many. This subject may be called "cacophonic"; like Poe's shadow it speaks a babble—Babel—of syllables, each of which belongs to another modality, another person or tone. There are, then, several features of such indeterminate voice: overcoming of everyday logical discourse; of sentence-based progressive thought; of one primary tone ascribed to one person. Now we may re-introduce the term *rhythm* as defined by Meschonnic (1982), which is the place in discourse where the subject position transgresses the domain of totality: "Rhythm obliges us to give over a sense taken as totality-unity-truth, and to take on a sense which is no longer totality-unity-truth."[2] When the primary pulsion of rhythm situates sense that way, it uncovers the oral, which he defines as "the internal plurality of unity, subject, and rhythm." Using Meschonnic to withdraw from such as Barthes and Foucault, we could on these grounds (yet to be validated, of course) rephrase the postmodernist critique of the subject. What if we spoke less of the subject's disappearance, and more about the dispersal of the very language used by the subject to formulate a knowledge about itself? Instead of a one-voiced subject, we have a polyphonic, even cacophonic subject. This subject describes itself in various ideological discourses; it does not cease to exist, but rather disseminates on the level of intonation and rhythm where it normally was never placed or imagined.

The work of Cyprian Norwid, the Polish super-exile of the mid-nineteenth century, may be read as a commentary on the loss of the bardic after Mickiewicz. Stanisław Brzozowski commenting on Norwid in 1905 says, "Do not be surprised that Norwid's work is so heavy, and each movement is like death. In order to say something one has to die in it; in order to see, one must part."[3] Brzozowski presents the poet's voice as "the speech of ruins." This is quite the opposite of the standard romantic critical point; instead of the inflation of the self, we have its diminution, fragmentation, de-tonation. Brzozowski implies that Norwid's voice has been invaded by death, the voicing itself a result of a clash of elements that changes a solid structure into a heap of ruins. The subject has to be ruined to be able to speak. This locates Norwid in the continuity of changes in thinking through the place of the subject, since the seventeenth-century scene of dying.

Norwid is no longer in the proud but anxious bardic situation of Mickiewicz or Słowacki, and not yet in the aggressively antimetaphysical situation of Nietzsche. He places himself by his own philosophy of history in the poem "Słowotwór," about a dying culture of the "printed letter" to be replaced by a society based on a Slavic national Logos:

> Druk, gocka litera,
> Litera umiera . . .
>   Tyś rzekł, o! Panie.
> Jehowo, Jehowo,
> Wracamy w twe Słowo,
> My bo Słowianie.
> To słowo w bez-mowie,
> Choć z niego przysłowie
>   I zmartwychwstanie![4]
>
> [Print, the Gothic letter,
> The letter dies . . .
>   You have said it, O! Lord.
> Jehova, Jehova,
> We're back to your Word,
> As we are Slavs.
> This word is in nonspeech
> Although proverbs derive from it
>   And Resurrection.]

The death of the letter, coordinated with the coming of print technology, does not for Norwid mean an automatic privileging of voice; what is liberated by this death is not breath, rather a de-toned voice, a toneless voice, nonspeech in which the word resides. Foreshadowing Heidegger's discourse of architectural terms, Norwid stresses residence: not only the word dwells in the nonspeech, but also the human being. "Wracamy w twe Słowo" contains the preposition "w" or "in," which stresses not only a mere coming back but also dwelling in the Word. This nonspeech is not, in Norwid, mere silence but a de-toned voice, deprived of personal tenor but also of the pressure of socially acceptable pitch. The freedom of this liberated voice is only to be actualized in and through de-tonement; one could say that the atonement of the subject and the death of a certain civilization, much to be hoped for, lies in the de-tonement of its voice.[5]

One of the constant subjects of Norwid's philosophy is the liberation of voice from personal and social restrictions. In "The Four Pages of a Social Song" (1848), social freedom is presented not as abolition of classes and the division of the worker's labor that prevents whole persons; but through the term *good will*, which manifests itself as phonic harmony of thought and musical tone:

> Wolność w Polsce będzie inna
> Nie szlachecko-złota,
> Ni słomiana wolność gminna
> Od płota do płota . . . .
> Wolność będzie z dobrej woli,
> Jak w pieśni rymowej,
> Gdzie i z nutą myśl swawoli,
> I nuta gra słowy.[6]
>
> [Poland will have another freedom:
> Not gentry-like golden,
> Neither like a type of straw common
> From one fence to another . . . .
> Freedom will be of good will,
> As in songs that rhyme,
> Where the thought plays with a note,
> And the note rings out in the words.]

Elsewhere Norwid writes that "Wherever the inner word [*wewnętrzne słowo*] suffered. . . /There walked the hyena of slavery" (3, 581): slavery comes either as forceful imposition of a tone, or as a unification of the plurality of toneless voices under one generally accepted tone. Polish romanticism, Brzozowski accurately summarizes, has as its fundamental law "the salvation of the nation which does not have anything else left except the word, the salvation in and through the word."[7] Polish romanticism, including Norwid, combines this philosophy of national survival with a linguistic-poetic etymology that bases the name of the Slavonic tribes in phonetic proximity to the Word (*Słowianie-Słowo*).[8]

Dropping the national motif, Derrida in the present day is equally straightforward about de-tonation as the only genuine method of poetry and philosophy. In the early work, *Speech and Phenomena,* Derrida states, "My death is structurally necessary at the pronunciation of the word 'I.'"[9] There is a linkage between subject, voice, and death: like Brzozowski, Derrida does not speak about physical death, but about its structual variant—that is, of the possibility of death necessary for the phonetic act *(au prononcé).* Derrida's reading of Western philosophy is in this sense like Donne's reading in poetry, a listening to the legacy of tones wherein each voice reaches us from a crypt. As executors of such legacies, they cannot fulfill their missions, because each of their pronouncements will be a legacy in its own right. As in the story by Poe, Derrida hears a plurality of voices, polyphonic and often multilingual tones which are pronouncements of "our long deceased friends." To be aware of these tones is to relive, forever, the horror of being buried alive and the dilemma of the vagueness of the borderline between life and death. It is not only "The Purloined Letter" that should be investigated in search of Derridian tenets, but also "Ligeia," "Berenice," and "The Premature Burial." Derrida himself refers to Poe in this early book, precisely in the context of death in life: "This is not an extraordinary tale by Poe, but the ordinary tale of language."[10] In the phonetic gesture of pronouncing, each word is separately spoken then cancelled, constructed then ruined. We have to remain within fragmentary utterances, verbal ruins, and changeable maneuvers. Somewhat later in his career, Derrida begins *Margins of Philosophy* (1972) with just such a formulation of a logos which undoes what it has pronounced by turning it into a sound or sounding board, a semi-articulate production of vocal cords, "a logos which creates itself and negates itself in letting its voice well up."[11]

Another route leading to Derrida from the previous century is Nietzsche's meditation on the aesthetic qualities that result from disruption of tone.[12] Nietzsche's philosophy of voice centers on the notions of tone and de-tonation. Tone of voice, for him, has as one property the ability to make the human subject unsure about the stability of linkages between thought and its verbal communication. In *Human, All Too Human,* Nietzsche speaks about the "danger in the voice," which he defines as a betrayal of "to mean" by "to say": "Sometimes in conversation the sound of our own voice [*der Klang der eigenen Stimme*) confuses us and misleads us to assertions that do not at all reflect our opinion."[13] The tone (sound, Klang) confuses and misleads the speaking subject and disrupts the process of reflecting mimesis which ought to hold between thought and speech act. This is not visual but aural mimesis; Nietzsche's English translators use the word *reflection* for his *entsprechen* which means the speaking of the tone (*sprechen* would be the speaking of the subject); for Nietzsche this particular, momentarily deluded speaking subject is deprived of its tone, ceases to be its own tone master. This emancipation of tone does not eradicate the subject itself, which must listen from a distance to the pronouncement which is not completely its own. This speaking subject may be misled, but plainly also is aware of being misled: can hear itself without being totally alienated from itself.

For Nietzsche, this form of aesthetic disruption has historical causes. He believes that the history of German is a slow process of the spoken being taken over by the written, to the extent that we get "the predominance of the literary style over the talk, and the formality and affection of an entire people [become] the basis of a common and no longer dialectical language."[14] The tone of German in the Middle Ages "was extremely rustic and vulgar," Nietzsche argues as he expounds this history in *The Gay Science;* "even at present . . . it still sounds very coarse, sylvan, and hoarse." The history of German is one of the "affectation becoming natural" through a slow appropriation of the "chancery style"—rustic tones replaced by the artificial tones of *die Kanzlei,* legal language, officialese. In the modern epoch Nietzsche hears "a similar striving after selectness of tone" [*Vernemheit des Klanges*] which wishes to replace the chancery style by "something mocking, cold, indifferent and careless in the voice" [*etwas hochnisches, kaltes, gleichgültiges, nachlassiges in der Stimme*]. The chancery has been replaced as a model by the Prussian officer, with his immodesty and inelegance.

So for Nietzsche, tone is a language too, or a kind of social notation, through and by means of which the subject speaks about itself and others. In *Ecce Homo,* a philosopher and physician is required to hear tones with delicate ears. In *Beyond Good and Evil,* Germans are deprived of this ability, read not for the ear but for the eyes, and thus they accept the detonation (but not disappearance) of the subject. Even at the high moment of the attack on the modern self, Nietzsche will believe that "at the bottom of us . . . there is . . . some granite of spiritual fatum"; "whenever a cardinal problem is at stake, there speaks an unchangeable, 'this is I.'"[15] Nietzsche's "I" is more multiple and physiological than Kant's. His speaking subject exists not less but more as it is disseminated, in ruined form, throughout all the segments of communication. For him, as for Norwid, this most effectively takes place in verbal art, where the aesthetic stance is characterized by "the extreme sharpness of certain senses, so that they are capable of understanding a totally different language of signs—and to create such a language . . . [and] the ability of being rid of one's self by means of gestures and attitudes, the ability of speaking about one's self in a hundred different languages—in fact a state of explosion."[16] Art-speech best brings about a detonation of the subject, and at the same time a rediscovery of its tone, even of its *tonus* or tension and elasticity of body tissue. Such an excess of subjectivity, due to a linking of this dispersal and proliferation of discourses with the body, produces in the intellectual sphere a high-intensity productiveness within language.

Nietzsche's statements on the social de-tonement of the subject constitute one early phenomenological analysis of the basic character of intentionality. In *Human, All Too Human*, he speaks of the release of the subject from its trivial concerns when we read aloud dramatic poetry: we "make discoveries" about our possible selves when Apollonian sense-making logic no longer entirely rules over sound. In the Dionysian logic, the word is interpreted by tone, music, melody; the subject is located, for the time, outside or next to articulation. The human subject steps aside from the everyday and inauthentic voice—but only momentarily. As always with Nietzsche, one conclusion undercuts another, and this subject through authentication by the tone is also exposed to all the manipulative maneuvers of the tone. The Dionysian subject, driven by melody and intonation, deprives itself of the Apollonian logical defense system against the forcefulness of the tones of others.

The Passage: Jacques Derrida

As we have said, this book (in itself a contorted undertaking as it attempts to "write" voice, but is it not a general predicament of someone who operates within a language incessantly to cross from one "dimension" of speech to the other, to penetrate through the dark holes of speaking to the side of writing and vice versa; did we not write, "as we have SAID"?) comes from the space between two places. It is a product of a separation (geographical, but also at the time when it was conceived as a research project markedly political), a difference, which was both personal and social. Each cooperation grows from the respect for this difference and is a homage both to the places that generated certain ideas and to the distance which intervenes. One could claim that in such a project the nominative case does not, cannot, exist as each statement is in part divided and in part shared (in the sense of the French word, *partage*); each sentence and each word begins "in the middle" of the other's discourse (does not begin as the subject's independent, individual production); each pronouncement is precisely a "dependent case," a case other than locatable and authoritarian nominative. This book continues as it began, as a word of transition, a statement of passage between places, persons, political systems, the spoken and the written. This is what Jacques Derrida calls "Schibboleth":

> This word I call hebraic, you are aware that it may be found in a whole family of languages, phoenician, judeo-aramaic, syriac. It is crossed by a multiplicity of senses: large river, river, ear of wheat, shoot of olive. But beyond this sense, it has taken on the value of a word of past and passage. We used it, during or after the war, to cross a guarded border.[17]

The scene is evidently one of danger, but also of domesticity which one tries to protect against a foreign incursion: double function of a frontier which, separating and dividing, has also a neurotically uniting power; the unity guarded by a border is "neurotic" because it is founded upon the identity of the "we" determined against any "them." But the problematic of division and partition is not only external. To begin with, it is an inherent question of language whose surface is wounded and discontinuous. (This terminology inadvertently circulates around the issue of violence as if to signal that language cannot be taken for granted as a straightforward manifestation of peace reducing all the differences.) If language problematized by violence animates the spirit of questioning, of what Hans-Georg Gadamer refers to as "hermeneutical consciousness,"[18] then we need a form of answer which would enable us to move freely from one territory to another. We need a password, or a schibboleth. Our effort aims then at providing a number of such passwords with a necessary proviso that each one of them—voice, speaking subject, the bardic—is nothing else but also a question, a calling out toward an approaching party, a way of finding out their identity. Thus, we must operate in the realm of "if" which inevitably precedes all our discourse and begins many of our actual sentences: we speak as if we had a voice, or this is what we would say if we had a voice. The whole project is, then, located in cases other than nominative. The subjunctive mood of the inquiry, as existential situation and as rhetoric, prefigures the dilemma of the subject, and the speaking subject in particular.

Return now to the passage we quoted from Beckett in chapter 1: "What would I say, if I had a voice, who says this, saying it's me?" The one who speaks is at the mercy of the Other, who belongs to the domain of death. The one who speaks is himself (or herself) taken over by death, and the voice resounds from the crypt or a vault, "the pit of my inexistence." And yet the death of the Other is not, so to speak, complete, as he/she/it (necessary confusion of pronouns) "feels," "says," wants to "kill." Similarly, the speaking subject is not fully dead either, he is "there" and turns to the mute audience demanding a "simple answer." What is dead in this subject that speaks is its voice, which has been removed to the realm of the conditional: "What would I say if I had a voice?" The subject speaks with a voice that has only a spectral "inexistence." Nevertheless, speaking is possible but only as a dependent case, that is as a detached phenomenon, the origin or matrix of which, the nominative, must remain unknown. The one who speaks presents itself as an "accusative," a direct object of the verb. We can see how the presence associated with voice and its authority crumbles and turns into the abysmal "pit of inexistence" and a play of reflections and images. The one who speaks is a companion of the "old stranger" who/which (no ground for a decision) defies a clear identification by the fact that he "is nothing." The speaking subject is then an adjunct, a dependent case, an accusative of nothing which denomination describes as not a mere vacuum, but a state where the binary opposition designated "reality" ceases to function. The Other is living and dead at the same time.

At the beginning of his career, Derrida alludes to these two essential facts of philosophy: (1) the demystification of the phonocentric presence; and (2) the impossibility of completely abandoning this concept. What remains is a certain Gothic version of philosophy which combines the motif of the encryptment or confinement with the yet-audible production of utterances. Thus, "It remains, then, for us to speak, to make our voices resonate throughout the corridors in order to make up for [*suppleer*] the break up of presence."[19] This resonating power bereft of the specific source and locatable origin, the power whose operation is based on the play of substitutions and echoes, is what the philosopher called "écriture." *Ecriture* is not, then, a form of notation but a version of the ghastly, vampirical speaking which is rooted in the secret, twilight zone between life and death. Hence, "As in hieroglyphs or rebuses, voice is circumvented [*circonvenue*]."[20] It follows that voice must lose its regulatory authority and become subjected to other systems. Writing on Antonin Artaud, Derrida notices that the word does not disappear from the theatre of cruelty, but is removed from the central position to be dissolved in the body of the actor: "The word will cease commanding the action but it will remain present there. It will occupy a place rigorously delimited; with function in a system that will control it"; Artaud's is a "system of signs wherein the institution of the voice no longer commands" (pp. 351, 287). Turning voice into script does not make the vocal vanish; rather it creates its nervous proliferation. The speaking voice multiplies its productivity to present a convincing argument for its own existence, to get out of the "pit of inexistence," and to cover up traces of its transgressive activities. If *écriture* spells an attack on the central position of presence and voice, then inevitably it must also criticize their most venerable attributes signifying the paternal and political authority—the Father; and must also denounce scientific epistemology as the only way of achieving truth. (Light as a chief metaphor for cognition is emphasized, for example, in Descartes' *Discourse on Method,* where the "light of reason," is always presented as the natural source of truth: *"la lumiere naturelle"* common to all people.) Hence in the *Grammatology* Derrida speaks of the writing gesture as a killing in which the victim is the figure of the Father ("Writing . . . which kills in a single gesture father and light").[21] As we can see, the scripted voice is very distanced from the reading of the purely spoken voice which presents it as a realm of integrity, identity, and unity. Now voice opens a new epoch: "Death of the Father inaugurates the reign of violence."[22] This movement in Derrida's thought brings the problem of the speaking subject closer to the tradition of the pre-Socratics, who believed in the conflict-based model of the world; Heraclitus, for example, held that "war is the king of all and the father of all." The speaking subject is, then, a disembodied voice which operates in the realm of "dark thinking," and whose world, as well as the subject itself, is an arrangement of various factions at war with one another. We should not falsify this image of the one who speaks by means of traditional representational motifs, with notions like 'harmony', 'identity', 'unity', 'totality'. The voiced subject is, in fact, the one whose speech comes after the murder of the Father and the fading of light, and since both attributes were crucial for the philosophy of speaking, then voice must cease to be what it was. It becomes voiceless. Hence Beckett's question, or rather schibboleth: "What would I say, if I had a voice?"

Still the question of the pronoun remains. Who is this "I" that Beckett shows as an I and not I at the same time? The foundational study, in which the subject lost its extralinguistic existence, remains Benveniste's "Subjectivity in Language." Benveniste begins the essay with the statement "The 'I' . . . does not denominate any lexical entity" and goes on to claim in the same sentence that the mere supposition that "I" could refer to a particular individual would be a linguistic scandal: "How could the same term refer . . . to any individual whatsoever and still . . . identify him in his individuality?"[23] In a traditional theory of grammar, pronouns substitute for nouns as a matter of convenience. James Beattie introduces his 1788 discussion of pronouns by the following riddle: "Suppose me to meet with a person, whose name I know not, and to whom I am equally unknown."[24] In such a situation, the very process of the exchange of information is disturbed:

"He knows not my name, and I know not his. I might point to myself . . . and to him . . . but this would be inconvenient in the dark, and awkward in any circumstances." It is the intervention of pronouns that solves the problem: "Instead of two proper names, substitute the two pronouns I and You." Pronouns are, then, the domain of clarity and determine the sense of identity necessary for the exchange of information. The very fact that they replace proper names testifies to their power as identifiers. The pronoun is another name given to what has already been identified as extralinguistically fixed. Wilhelm von Humboldt (1836) seems less decisive on this issue. He believes that "true individuality resides only in the *speaker* at any given time,"[25] but this claim assumes the existence of an individual in whom language receives "its ultimate determinacy," which in turn establishes the I as fundamentally extralinguistic. For Benveniste, "'I' refers to the act of the individual discourse in which it is pronounced, and by this it designates the speaker" (p. 226). Thus, the speaking I is "exclusively linguistic" (p. 226), and instead of the traditional relation of substitution or sheltering residence, we obtain that of designation, that is of the pointing earlier writers wanted to avoid: of marked difference.

No matter what we say (again the fated verb; but does not Beckett himself list it as one of the three key verbs inaugurating his text, to go, to be, to say?) still, somebody speaks, at least, somebody speaks in our name. The question is to determine his/her/its/their identity. However, this has to fail for two reasons. Even if we did succeed in our mission, all we would learn is who speaks on our behalf, who pretends to be us. Then, too, this task is nothing new, it has been undertaken many times before with the same result. All we can diagnose is the presence effect of "the same old stranger." But the word *presence* is not correct either; the presence of the Other is posited and not noticeable to the degree to which he/she/it/they feel the essential incompleteness of their being. The "old stranger" is "looking for me," "wants me there . . . with a form." The old stranger is one who speaks in our name, but who can exist only because our name is denied to him/her/it/them. The speaking subject is then conceivable in our project not so much as a disintegrated self but as the one who seeks and is sought, a picaresque subject whose voice belongs always to the Other—the speaking subject, the passing subject (one *in statu viae*, and one living and reliving its death), the looked-for subject.

Voice does not bring up notions of security and identity, but those of the end (understood both as the final point, the destination of the quest, and the purpose and goal) and violence (as a show of force used against me by those who speak for me, and as used by me in my efforts to resist this ventriloquism). Derrida in his later texts brings back the very term *voice* so dramatically criticized in his earlier writings. What matters now, however, is less voice itself but its subtlety and intonation. What is at stake is the physical underpinning of the voice—the tone. Derrida advises us to take heed not only of the differential multiplications within voice, but also of the divisions within divisions which intervene in the voice in order to open spaces beyond any possible pluralism or specifications.[26]

Voice loses its solidity and becomes a cracked surface, which opens fissures leading underground: toward the romantic epistemology of the chasm and descent, as in S. T. Coleridge's "Kubla Khan," essential for "thinking darkly," the phrase to which we shall recur. This in turn makes the ground of the truth of voice useless as a place of foundation for the edifice of self-knowledge. Derrida's recent interest in architecture, particularly in the work of Peter Eisenman and in the cooperative venture with Bernard Tschumi in Parc-de-la-Villette, shows that what is at stake is a new art of building. This art would leave behind Heidegger's studious elaboration of the linkage between the foundations (earth) and a sense-abandoning structure (sky). Derrida takes up the motif of an architecture without foundations, the architecture thus cosmic and chasmic in its character. In a 1989 text, Derrida begins a P.S. to his letter with overtly Heideggerian terminology ("I thought of the Heaven and of the Earth"), but abandons the Heideggerian trajectory since the missile/missive of his thought now tries to consider the necessity of leaving earth (*quitter le sol terrestre*): "Would one say about the architecture of a rocket and of astronautics in general . . . that they dispense with foundations and hence with keeping standing, with standing up, with the *vertical position* of humans or with *building* generally?"[27] Derrida comes back to voice to demolish (de-tone) the original project of presence and solidity, but also of linear, Darwinian development. The voice can no longer function as the guarantor of verticality and erection (*tenir debout*), no longer evolves but de-volves and re-volves.

The apocalyptic tone of which Derrida writes, following Kant, deals not with the prophecy of the end but, rather, with the impossibility of such a prophecy. The end, that is, the truth, for example the truth of the speaking subject—"truth itself is the end, the destination"[28]—is always on its way; as such, it is happening right now and here. If the subject is a being *in statu viae*, then necessarily this state must coincide with the state of death, the end, always on its way, a picaresque encounter of existence. "The end is soon, it is imminent . . . I see it, I know it, I tell you it, now you know it, come." Derrida's own tone here shows he is mocking the philosophy of endings. We hear the same call in the Beckett passage where the speaking voice looks for its source, author, and mouth with the same apocalyptic project of becoming either an agent or an object of the act of "voiding of existence," of "having [one] dead." In both Derrida and Beckett the project is aborted, thus ended, but did we not say that the end is always on its way? because the identity of the one who speaks and the one who hears is unclear. The voice who says "me" does not have to be "me." Beckett begins with a question and a call for a "simple answer" and obtains, as a result, a long and meandering shifting of roles between speaking and hearing, the shifting which poses more problems without solving any of them. Derrida confesses that this amorous and deadly "Come on" ["Viens"] need not come from the voice which signifies me, neither does it originate in the tone which means me: "'Come' cannot come from a voice, or at least from a tone signifying 'I' or 'self.[29]

The point of destination is equally questionable:

> "Come" does not address itself . . . to an identity determinable in advance. It is a drift [*une dérive*] underivable from the identity of a determination. [*"C'est une dérive undérivable depuis l'identité d'une détermination."*] "Come" is *only* derivable, absolutely derivable, but only from the other, from nothing that may be an origin or a verifiable, decidable, presentable, or appropriable identity.

This philosopher's "tone," not that of the linguist or literary critic, is no more than a sign of the me which remains undecidable. This notion of 'tone' is one which bursts the discreteness and discernibility of speech and its elements. Derrida disrupts a long tradition of thinking about voice as the seat of the subject, the tone directly linked with the emotional structure of human being. To entertain this earlier position on tone has consequences. First, discreteness and singularity of the units of speech production has always been considered a major feature, distinguishing human language either from animal sounds (with the exception of birds) or a difficult and problematic area of the human being's spontaneous responses to various life situations. Since the early grammarians, voice has always been considered fundamental but also troublesome, subject to strict rules of conduct and control. The classical grammarians, carefully distinguishing between *vox articulata* and *vox confusa*, emphasized as the essential disposition a divisibility and hierarchal order within the former sphere. This ordering progressed from the *littera* through the *syllaba* and *dictio* to the *oratio*, and in a striking way a discussion of voice (*de voce*) became, long before Derrida, intrinsically linked with the question of writing. Hence Donatus will establish a clear gradation of production (*facit*): *"Vox enim facit litteram, litterae faciunt syllabam, syllabae faciunt partes orttionis."*[30] The link with scriptability necessarily means a liaison with rationality. Thus we read in Diomedes that *"omnis vox aut articulata est confusa.*

Articulata est rationalis hominum loquellis explanata. Eadem et litteralis vel scriptilis appelatus. . . confusa est irrationalis vel inscriptilis, simplici vocis sono animalium effecta, quae scribi non potest" (18). Of course Derrida denies the possibility of such a segmenting. If one denies such distinctness, then one has to launch a decisive attack on the written and literary character of culture, and on the rational origin of culture. If then Derrida, in his "spectrography of tone and of the changing of tone,"[31] makes us aware of the problematic character of the speaker and listener, he does that with an eye on how to rethink the foundations of Western culture.

Beckett has a similar task. Beckett emphasizes three crucial elements of the positioning of the speaking subject.

1. Voice is irrational: the speaker in Beckett will admit that "it's not with thinking that he will find me," stressing the illusory character of understanding ("it's easy to understand . . . but he does not understand").
2. Operations of voice are ahermeneutic: something easy to understand is, in speech, therefore closed to understanding, where what is at stake is not the concealment of meaning but rather its erasure or transference to the area of "nothing," where the subject cannot act unless everyday life logic is suspended; hence "mad, mad, he's mad" in Beckett.
3. Voice is made bestial or monstrous: the "he" who is also the "I" is a "nothing," but this nothing, to be represented, must be supplied with representable features which allude to something which is representable and defies representation at the same time: a monster, a shapeless old stranger.

There are some less obvious, nevertheless essential, references to voice and its relation with the subject in the passage. The "me" admits that the "old stranger" wants him "there, with a form and a world." This need of a speaking subject to have a spoken form and world, for a central self, is not new at all, of course; what is relatively new, as Beckett records, is the partition of suspicion between the speaking and the spoken. In 1836, Wilhelm von Humboldt begins his inquiry *On Language* by putting in one sentence all the beliefs concerning the centrality of voice and its associations with reason, logic, unity, and understanding:

> Just as thought at its most human is a yearning from darkness into light, from confinement into the infinite, so sound streams outward from the heart's depths, and finds a medium wonderfully suited to it in the air, the most refined and easily movable of

> all elements, whose seeming incorporeality is also a sensuous counterpart to the mind.[32]

Humboldt goes on to claim that the role of sound grew out of its discrete, distinct use, out of its articulatory qualities. Hence, we read about words as "the signs of *particular* concepts" (70), or about "the cutting sharpness of the vocal sound" (55). The distinctness of sound in making a language into a process rather than a fact, *energeia* rather than *ergon*, is for Humboldt conducive to and most strikingly present in the form sounds give to thought. If "language cannot be indeed regarded as a material that simply sits there . . . but must be seen as something that eternally produces itself" (58), then the notion of the 'form' must acquire a particular importance as it stabilizes and shapes the otherwise fluid stream of linguistic becoming. The form in Humboldt's theory is primarily the "sound form" [*Lautform*] which is "the expression which language creates for thought" (76). If the voice in Beckett's text is to provide the old stranger with "a form," we can understand this form as a call for meaning and truthful representation—that is, for the undisturbed and reliable link between sound and meaning. Humboldt claims that the "connection . . . between sound and its meaning, seems certain" (71) and later on emphatically states that the meaninglessness of sound would be a major incursion upon the major mechanisms of language production: "The crux of the matter is that significance should truly permeate the sound; that nothing in the sound but its meaning should appear, at once and unbroken, to the ear that receives it" (76). Thus, the evasion of articulation and the role of the speaking subject can be presented now as a voice which must necessarily possess some form, but we, listeners or readers, know from what the voice says that this form is without its meaning, to use Humboldt's categories, because it is spoken in somebody else's voice, somebody who is a "nothing." So at the same time this highly questionable form is created by the Other, the old stranger who desires it with a deadly passion. The speaking voice is, then, a form wished for and made by the Other and constantly doubted by the one who speaks. By this route we arrive at a peculiar resaying of Bakhtin's theories of dialogism and heteroglossia—of the concept of our 'word' that always half-belongs (or worse: more-than-half-belongs) to somebody else.

The situation is similar with the concept of the 'world' ("he wants me there, with a form and a world"): for Humboldt, language presents a good example of intersubjectivity. What language presents is subjective as far as location, but these sounds turn back on their maker. In language, the "mental striving breaks out through the lips . . ., the product of that striving returns back to the speaker's ear. Thus, the presentation becomes transformed into real objectivity, without being deprived of subjectivity" (56); and accordingly, as we may illustrate with the present-day phenomenon of slight estrangement at hearing played back to us our tape-recorded voice, the language becomes another world, "a second world that man has objectified out of himself" (70). This desire for "a world" in Beckett's monologist, in Humboldt's theory, and in the response to tape-recorded voice is in fact yet another, more emphatic, version of the yearning for a reliable link between sign and concept, representation and meaning, sound and sense—which is precisely the longing that the speaking subject must deny and leave behind.[33]

The speaking subject is that mode of voicing one's being which disturbs a clear connection between sound and sense. In so doing, the speaking subject must then operate on the boundary separating the articulate and the inarticulate—in the terms of classical Roman grammar, the boundary between the *vox articulata* and the *vox confusa*. This strengthens what we have claimed above concerning the monstrosity of the speaking subject, as *vox confusa* is traditionally ascribed to beasts, the creatures that cannot write, or to the inanimate objects used as vehicles in human hands. (*"Quae est confusa? Quae scribi non potest, ut puta velut ovium balatus, equi hinnitus, mugitus bovis"* [Victorianus]; *"inanimalium autem est ut puta cymbalorum tinnitus, flagellorum strepitus, undarum pulsus,"* Probus).[34] Beckett's "all the confusion" refers to this dilemma in which the speaking voice, rather than the speaking subject, is strangely disembodied, stripped of specific forms in its wandering between the me and the old stranger; the speaking voice is an egregious nonform outside, and in between, whatever is beast or thing or human being.

To think of the speaking subject must mean to think from within these differences, and thus a mere restricting of the voice to *vox humana* is no longer tenable. For the later work of Derrida, such a thinking and a readmission of voice into the canon of his philosophical terminology takes place in the realm of sound and tonalities. *Vox confusa* of the ancient Roman grammarians and the "confusion" of Beckett become, in Derrida's interpretive practices, sounds operating on the borders between languages, circulating among various speeches, and denying easy national identification. In his respectful reluctance to approach James Joyce ("I've never dared write on Joyce"), Derrida decides to use a fragment which refuses completely to identify itself as language, nation, politics. He reads Joyce by means of a schibboleth, a password which passes and lets pass, a sound without residence."He war" are the title's *Two Words for Joyce*: "These are only half English, if you will, if you truly wish to hear them, that's to say to do a little more than hear them: to read them."[35] Thus, when making a decision to pronounce a word, and this is always a matter of will [*voulez*] but also of manners, kindness, and care [*si vous voulez bien*], the individual enters the realm of the freedom of language. Now the sounded words are no longer restricted to the reader's idiosyncratic semantics, but operate on the level where human meaning is only partially true [*à moitié*]. Such a voiced language is then, by half, appropriated by the Other, and this appropriation is a constituting power in the speaking voice. On the one hand, voice represents what is uniquely individual; voice dismantles through metalepsis and paronomasia its individualizing and identifying function. The human regional intention, understood here as mere volition, is treated with philosophical irony: we may wish something but the ultimate result of our wishing [*si vous voulez*] is activation of power that does not take our wishing into account.

Humboldt makes a similar point in chapter 9 of his essay, where he wonders, "How small, in fact, is the power of the individual compared to the might of language?" (63), but Humboldt will admit that "true individuality resides only in the speaker at any given time" (63). Humboldt's claim is based on the principle that "only in the individual does language receive its ultimate determinacy" (63). Plainly this disagrees dramatically with more recent thinking: with Bakhtin's philosophy of cocreative dialogism, and with Derrida's response to "He war," in which our polite wishing [*si vous voulez bien*] is precisely a plunge into penultimate indeterminacy of language. (We say penultimate, because "ultimate" without the prefix would again turn us toward determinacy). "He war," a phrase divided among languages, when voiced reads "he wars" in the sense of waging a war, but also appears to be partly German ("war" as past tense of "to be"), and through this confusion the phrase introduces the motive of Babel, itself a contorted production, "difficult to say if this was a noun, a proper name, or a common noun spreading confusion."[36]

Hence the speaking subject can no longer isolate itself in the certainty of the ownership of its own voice, but has to remain a vigilant listener to various tonalities. In the terminology of deconstruction, one could say that the one who speaks does not reside in the domain of the same, but just the opposite; that one operates in the territory dominated by the difference. This implies that even a singular voice is from the start implicated in the proliferation of timbres and tonalities. The final pages of Derrida's meditation on Joyce bring back all the phonetic terminology of discourse:

> A differential resonance of several tonalities, several degrees of laughing agreement [*oui-rire*, literally, hearlaugh] which do not

> let themselves get fixed into a single dispatch from one self to another, or a single password; rather these call out to the countersign of the other, to a YES which resonates in an entirely different writing, another language, another idiosyncrasy, with another quality of tone [*timbre*].

Derrida's move is toward the Other of the voice—toward such a vocalization of discourse which would unconceal the *vox confusa* underneath *vox articulata*, which would demonstrate the inhuman in the speaking apparently totally subjugated to the human. If we can say about, and after, Heidegger that "the soundless voice of Being is an inhuman voice, and the role of the poet is to preserve its silence" (Steven L. Bindeman), then Derrida's reading of the same problem would emphasize its consequences for the construction of the speaking subject.[37] The voice of the individual is always broken and shattered, multitimbred, and the role of the philosopher is to try to find ways in which this situation can find a representation in human sounds. In Heidegger the yes-saying assumes the form of silence; in Derrida the *oui-dire* becomes the *oui-rire*, hearlaugh becomes hearsay.

The *oui-rire* or *vouloir-rire* brings in the element of monstrosity, or inhumanity, inevitably constitutive of the speaking subject as envisaged in the present book. Beattie in "The Theory of Language" (1788) distinguished between human and animal sounds precisely in terms of discreteness and articulation. Beattie claims that "the voices of brute animals are not broken . . . into distinct elementary sounds, like those of man when he speaks," and, what is more important, that human speech is not grounded in instincts but in "distinct ideas."[38] Such a grounding implies that laughter, like other similar reactions, must be related to humanity's animal and biological aspect. Thus, according to Beattie, animal sounds are "analogous, not to our speaking, but to our weeping, laughing, groaning, screaming, and other natural and audible expressions of passion" (5). To take into account laughter as a variety of voice, as its tonality, recovers the value of desire—"those peculiar tones of the voice, which all men know to be significant of certain passions and sentiments," says Beattie (10)—and thus designates the realm of voice as the territory of freedom of desire or its transference to the level where the subject does not restrain it. According to Beattie at his most conventional, "Anger, Joy, Sorrow, Hope, Fear, Scorn, Contentment, Pity, Admiration, when under no restraint, appear in the voice" (10). This freedom is not absolute, for there are limits determined by congruence of subject matter and its representation: lamenting by laughing would be, for Beattie, "ridiculous." Other limits are given by social convention: "in polite conversation, no voices, looks, or attitudes are allowable, but such as betoken kindness, attention, good-humor, and a desire to please" (13).

By contrast, the *vouloir-rire*, or will to laughter, in recent texts by Derrida, has the sounded word as a schibboleth circulating to and fro between various languages; and this must leave behind the tradition of interpretive and semantic clarity and luminosity, which are now replaced by opaqueness. This move is also representable by a shift from the pleasure of the eye to the pleasure of the ear: "the primitive scene, the full authority of the father, the law, pleasure through and by means of the ear."[39] To speak is then to think. In this Derrida follows Humboldt: "Language is the formative organ of thought,"[40] but the similarities do not extend further back to the Cartesian paradigm of light. Charles Winquist, writing on deconstruction in theology, refers to such pleasure-of-the-ear theory as "thinking darkly," by which he means operating on the level of desire rather than of well-articulated thought. To think darkly would be, like laughter in Beattie's discussion but in a positive sense, related to the inhuman. It means redirecting thought in such a way that we may deal with both the determinate and the indeterminate meanings. "Thinking darkly," as Winquist puts it, "begins with the recognizable experiences, tangible feelings, and active fantasies," and characteristically mixes the archetypal images of circulating sound and schibboleth, and the familiar figures of everyday life, which intertwine with each other in "the darkness of language."[41]

The Periphery: Henri Meschonnic

For Marshall McLuhan, voice (along with radio, its modern technological avatar) belongs to the paradigm of memory. However, this voice is not a private memory of intimate moments in which the individual is separated from others; voice for McLuhan is rather the memory which reconstitutes links between person and society: "Radio is not only a mighty awakener of archaic memories, forces, and animosities, but a decentralizing, pluralistic force. . . . Centralism of organization is based on the continuous, visual, lineal structuring that arises from phonetic literacy."[42] Meschonnic in a series of books will advance a similar point: "To speak is to keep being born."[43] For Meschonnic, word of mouth is constitutive of the human condition, but it is not by this word that this condition is fulfilled. Disputing the very concept of 'postmodernity', Meschonnic rejects Jean-François Lyotard's claim that the function of the oral form is anamnesis. Speaking does not exhaust itself in the act of recitation, as Lyotard maintains, but belongs to a wide network of relationships which regulate human conduct in the world. African cultures, in their oral tale telling, not only commemorate the moment of community at the telling; they also establish a very clear link between the present and the past. Meschonnic comments: "A very peculiar error, to state that such a culture does not have a need of remembering its past."[44]

But then voice, in Meschonnic's theory, must mean something else or something in addition to sound production. There has to be an element which transcends empirical voice, delegates its various modulations (or tonalities, as Derrida would say) to various segments of reality, various circumstances, various times of day and night: "Feasts, burials. Initiations. Tales by men, or women. What is told by day. What is told by night." This segmentation already implies certain regularities, certain foreseeable dispositions into which changes of voice will have to be fitted. Hence, to speak of voice(s) is to unravel important historical processes which conditioned the circumstances of voice. What is at stake is a question of *rhythm*, to bring in Meschonnic's key term which is not only technical but calls upon the social memory of a speaking subject: "rhythm is a historicity of the text; it implies a sociality, a sharing of time between subjects, potential updatings. Meter alone is without memory." Thus, the oral (*oralité*), we are warned, is not to be identified with the spoken. (Meschonnic's distinction resembles Heidegger's between *Sprechen* and *Sagen*.)

> No, the oral is not primarily sound. When you hear the oral, you do not hear sound, you hear the subject, from the physiological to the historical and cultural elements that compose the continuity of rhythm that constitutes that specific mode of signifying. When the subject prevails, whether it be in written or in spoken language, there is the oral. The oral is quite a different concept from that of the spoken.[45]

So the oral resides where "the subject prevails." This, however, has to be understood with utmost care. Meschonnic's "subject" does not overlap with a single individual; just the opposite. The subject is one to the extent to which it is not enclosed in its individuality, to the degree to which it has been formed by reciprocity with the Other. Hence Meschonnic warns, in his interview with Gabriella Bedetti, that "rhythm cannot be reduced to discrete units of measure since it works out meaning as a continuous matter of intersubjectivity. Romanticism confuses the subject with [the] individual" (102).

Like Derrida in *Of Grammatology*, Meschonnic the antiromantic will attack the dialectical structure of the opposition inside-outside; but, unlike Derrida, the present critique serves not to weaken the position of the subject but to redefine its boundaries. Thus voice, without losing its essential character (once again: "to speak is to keep being born"), becomes "mine" to the extent to which it belongs to the Other. Meschonnic cites Mondrian's statement that "abstraction is interiority at its clearest; or exteriority at its innermost,"[46] as a gloss on the discovery of primitive art early in the twentieth century—in itself a profound philosophical experience of the Other as an integral part of the individual: "The primitive is what reveals, what produces identity through alterity." Such an individual ceases to be the self or ego and becomes the subject (*sujet*). In Meschonnic's theory it is this invasion of the Other which turns a person with a biography into a speaking subject and thereby helps to determine the shape of modernism as an epoch and a style: "The Primitive is no longer primitive. But within modernity primitivism has triggered an effect of otherness. It now leads its own history. There can no longer be any modernity without it." The subject is what spills over the individual and thus must, in one way or another, become formless, independent of the organizing centers which impose contours and restrictions. This movement of "spilling over," "going over the top" *(débordement)*, is what disturbs the conventions and schemes of reality and what places the subject in a peripheral situation. The speaking subject is peripheral in the sense that it is closer to the boundaries separating it from the Other who has already stepped onto its territory. Using a metaphor, we could say that the subject is a dweller not of a metropolis but of a small provincial border settlement with constant traffic and smuggling going across the frontier. Hence also in Meschonnic's thought there is a place for a password, a schibboleth, whose function in Derrida's philosophy we have already stressed. Meschonnic names this mysterious factor which "goes over the frontier" rhythm, and attributes to rhythm precisely the power of transgression, bordercrossing: "What spills over beyond this outline [*déborde ce schéma*] is rhythm. Modernity. An atheology of the subject. Irreducible to teleologies." In his *Critique du rythme* (1982), Meschonnic ascribes to rhythm the hermeneutic power of pre-understanding: rhythm is what prepares sense and makes it possible. So the oral (again not to be confused with the spoken) is a deep foregrounding of sense, and the subject emerges at the junction of numerous discourses both intimate and social. "Rhythm is not meaning, not redundancy or substitute, but rather material for meaning. . . . If it emanates from a subject, it is a set of subjective-social relationships that make up discourse."[47] The subject is not a result or a passive plaything of discourses, but neither is it a master of a discourses or discourse-dispenser. Rather, the subject is the organizer of various discourses but simultaneously is itself organized by the discourses it is organizing.

"Rhythm, . . . as inscribed within the sign, became the organization of a discourse by a subject, such that the whole discourse lets that subject be heard, and that that subject is organized by this discourse."[48] Voice cannot then be defended on the ground of traditional concepts purporting its intimacy with the subject, who is the master and owner of a vocal mechanism. Voice is what has already been invaded by the Other, for example by history, and this is true even if the speaking subject is unaware of being formed by a symbolic order of discourse. "Voice, which may appear the most personal, most intimate thing, is, like the subject, immediately traversed by all that makes an age, a milieu." Meschonnic also says, "Rhythm, the subjective-collective organization of a discourse, is its orality."[49] *Voice, rhythm, orality,* describe a construction of the subject which precedes a complete "grammaticalization" of the subject. As Meschonnic points out elsewhere, a degrammaticalization does not mean irrationalization and cannot be subsumed under the opposition of the rational versus irrational ("voice is nonetheless not an irrational that would be opposed to the rational in language"[50]). 'Voice' and 'rhythm' are concepts which aim at introducing us into another view of language than the usual. Through these terms, we are to descend or go over the limitations of the word and its oppositions. Rhythm is to a certain extent an equivalent of Derrida's "trace," for it works to dismantle the structuralist vision of the world as organized along the rule of binary oppositions. Meschonnic carefully emphasizes this movement, a continuous drive which rearranges the schemes and boundaries of language. Rhythm is a spilling over of language into language. Such spilling over or transgression operates exclusively within the linguistic medium; it is, as Meschonnic writes in a poem, "language within language."[51] Thus the oral is not a mere opposition of the written:

> Thus we can, no longer, think of orality as the absence of writing and the only passage from mouth to ear . . . ; rather as an organization of discourse ruled by rhythm. The manifestation of a gestural mode, of a corporality and a subjectivity within language. With the means of the spoken within the spoken. With the means of the written within the written. And if something shows there's the oral within the written, and the oral is not spoken, this something's literature.[52]

Orality is not what is spoken, but what allows one to speak. Orality forms the speaking subject, and rhythm takes the most active part in this work with language. The subject described by the pronoun *I* not only reveals but also hides all the junctions where the I is traversed by other pronouns. Thus, recognizing the groundbreaking role of Benveniste, Meschonnic admits the position of the subject is that which cannot be defended on the ground of the first-person singular pronoun. He also admits that literature, as the traditional home of the subjective and the oral, is an impossible genre. Literature defies a three-way division into a lyrical I, a dramatic You, an epic He-She.[53]

Voice defies any reductive approach, either from the side of presence or the side of writing. In this Meschonnic resembles Ong, who maintains that the crucial datum of man's cognitive experience is not "only . . . initial spoken existence, but also the permanent irreducibility of the spoken word and of the sound itself."[54] Whereas Ong differentiates between the primary orality ("pristine orality of mankind untouched by writing or print") and its secondary variant induced by radio and television ("by no means independent of writing and print but totally dependent on them"), thus fundamentally supporting McLuhan's vision of the spoken as juxtaposed to the written or printed, Meschonnic defines *oralité* upon a refutation of such an argument. Meschonnic does not present his case as the primacy of the oral, but only as the separateness of the oral as a category independent of the written and spoken. Absence of writing does not tell us anything about the status of speech: "The absence of writing says nothing about the specificity of the oral. The border between oral and written is no longer as certain [as it was]."[55] Ong comes close to such a vision when he claims that in contemporary technology both kinds of orality are twisted together with the new electronic scriptability of the world: "Primary orality, literacy, and secondary orality are interacting vigorously with one another in confusing complex patterns in our secondarily oral world"; then in his qualification, elsewhere, of literature as "more interesting, although less noble than speech," Ong will ultimately revert to the binarism and privileging of voice.[56]

Meschonnic, on the other hand, evades a narrowly sociological orality, one restricted to the question of the mode of transmission. Instead, he creates a poetics of the oral by establishing a division into the written and the spoken, and the oral as an attribute of both:

> To surpass the duality of oral-written by means of a triple resegmentation between the written, the spoken and the oral: this permits us to rethink the oral as an essential of rhythm and prosody, with its own semantics, subjective and cultural organization of discourse—an order that can realize itself either in writing or in speaking. There's orality in Rabelais—also in Joyce. Intonation is a mode of speaking orality. The imitation of the spoken in writing is something distinct from the oral. The historicity of punctu-

ation in texts is a question of orality. Translation is a practice in the process of transforming itself by researches into orality.[57]

We have quoted this long passage in part to show differences between Ong's meditation on voice, based on mechanisms of dialectical opposition, and Meschonnic's thought. For Meschonnic, orality is a study of nuances which condition texts and are hidden in them; it is an exploration of the Derridean archaeology of the frivolous and its tonalities and intonations of thought, a defense of literature which concentrates on the peripheral and hidden and thus decenters the main project of the edifice. Accordingly, Meschonnic designs a very specific architecture of thought for those who want to study voice and the oral. However, such research cannot be understood as a mere shift in study preferences. As in Derrida, in Meschonnic's writings the whole formation of Western culture blocks such an undertaking. Both Derrida and Meschonnic realize that it is impossible and strategically wrong to postpone the question of sign. Derrida liberates the signifier but agrees with Charles Sanders Peirce that even things are also and only (or as much as) signs. Meschonnic goes a step further and tries to subvert the whole semiotic foundations of modern thinking. If in *La rime et la vie* he speaks about the "poetic effect" of the study of orality, then such an effect can be brought about only by a dismantling of "the effect of sign" which has dominated Western culture. It is the sign itself that poses problems for the study of orality, and that is why rhythm can be the standard-bearing concept that can overcome the tyranny of the sign: "The very conception of the sign opposes it. That's why rhythm, as an organization of discourse, can renew the conception of orality by taking it out of a dualist conception." The oral has, for Meschonnic, a power of dissidence which undermines the ordered world of the sign. The sign is the domain of rationality and logic, and if there is a kingdom of reason, it is located in the palace or cathedral, the twin towers of which are *signifiant* and *signifié*. This rhetoric of religious and political authority is not an ornament; Meschonnic himself will reproach semiotics for its generalizing projects which attempt to formulate theses in which all the possible versions of reality will be contained. Thus he says, "Semiotics is constantly drawn toward transcendence, toward the cosmic. It turns the sign into an order. It makes the temple and denies that it has done so."[58] Rhythm, orality, intonation, and punctuation are all subversive ducts leading toward the temple of the sign which is the center of power; "the sign is a contract, which rhythm denounces." They are not, as we have seen, irrational. They are other operations—reason in a new territory which has so far been abandoned as the area of mute barbarity. Thus, rhythm is presented as "perirational" or "the dissident radical of sense" which, disrupting the unity of the word and sense, is a force that defeats unity and totality.[59] Rhythm and orality are then peripheral forces of the margin, the frontier territories where one needs a pass-word, a schibboleth. This password, however, opens only a necessity of another schibboleth, does not inaugurate the entry to the realm of truth and meaning.

For Meschonnic, the oral is a realm of "signifiance" rather than of meaning or sense. In his introductory essay to Charles Nodier's *Dictionnaire des onomatopées* (1828), it is precisely sense that is diagnosed as the paralyzing operation of the sign: "By privileging sense, [the sign] has produced an artifact of form. . . . To the mandate of sense responds the mandate of language, and all is forbidden the subject but the use of signs."[60] Signifiance is "the specific production of elements that contribute to both meaning and signification without their knowing it."[61] Signifiance acts on the thin line dividing the conscious from the unconscious; it must go beyond the sign which represents exclusively consciousness. This implies, in turn, that the oral can be neither explained in terms of the symbolic (like the analysis of the unconscious in Freud), nor signed off with the help of everyday life logic. The oral feeds off both but subscribes to neither. Like Derrida's "supplement" or "dissemination," the oral must remain locked in the circle of undecidability. Meschonnic's orality is the sphere which, rather like Derrida's reading of Joyce's "he war" phrase, is suspended between two languages, two operations: "This orality shares with hysteria: to be neither a saying nor a said, but a doing."[62] Orality, voice, rhythm, punctuation, and tonality are not then signs but functions, and they do not represent but show: "Rhythm is not a sign. It shows that discourse is not made up solely of signs."[63]

The oral is, at the last and primarily, a bodily surplus of the sign. In its role as rhythm, "exceeding [*débordant*] signs, [it] aligns language with everything that can be compassed by the body." Orality is what uncovers the unconscious in the conscious; we remember the uncanny similarity that amazes Meschonnic between the oral and hysteria. Orality is also, as we have seen in Meschonnic's own paradoxical phrasing, language within language; the nonlinear within the linear; the internal plurality of unity, subject, and rhythm; and the nonlanguage that is the body. The negatives in this list of terms are not the result of a fault in the oral. The oral is nonlanguage, not in the belief that it underlies language; rather it is the dissident radical within language. The oral is the ability of the body to run against language within language, "counterlanguage, the presence of outside-language, prelanguage within language." Voice opens the possibility of chaos, a way of knowing which does not preclude sense but contains all imaginable senses. "Voice without meaning. Lack of meaning is an allegory of meaning in language."[64]

Derrida: the passage. Meschonnic: the periphery. The classical assumption of a centered subject is plainly ruled out by such accounts of voice. Neither deals in positivities, but Meschonnic offers certain openings for agency and possible intentionality. A nonfoundational theory must, it would seem, head in the direction of a much more detailed understanding of the discourses of various subject positions such as race-class-gender-nation, in addition to examining specific, biographical subjectivities in the well-known way. That is why we propose, as a corrective, cure, and supplement, in addition to biographical subjects, the idea of the speaking subject.

CHAPTER 6. Reading the De-toned Text

Voice Determinate and Indeterminate

When he stopped running and apologizing, Jonah preached Apocalypse Now. His rhetoric of apocalypse is profoundly ugly, but also fluent, without syncopation; the language of last things is bardic, betrays no breaks in the voice, no stuttering, no ironies, no awkward silences. Perhaps that is why we are so attracted to this language, even in the midst of denouncing it. We are drawn by Jonah and appalled by him. Who would be Jonah? Who would not? We would both be both. Derrida and Meschonnic, so different in so many ways, are united in their attitude of fascinated repulsion toward the easy sonorities of the sacred, the apodictic. The Language poets, fastidious in scouring the bardic from the house of poetry, seemed at the start of their project afraid of literary voice, and they set up a whole school to practice their hygiene. Now most of us are preachers of postapocalypse. We are antivoice nonfoundationalists—formed and deformed by what we wished to avoid.

Apocalypse is perhaps the most presumptuous of all the meta-narratives, grander even than the Marxist one, and only a speaker possessed of massive righteousness would take on its rhetoric in a post-modern era of, as Lyotard has famously said, "incredulity toward meta-narratives." Postmodern as an artistic practice and postmodernity as the overarching cultural condition are the topics of many current studies attempting to define, date, and politicize: Lyotard's *The Postmodern Condition* (French, 1979; English, 1984) with its defining phrase and many others challenging notions; Ihab Hassan's comparative table showing thirty-three differences between modern and postmodern (1982); studies of postmodern architecture by Paulo Portoghesi (1982, 1983) and Charles Jencks (1984); Fredric Jameson's landmark essays (1984) on postmodernism as the cultural logic of late capitalism and on the limitations of Lyotard's account of the postmodern (introduction to the English translation of *The Postmodern Condition*), his *Flash Art* interview, often reprinted, and his recent book (1991); the book Douglas Kelner edited on Jameson, part system-building eulogy and art critique (1989); and books by Linda Hutcheon (on narrative modes, 1988), Steven Connor (survey of several fields, 1989), and Edith Wyschogrod (theology, 1990). We have a left attack against postmodern thinking from Jürgen Habermas and a right attack from Hilton Kramer at *The New Criterion*. There are grounds for doubting that the terms *postmodernism* and *postmodernity* will ever gain conceptual coherence, but of course this has been a reason for writing more studies. We do not comment here on the origins of the postmodern, or on the degree to which postmodern writers and works are reactionary, or on the relationship of postmodern theory and feminist art practice, or on artistic expressions outside literature—all open ideas that have a bearing on literary voice and the role of Jonah in our time. For now, we must narrow to the one question our examples may help us to clarify, if not settle: In postmodern philosophy and practice of voice, what is incredulity toward expressive intention taken to the furthest power?

Postmodernism, from the point of view of philosophy of voice, is the furthest state we know of the critique of expressivity. To periodize in broad terms, postmodernism is modernism minus romanticism, and postmodern philosophy of voice is modernism minus expressive intention. There is a countertendency toward neoromanticism in certain important writers, such as Robert Bly, Toni Morrison, Ted Hughes, and Margaret Drabble, who have far greater popular acceptance than writers who efface self, intention, expression. Writers like Toni Morrison are no doubt postmodern if we place them chronologically, but they rarely exhibit the attributes Jameson lists for the emergent aesthetic: new depthlessness, or lack of interiority; the historicist effacing of history, through a jumble of styles; a waning of affect; the decentering of the self—schizophrenia as a breakdown in the chain of signifiers, emblem of the new condition; a sense of placelessness, of being diffused into space; new communicative technology of electronic media, with selves dissolving into networks of electronic impulses; infinite play of the signifier; and abolition of critical distance, so that society is aestheticized, barriers between popular and high art dissolved. In the most advanced postmodern work of verbal art, lack of the distance-with-connexion of *social* articulation baffles *vocal* articulation—to produce a free-floating speaker and a free-floating listener.

Some commentators on the postmodern argue in exactly these terms, which for them are not hyperboles but statements of the way we now operate within the writing of our era. We move into a printed page "free of evaluative constraints the text might pretend to have," with "no discourse on value, no ascription of value toward which the writing strives," so that both writing and reading are a pursuit of the Beckettian unnameable, "a free play of textual person, . . . [an] absolute undermining of textual self." The writer avoids the upright pronoun, in "fear of the accidental name." And crossing beyond the "liminality of voice as a mark of self," the reader enters "vertiginous possibility" which "frees voice and character and reader" to the degree that "you literally float away from the text." The result is that the reader "won't go unassailed," and when the amorphous readerly self cannot know how to proceed it moves among the play of surfaces in the text, coming to "posit in the language itself a power." For several students of contemporary writing, this is textual person in the postmodern poem, novel, and play: finding power in the language itself, its materiality; a mode and method antagonistic to the older literature, which set the allegorical power of the artist over against a diminished reader.[1]

One method of disowning the authorial agency or voice is to give agency to the reader as co-creator, as in the theories of Ron Silliman and Antony Easthope. Another method listens for the author as a radio for messages coming from the culture, or from the unconscious, as in the work of Jack Spicer and Hannah Weiner. These are claims of postmodern manifesto discourse, and there seems no way to square them with the equal and opposite claims, from others within postmodernism—Charles Bernstein and Victoria Forrest-Thompson—that the work's language-as-material emphasis is consciously, proudly artificial. Can artifice constitute a poetics without an intentionality at least regional? Can there be a sharing of meaning making between author and reader that is not intersubjective, not a relationship between minds by means of marks on the page? Can the undermining of meaning, value, voice, intention, agency, be as absolute as the manifestos claim? Through de-tonation of many sorts, some of which we describe below, postmodern practice will answer such questions in the affirmative. Still, the practice is not as radical in de-tonation as the manifestos, and the practice in fiction is not as radical as that in poetry. Within poetry itself, even within the work of a single writer like Lyn Hejinian or J. H Prynne, some works yield themselves more to voice, autobiography, a joyous or wounded agency.

This can be shown through examples, but let us first consider what determinate tones are being de-toned. Indeterminate voice in twentieth-century literary practice is consciously the focus of an interminable debate, most recently raised to higher polemical explicitness by the language theory of deconstruction in the late 1960s. Derrida sharply criticizes our willingness to be tempted by a phonetic illusion, but that temptation seems rather a pleasure than an error. The temptation by our desire for vocal sound is philosophy's name for the undecidable ambiguity of empirical and lyrical voice which is literature. As one wry antagonist has recently pointed out, Derrida's own reading of John Searle, characterizing Searle's language by adjectives, engages in the practical reading of speech tones in printed voice—something Derrida in his fiercest antiphonocentric moment would have called impossible.[2] In 1982, Derrida himself wrote a sustained meditation on the concept of 'tone', moving from the history of philosophy in Kant's use of the notion through the etymology of the term, concluding with Heideggerian and biblical meanings of voice, trying at last to get beyond "onto-theo-eschatology": "Now here, precisely, is announced—as promise or threat—an apocalypse without apocalypse, an apocalypse without vision, without truth. . . . But what are you doing, all of you will still insist, to what ends do you want to come when you come to tell us, here now, let's go, come, the apocalypse, it's finished, I tell you this, that's what's happening."[3] The Jonah-like, excited sentence (we too cannot resist the impulse to identify tone) that asks "What are we doing?" is the last in Derrida's 1982 article, so at closing he leaves open a space for the reader to ask for the reason behind his skepticism; then he stops without answering, having revolved the issue and then posed it at the last with his singular and plural pronouns of vocal agency.

Tone in literary studies is a metaphor, from "tone of voice," a rhetorical concept which refers to the relationship between the writer and the reader. Defining tone is difficult, just as it is difficult to describe precisely any human relationship. We might ask a student how he or she would define Robert Frost's relation to the reader in the last stanza of "Provide, Provide":

> Better to go down dignified
> With boughten friendship at your side
> Than none at all. Provide, provide![4]

How does one say the last two words of the poem? The words, at the least, are cruelly ironic, friendly, and hectoring, but to get even that far is to begin to interpret the whole poem. Such questioning makes helpful indication of a norm and so places the tonal level. With this Frostian kind of mimetic voice, which directly pretends to be genuine speaking, there has to be a belief that there is a norm.

Twentieth-century writing has, though, specialized in a more anonymous kind of voice which yields less readily to determination of tone. This removal from any identifiable speaker is the textual voice.[5] Two examples so familiar they require only a mention are the dead Addie Bundren who uncannily speaks a whole section in Faulkner's *As I Lay Dying* and the aria-like three-page-long unpunctuated speech in Beckett's *Waiting for Godot*, where deliciously random cultural allusions pour out of Lucky's mouth from where we do not know. Even after the first shock of nonrecognition of an unplaceable voice, the reader is still, relaxing with the run of language, engaged in the frantic quest to *identify the tone*. The reader in some particle of readerhood refuses to believe that the author has disappeared into the words, or has, oracle-like, received the words along the nerves of the typewriter fingers from an outside agency. But these are still properly speaking modernist examples, dating perhaps from an era before readerhood has experienced its sea-change.

Since speech in literature is always an artifice, even within mimetic voice the norm must be desecrated as it is being observed. Otherwise we get the excessive adherence to vocal realism in the dreary free verse of many poets we could name, in weekly television dramas for mass audiences, in newspaper writing. Even within mimetic voice there needs to be that principle of unrealism García Lorca defined with the flamenco term, *duende*. Lorca describes a singer who, after a storm of applause for her performance, was exasperated to hear an old connoisseur of flamenco say softly, "Viva Paris." She sang for her encore, "without a voice, without breath, without nuance, throat aflame. . . . She had to *mangle* her voice" to achieve not form but the marrow of form, "so that her *Duende* might come and vouchsafe the hand to hand struggle. And then how she sang! Her voice. . . . jetted up like blood, enabled by sorrow and sincerity."[6] In Lorca, César Vallejo, Wallace Stevens, and others among the modernists we may have mangling of meaning and of sounding to quite a degree, and yet this unrealism would still be attributable to a speaking subject.

This unrealism of voice is emphatically not a high modernist or Ibero-American phenomenon, but has some of its origins in English Victorian poetry—in Browning's quirky voices in dramatic monologues like "Soliloquy in a Spanish Cloister" ("Gr-r-r"; "*Hy-Zy-Hine*") and "Fra Lippo Lippi" ("Zooks . . . a wee white mouse, / *Weke, weke*"); in Tennyson's Lincolnshire and Barnes's Dorsetshire and Kipling's Cockney dialect poems; and strangest of all in Swinburne ("The pulse of war and passion of wonder, / The heavens that murmur, the sounds that sin," and so on in "The Triumph of Time"). Swinburne sets up a lyric drone of prefabricated parts, all effortlessly joined together and received effortlessly by the reader caught in the immense tracery of his extended poems. "I" is a flag of convenience, a way to evoke verbal behavior and begin to push around the counters of roses and waves and skies and flesh and spirit and wonder and thunder. It is a brilliantly artificial style designed to keep the reader from leaving the text, an attenuated coercion. Swinburne's language is opposite to the supersaturation of devices and hyperbaton of syntax in Gerard Manley Hopkins; Swinburne's exaggeration is the monstrous development of the voice of ease.

Mimetic voice shades into anonymous voice. Much depends upon our tolerance for anonymity and randomness in writing. John Ashbery wrote his poem "Europe," he says, by opening *Esquire* magazine, getting a phrase from it, and then writing on his own: "When I ran out, I'd go back to the magazine."[7] Such procedures make for a dispersion of the speaking subject. One of the differences between the modernist era and today is the increasing recent preference for the new voices, new emotions, or textual emotions, which are produced by the dispersion of the subject.

Ashbery has four methods of writing, which do not change from his earliest poetry to his most recent. The first method is pseudonarrative, where false leads and snatches of story are thrown out to catch and frustrate the reader's expectations of development; the second is play with personal pronouns, which never refer to one speaker but to all possible mentioned persons; the third is parody of cliché allusion and language, where fashionable or received phrasing is used on a vast scale, always with one intent, to delectate the badness in the process of dismissing it; and the fourth is genial disregard for the concisions and euphonies of American English, a lack of interest in sound play which is evident, too, in the way Ashbery suppresses voice color when he reads aloud. The long poem "Litany" is an extension of all these methods. It runs in double columns down wide pages; according to the author, the ideal reading of the poem is with two voices following the two tracks at once. For the listener, then, there will be sometimes antiphony, sometimes noise, rarely snatches of sense. That is a valid technique to achieve subversion of voice. Derrida uses it in *Glas* (English version, 1987) by running in parallel columns separated by a line two treatises on different topics and levels of generality.

In Ashbery, neither the writer nor the reader is in the poem in the old Frostian way, though clearly these poems hope to be communications and have been read as such. The intent is to bring into poems the mind's random workings, fantasies, language play, notations of inner and outer climate, the very aimlessness of thinking. Thus Ashbery forgoes some of the resources of the old speaking subject and of sound, in order to become the specialist of chance thoughts on the mind's surface. (Ashbery's agile mind is packed with many things and ideas.) He leaves lines tonally neutral, without any indications of how they should be said.[8] It is what Ashbery himself calls "all-purpose" poetry, a "hymn to possibility," where the reader fills in the meaning. When, in the early eighties, Ashbery's work seemed one extreme of the intransitive in poetry, a Derridian poetry where utterance is not bound to personal consciousness, it now seems familiar, a playful attenuation of links between speaker and listener, a meditation approachable if not predictable.

Ashbery's work has been a permission to a group of American writers, somewhat younger, who have invented many new methods of de-tonation. White spacing, choral return of short phrases in new contexts, short sentences that are perpendicular to one another in meaning, self-conscious punning on cliché phrases, taking the literal for the metaphorical and vice versa, and running logic programs that go off the skids in imaginative ways are a few of these methods. The attempt goes further than Ashbery, because not only do Language poets wish to see what happens when metered verse and logical or narrative sequence are distorted or abandoned; they wish to experiment with the breakdown of logic and the English sentence, and thus some of them are dethroning what may well be the final notations of tone. For them poetry is language, but apparently they cannot eliminate the marks of voice, person, or narrative sequence altogether.

Language School writing is descriptive in the sense of recording impressions from the world or the mind, emphasizing the physicality of language itself and the very act and materials of the scene of recording. Writing is taken as more authentic than speaking, because speaking is associated with so many overstatements, so much that is overpersonal, sloppy, soaked in feeling, delivered in an apocalyptic tone. These writers persuasively argue, in their poems and essays, that their work does intend to pass over to an object: to designate a physical world and to communicate a social world, and to do all this with some humor.

A question remains about how many eliminations are possible in the sphere of voice-person-narrative before these disappear even as spectral norms or hypotheses. When that happens, even in one leading segment of current work, literature will undergo a shift as decisive, perhaps, as romanticism, because every belief of the romantic culture in which we still subsist will have been cancelled.

To accommodate the poetic and theoretical writing that de-tones voice, there will have to be, as Jerome Rothenberg says, "some willing surrenders in the area of understanding."[9] With Joyce, Eliot, Beckett,

Lorca, Vallejo, Césaire, Ashbery, Davenport, the Language poets, certain Russian postmodern writers, Prynne, and with Rothenberg himself when he translates even the nonsense vocables from the Navajo in his *Horse Songs*, we make those surrenders gratefully. There will also be occasions when readers will resist writing that estranges itself "from the common language of daily life, its syntax, habitual sequences, and processes of association."[10] For such occasions, the idea of tone of voice, a social function, will serve as a means of defending judgment, but no longer is it possible to argue that because tone has been suppressed from a line or poem or poetic oeuvre the work is unreadable, unliterary, unsocial. In each case, the literary voice must be tested by reading attentively all the printed-voice notations that are undecidable as between person and text. Our point is that voice in this definition resists being taken all the way over into empirical speaking, or all the way over into sheer text where everything sounded is off key because there is no key.

Apparently, if you put straight the situation in modern philosophy, and entirely undo the thinking of presence in literature, you undo something essential. A residual or imaginary presence is necessary to preserve the ambiguity of text and speech.

Postmodern Indeterminate Voice

To examine the language of the de-toned subject, we might inspect the Russian work of our contemporaries in Moscow and St. Petersburg, for instance the poems of Arkadii Dragomoshchenko; or we could read works considerably earlier, the poems of Veniamin Vvedenskii and others of the Oberiuty group, and earlier yet the works of Alexei Kruchonykh and Velemir Khlebnikov's loopy long poem *Zangezi*. Polish, French, and Italian all have their modernist equivalents, and Spanish in Latin America has Huidobro and Vallejo. For the American tradition, the Rimbaud line has been surveyed in Marjorie Perloff's path-breaking book (1981) *The Poetics of Indeterminacy* in sound, imagery, narration.[11] Perloff offers satisfyingly close readings of difficult texts by Stein, Williams and Pound, Beckett, Ashbery, and Cage and Antin. We are indebted to Perloff's insistence on studying what she finds Northrop Frye calling "associative rhythm" in prose and verse, namely short-phrase writing "largely innocent of syntax," with repetitions as rhythmical filler (40). There is no way to prove the claim of Perloff's last page, namely that "when . . . the poetry of indeterminacy, of anti-symbolism, has reached its outer limit, it comes back once more to such basic 'literary' elements as the hypnotic sound patter, the chant, the narrative account, the conceptual scheme" (338). Will the poetry of the future return to more conservative methods? Does poetry of the present come to a limit and then draw back from it? Defining the limit is a matter of the greatest tact and difficulty; what was an apparent outer edge, a scant decade ago when Perloff was writing, has now been dramatically exceeded by drastic eliminations of syntax and person. Nonetheless, her book emulates the poets themselves in pushing de-tonation as far as may be to see what might happen at all the levels in the poem, from the disposition of the typography and the syllables to rhythmic phrasing to the interpretation of the whole as narrative, as concept; and in this we would emulate her.

To read our own choice of new American and English works in drama, fiction, and poetry, we will discuss these interrelated features of printed voice: (1) the image of the writer, as speaking subject in the writing; (2) the implied, indeed now required, reader's role in the writing; (3) the role of rhythm in constituting writer and reader. To explain the third of these: as long ago as Longinus's fifth factor contributing to sublimity, the effect of rhythm was considered an essential component of new forms of subjectivity. Longinus rearranges the order of words in a dactylic phrase of Demosthenes and shows how an effect "noble and grand" is mutilated, in his word, by removing or adding a syllable: "It still means the same, but the effect is different, because the sheer sublimity is broken up and undone by the breaking up of the run of long syllables at the end."[12] Longinus is mistaken to confuse meter with rhythm, an error strenuously resisted by Meschonnic, who takes rhythm, in all the ranks from the syllable on up, as literature's primary fusion of the personal and the social. For our purposes here, the issue of meter is moot because postmodern poets have typically progressed far beyond the elimination of meter and lineation, to the point where the primary exclusions are of the English sentence, cause-effect logic, narrative order—namely deletions or scramblings of nearly all the elements of a text which constitute, or at least suggest, the unity of person.

Reading for rhythm in the widest sense as constituting the speaking and the reading subject, we take up works according to an order of increasing difficulty: (1) works that show *de-tonation*; (2) works that show *strong de-tonation*; (3) works that show *uncanny de-tonation.*

This is not an order of increasing literary value—or disvalue, though in this book we must struggle to be fair to works in the *uncanny* category when we see in them the near total dissolution of the person and the Bakhtinian dialogic. Entirely to dissolve these is to make fade the problematic of literary voice, the aforementioned ambiguity of text and speech; and yet, admittedly, to begin to dissolve person and dialogic is to create a new literary opportunity through de-tonation.

Conceivably, a single work could exhibit all three of these distinguishable types at the same time, in different parts of itself. Or a single work might step down or up the scale, over time as circumstances change, over different groups according to knowledge and reading attentiveness. Below, we define the categories separately for the sake of placing our examples where they primarily belong. However, blends and shifts are likely, and further fine tuning of the categories would display them as mappings of gradualities. This is one of those cases where Coleridge's prescription, for a logic that would distinguish without dividing, is exactly pertinent.

De-tonation

De-tonation has been discussed above without any regard to type or intensity. Now we take de-tonation as a first stage of indeterminancy, whose textual markers displace personhood by making it seem multiple, by making it both active and passive, by deterritorializing it, by processing it through various telephonic or cybernetic functions, by syncopating and breaking rhythms. The textual markers of nonrealism might be puns, varying lengths of segments, sounds of nonequal phonic value, rhyme and meter and their avoidance, nonsense sounds and body sounds, switching in and out of dialect, play with tense and pronouns, use of typography and visual emphasis or de-emphasis, punctuation or nonpunctuation. The more these regional intentions and speaking-subject practices are used, the more de-tonation shades into strong de-tonation. This is the beginning of what we have, in chapter 2, called the "shatteredness" of self, a syncopated subject that loses its solid rhythms due to the oscillating power of "there," the outside, which both promises and denies the Other. The reader is theorized still as a reader, a passive recipient of text. With de-tonation we enter the detour of the inarticulate.

Many of the most daring modernist poems are now in the category of simple de-tonation—for instance much of Wallace Stevens, though during Stevens' life for many readers these texts were strong or uncanny. One instance might be Stevens' "Oak Leaves Are Hands," which begins "In Hydaspia, by Howzen, / Lived a lady, Lady Lowzen"—a modest little poem which de-tones by sound effect and by pseudonarrative; stubbornly modern in its methods, the poem stands as a measure of the degree to which other writers perform a more radical de-tonation. Until Marjorie Perloff and others in the seventies and eighties analyzed the language of postmodern poets, giving hunches and expressing amazement at the reading processes needed, certain works like Ashbery's "Litany" seemed impenetrable; now these works begin to seem familiar. Statistically speaking, most Anglo-American poetry published in the past generation is extremely sparing in its detoning and so would fit into or below this low end of the range.

Since most drama and fiction never reaches into the strong or uncanny categories at all, we take our examples from a television play and three science fiction novels; this shows that de-tonation does penetrate into popular works, especially in these forms and at this end of the range. Poetry occupies the more difficult, specialist, and elite categories at the other end of the range.

DENNIS POTTER: *THE SINGING DETECTIVE.* This play was first broadcast in six one-hour parts on BBC Television, in November and December 1986. The published version takes up 249 pages and is heavily scripted with stage instructions, explanations, cues on how speeches are said, and hundreds of orthographic equivalents for phatic and nonsense utterances, and for the sounds of class dialects. Philip Marlow, the main character, is wheeled into a hospital ward with a terrible psoriasis over his whole body—the skin disease is a breakdown of his relationship with the world at its most sensitive physical place, and this is the outer sign of mental disturbance too. This author of hack detective stories, who has the same surname as an Elizabethan playwright and the same full name as Raymond Chandler's fictional detective, is suffering an acute disturbance of the dialogic function. He is unable to connect with himself, with the world, with his wife from whom he is separated, with his work. He is imprisoned in his incompetent body, immobilized, turned into a object by some but not all of the hospital staff. So he can live, and eventually find a kind of health and freedom, mostly in his mind. Parallel to the story in the hospital ward are two others: a real-life memory account of growing up in the Forest of Dean with a beautiful mother who is not faithful to his lovingly idealized working-class father; and a fantasy tale of a detective (without psoriasis, without regional class dialect) who sings forties classic songs with a big band and who is seeking the murderer of a Russian tart drowned in the Thames. Marlow can switch at any time from one of these three tales to enter any of the others, and sometimes there are irrational intrusions and blends, narrative overlays. (In the BBC version, actor Michael Gambon plays both Marlow in the hospital and Marlow the singing detective.)

Why the metaphor of detective fiction? There is a psychiatrist in the hospital who through discussions brings out the author's disgust with his body, and this makes an opening to other recognitions about what he witnessed and did as a boy, for instance coming upon his mother's infidelity with a local man in the forest. Hauling memories out of the muck of time is detective work, too, and helps bring Philip toward physical recovery and escape from the hospital. Why, then, a singing detective? This is where period significance comes in: the lip-syncing to old songs sets the tone of the whole play, creating a retro postmodern scenario where the researched flavor and pop music of one era become the escape fantasy of a contemporary invalid. The ugly, evil memories are transposed into glamorous unison band music and jaunty lyrics of love, Ronny Ronalde's "Birdsong at Eventide": that is the avoidance narrative, in which fluent singing of the detective is welcome proof that he has grown out of his provincial dialect. There are songs in the Forest of Dean childhood segments, too, but group singing in a working-class club, by people like the lad Philip and his father who are marked by local dialect; and that is the confrontation narrative.

At the beginning, when he is at his worst in mind and body, Marlow speaks the scene of writing and writes the scene of speaking; the text is the camera and the camera is darting out of his mind and back in:

Dr. Finlay: Are you having trouble with this fellow?

Ali: (*Beam*) Oh yes, my God yes.

Dr. Finlay: Has he been making offensive remarks about origins?

Ali: (*Puzzled*) Origins?

Dr. Finlay: Your-ah-race, or-?

Ali: Race?

Dr. Finlay: (*Irritated*) Yes. Your race!

Marlow: Go on. Tell him. You brown bugger.

Ali gives a whoop of laughter. Dr. Finlay, taken aback, goes to say something but-*bleep-bleep-bleep*! goes his bleeper, and he turns on his heels to stride away, angrily flustered.

Jumped up little snot. You get out of bed when you want, Ali old pal.

Ali: No, no, no.

Marlow: Well—why not? What's the point? What are we waiting for? Why endure one more moment than you have to? Go on! get out of bed, Ali! Jump up and down! and then hold a pillow down over my face! Come on!

He stops abruptly, like one suddenly aware of the true extremity of his feelings, and the depths of his bitterness or despair. Very close on Marlow. A beat. Then-

(*Whisper*) At first comma the only sound is the slap hyphen slap of the water against the boat comma which has its engine switched off double space The other comma natural noises increase as the-

On the cold river, at dawn, the struggling, grunting policemen slowly pull in and up on to the deck of the launch the naked, drowned body of a beautiful young woman.

On the screen of a word processor, a bright glow of letters softly blip-blips across the monitor-

> *The other, natural noises increase as the struggling, grunting policemen slowly pull up on to the deck of the launch the naked, drowned body of a beautif-*

In the hospital ward, an attractive young nurse, Nurse Mills, is suddenly, on the uncompleted word *beautiful*, standing at the foot of Marlow's bed. Marlow jolted out of reverie, stares at her.

Marlow: The naked, drowned body of a beautiful woman.

Nurse Mills: What are you talking about, Mr. Marlow?

Marlow: I had on my best pajamas, the ones with red stripes and blue forget-me-nots. I was all dressed up and talcumed and the armpits. A million dollars was about to call. I was ready for it.

Nurse Mills: High temperature again, have we?[13]

The reader like the camera is "Very close on Marlow." The scene in the ward with Dr. Finlay and Ali moves to an unbearable moment and then toggles over to the fantasy detective story and the image of discovering the naked, beautiful corpse. This occurs in exaggerated slo-mo voice, where the writtenness of the language is signaled by speaking the punctuation. Then the language slides into the fantasy scene of the "grunting policemen," and we have made it all the way into another discourse—but only for a moment, because writing insists again on its artificiality by means of the camera looking at wordprocessor language: this we read, not hear. Then we toggle back to the hospital ward by means of associative logic on the word *beautiful*, and the connection between the dead woman in the forties fantasy and Nurse Mills, whom Marlow cannot relate to, at first, without writing her in a style Potter himself, directly below, calls "Chandleresquerie." All these times, places, and styles coexist within Marlow. When they are on display, in sequence, with their varying sociolects, voices in conflict with each other, it is hard to imagine there is a Marlow. This is the broken rhythm of an impossible person who is fighting for health and sanity. The rhythm relies on the quick cut of motion-picture editing, but in one line here the cut comes by Potter's command only after "a beat" of time on the close-up frame; it also relies on voice-over to project writing in the guise of whispered speaking. These add technological powers to Potter's representation of the broken rhythm of self, and yet any explanation of his dramatic action will still rely on highly traditional habits of association (corpse and Nurse Mills connected by means of the idea of beauty), and ultimately on a Freudian metanarrative.

WILLIAM GIBSON: THREE CYBERPUNK NOVELS. Cyberpunk, projecting certain late-century lines of thought into the future, is in its use of time the opposite of Potter's retro postmodern. Three of Gibson's novels, *Neuromancer* (1984), *Count Zero* (1986), and *Mona Lisa Overdrive* (1988), employ as characters cybernetic biological organisms, cyborgs. These human space jockeys have remarkable physical and mental capabilities, given by mechanical enhancement, but the great cost of the machinery is borne by multinational companies driven solely by relentless quest for profits. So characters are as often run by the companies as they are able to circumvent the bosses, to use the enhanced powers for more humane purposes:

> Case was twenty-four. At twenty-two, he'd been a cowboy, a rustler, one of the best in the Sprawl. . . . He'd operated on an almost permanent adrenaline high, a byproduct of youth and proficiency, jacked into a custom cyberspace deck that projected his disembodied consciousness into the consensual hallucination that was the matrix. A thief, he'd worked for other, wealthier thieves, employers who provided the exotic software required to penetrate the bright walls of corporate systems, opening windows into rich fields of data.[14]

Case travels as a passenger behind Molly's eyes:

> Then he keyed the new switch.
>
> The abrupt jolt into other flesh. Matrix gone, a wave of sound and color. . . . She was moving through a crowded street. . . . Her body language was disorienting, her style foreign. She seemed continually on the verge of colliding with someone, but people melted out of her way, stepped sideways, made room.

> "How you doing, Case?" He heard the words and felt her form them. She slid a hand into her jacket, a fingertip circling a nipple under warm silk. The sensation made him catch his breath. She laughed. But the link was one-way. He had no way to reply.
>
> Two blocks later, she was threading the outskirts of Memory Lane. Case kept trying to jerk her eyes toward landmarks he would have used to find his way. He began to find the passivity of the situation irritating.
>
> The transition to cyberspace, when he hit the switch, was instantaneous. He punched himself down a wall of primitive ice belonging to the New York Public Library, automatically counting potential windows. Keying back into her sensorium, into the sinuous flow of muscle, senses sharp and bright.

Case occupies a mental space separate from his physical body when he is a rider on Molly and takes over her sensorium. But there are limits: "He had no way to reply." Then he may enter still another modality, cyberspace, where he has more control, but in either mode he has to a degree separated from himself, dissolved either into sensation or into networks of data. In either mode he suffers diminished autonomy, becomes passive, must doubt his identity even as he extends it.

Neuromancer is new romancer, of course, project for a new fiction, but also neurofiction, telepathy tales. Case says to the strange self-destructive clone woman 3Jane: "I met Neuromancer. He talked about your mother. I think he's something like a giant ROM construct, for recording personality, only it's full RAM. The constructs think they're there, like it's real, but it just goes on forever" (251). Case, in his last battle with the destructive forces of amoral Capitalist combines, needs more than his machinery—needs person to a higher power, needs to add hate to all his information:

> He came in steep, fueled by self-loathing. When the Kuang program met the first of the defenders, scattering the leaves of light, he felt the shark thing lose a degree of substantiality, the fabric of information loosening.
>
> And then—old alchemy of the brain and its vast pharmacy—his hate flowed into his hands.
>
> In the instant before he drove Kuang's sting through the base of the first tower, he attained a level of proficiency exceeding

> anything he'd known or imagined. Beyond ego, beyond personality, beyond awareness, he moved, Kuang moving with him, evading his attackers with an ancient dance, Hideo's dance, grace of the mind-body interface granted him, in that second, by the clarity and singleness of his wish to die.
>
> And one step in that dance was the lightest touch on the switch, barely enough to flip—
>
> —*now*
> and his voice the cry of a bird
> unknown,
> 3Jane answering in song, three
> notes, high and pure.
> A true name. (262)

This is a fictional language of metaphors ("the shark thing"; "alchemy"; "dance"), spacings such as the gap of silence-doubledash-indent between "flip" and *now*, rhythmic emphasis such as the long periodic breathless sentence beginning "Beyond ego" and the italics on *now* and the indentation of the crucial lines on voice and answer: all devices straining to suggest what cannot be represented. Unspeakable is the idea of the beyond-personal, the mind-body linkage when all the conditions are right. Case's voice, too, is estranged, "the cry of a bird / unknown"; Case will live and succeed only through "the singleness of his wish to die," so of course his voice is de-toned. And yet it is still his voice, and it earns a reply of great worth, "a true name" that seems to elude all the dilemmas of phonocentrism. Voice and fragmented voice are heavily thematized in the final chapters of Gibson's other two novels, voice as value, lyrical calling of person in a future society where person is variously empowered, divided, and snuffed out by technologies. Reality bends and breaks along with the language in this fiction, estrangement effects coming with the spatial and mental reach of the multinationals, and with the involvement of sensoriums with imagined technologies, the abundant jargon, but also with the use of the metaphor of voice as regional intentionality. Voice is Gibson's leading metaphor for a coherent if oscillating guise of person: "grace of the mind-body interface" that may be stolen anytime through plastic surgery, gene cloning, flipping a switch, pulling out a bionic jack.

Strong De-tonation

Strong de-tonation is a marked shift into a speaking subject that flickers at a far higher rate of speed. Some of the finest works of seventies and eighties postmodernism, such as late Beckett, Ian Sinclair's *Lud Heat* (1975), Edward Dorn's *Gunslinger* (1968–1972, reprinted 1989), Lyn Hejinian's *My Life* in its two editions (1980, 1991), and J. H. Prynne's *Poems* (1982), all detach sonority from presence in a way that is systematic but not thoroughgoing, leaving pockets of recognizable selfhood, the flash of person and whirr of interesting sound. The solid rhythm of the recognizable selfhood has been lost by means of textual methods listed above under de-tonation, but in addition now temporal sequence, spatial placement, and hierarchical perception are under question. Sentences do not cluster around a coherent speaking subject; imaginary persons tend not to interact with each other; the foundations of a stable irony are to some degree washed away; and the reader ceases to be a reader and becomes a collaborator.

Lud Heat, for instance, is a first-person retelling of many occurrences during one year as shadowings of evil design; the Sinclair-I relentlessly searches information on London's deep history of violence, and he finds patterns everywhere. The poem's coherent fantasy takes it out of all known genres, including personal narrative, giving de-tonation by context, not by device. The speaker needs a psychoanalyst but instead tells the obsession to the reader, who is trapped within a perfect circle. The fluent rhythm is that of perfectly rounded fantasy. The book unleashes an imagination of violence so ugly, history deep and city huge, even while focused on one person's studies and daily life, as to unsettle, for the time of reading, any notion of the moral life. The poem is evidence that it is possible to be bardic and indeed Delphic, and still be postmodern. Sinclair has a direct line to his own bizarre Yahweh, or antichrist, in whose service he performs de-tonation as obsessive cohesion.

Gunslinger in four books is a retelling of Western U.S. myths of the man of absolute accomplishment, now in the era of drugs of preference, multinational companies, kitsch culture, university pretention, casual violence, and other delightful abominations. The slinger is mythical, perfect; his speed and wit are the measure of the other speakers across many sociolects, including a person called "I" who is killed off and later resurrected. Markers of person and story are obscured, ambiguated, but not entirely. The poem is de-tonation as irony directed at all presumed stabilities of meaning, belief, value. Behind the irony is an implied ornery High Plains set of values—similar to the values that permit satire in Jonathan Swift, but here an affiliation not with dominant values but with victims, outlaws, Indians, drug-users, all those persons American Vietnam-era society has forced to the margins.

We would give more space to Prynne and Hejinian, who also want to expand, contradict, internally de-tone the monologic lyric that is still the standard poem in English. As in Sinclair and Dorn, these writers wish to fill the lyric with theory, to cross autobiography with scholarship, to suggest and withdraw the lure of storytelling. However, in Prynne and Hejinian the syncopation of subject is stepped up to new levels of opacity; this forces the reader to struggle with the poem.

> *Any photographer*
> *will tell you*
> *the same*
>
> Somewhere during the transition from childhood to womanhood, a girl is likely to become interested in religion. It would become appropriate to call this not intuition but preknowing, or paranoia. They asked my mother to correct my views or to keep me at home. Blindmen sell brooms. From hypochondria come sentences and memory. In California during the summer the shadows are very dark and cool, the sunlight hot and bright. But, because we have only seven days, the light seems to be orderly, even predictable. A pause, a rose, something on paper in the fragmentary text. The Mayan calendar has more days. The plump but uncertain girl grew righteous with love of the puce horizon. It is hard to turn away from moving water. Often gruff and bellowing, always female, but not always feminine. I imagined the pre-absence that occurs before one is born and thought that was god. Preparation. I would not allow myself to fall asleep during the long drive to the country until we had passed through the town of Alviso, where the migrant workers lived, so that I could see the rows of outhouses that lined the edge of the fields. The squirrel had knocked over the Dresden figurine, where my grandmother came from. We can "plan the weekend." As for we who "love to be astonished," you would say these are its ghosts. In New England, the weather builds character. I discovered that I could never quite remember how my favorite songs went. Irritated by motorbikes. After a certain point, one no longer hears any new ideas, must make do with new facts.[15]

She wrote the sequence in thirty-seven sections of thirty-seven sentences when she was thirty-seven, and a decade later increased the numbers of sections and sentences accordingly—not by tacking on sentences in segments already written, but by fitting them in; the new extra segments were entirely new. A new version, bringing the poem into her fifties, is already in progress—the endless poem. Its later sentences and segments are less perception-based, more gnomic, more like wisdom writing, more about writing as writing. Every sentence is a new stripe of color, laid on, sometimes perceptual, memory-based, family related, opinionated—and now and then, at intervals of changing length, is a recurrence of the quotation about those who "love to be astonished" and of the rhythmic list, "A pause, a rose, something on paper." The autobiography and opinions are claimed by a speaking subject possessed of charm and variety, and that is a primary continuity for the reader to rely on. The sentences themselves are infinitely various in structure, sometimes containing rhyme and even insistent measuring, and the sentences are also entirely unpredictable in content—nearly always perpendicular to the sentence coming just before and the one coming just after, so narrative coherence is always disrupted from sentence to sentence. Still, the rhythm of recurrence is there, as categories of sentences which recur: perception sentences on landscape or feeling tone of place or color which might have been written by Wordsworth, idea-sentences about writing or cognition or mutability, family history materials roughly in the order of personal growth to maturity, exclamations, analogies with "like" and surrealist jumps of logic, and so on. When the categories come back in changed contexts, the reader has a little salute of recognition and is pulled further in, kept alert. At any given moment, then, de-tonation occurs as fragmentation of self and of reader's developing sense of narrative at the local level; but also an image occurs of a larger project that has been divided into these categories and then reshuffled. The reader must encounter what has been reshuffled, but then imagine a more linear order. A life and opinions may be reconstructed from the well-polished parts, so that the title of this series poem in prose is fully justified, even as it is ironized, made fun of as a possibility. (Isadora Duncan wrote a *My Life* of romantic assertion, bold feeling: such projects are here by and large mocked, but not a little imitated.) The poem hints at the possibility of new orders of subjectivity, new methods of autobiography, and follows that possibility bravely to quite a distance, but turns back from uncanny de-tonation.

J. H. PRYNNE: *POEMS* (1982). Prynne has published all his poems in limited editions with small presses, except for the collection of 1982 which brings all the items to that date into one volume in a trade edition. Prynne does not read aloud in public or give interviews. The work has a studiously impersonal sheen, achieved largely by appropriating clashing discourses from many sites in British culture since the 1960s—principally biological and chemical sciences, the history of metals technology, economics, ecology, specialist cognitive science. Very occasionally Prynne has resorted to literary and popular culture and to personal experience that seems direct though may not be. A careful, lexically abstract language of control, partly parodied by exaggeration, is marshalled as one primary way to ward off, hold at a distance notions of 'wounding' and 'pain'. One habitual tone is that of abrupt negation:

> at all
>
> anyway
>
> whatever
>
> even so
>
> rubbish[16]

This is maximal closure, footing pulled out from under cliché talk by the last word. Usually ordinary language is not even quoted to ironize it. The Prynne method is austere: ordinary phrasing is an abomination, to be used only for shock value within a texture forbiddingly high in level of generality. "Chromatin" is typical:

> The prism crystal sets towards the axis
> of episodic desire: lethargy and depression
> cross the real-time analogue: currents level
> and historic matching blurs into locked-on
> receptor site blockade. Stable mosaic at
> adrenal print "you" are in white "I" see a
> moving shade by the door it is *my wish* to
> be there running on ("mental confusion,
> tremors, anxiety") and breaking the induced
> blockade I truly am by the door shaking or
> the frame goes to gel. Visual sonar
> arrhythmia blocks fading brocade made
> pressure crisis you and the flowers in
> pliant flicker real time! I surmount
> the uptake gradient, cognition by
> recount, the homeric icefields unfold.

The chromatin in tissues makes them change color on contact: an analogue for interanimation, and thus the constitutive metaphor. Prynne runs a denotative program in nominal style, scientific language with its buildup of nouns modifying nouns, "locked-on / receptor site blockade": this discourse is the running parallel and commentary on the elements of person in the scare-quote pronouns *you* and *I*, who are in some "real-time" scenario of desire. "Visual sonar / arrhythmia blocks fading brocade made / pressure crisis you and the flowers in / pliant flicker real time!" That is the sentence with the exclamation point and the lyrical internal rhyme, because it shows in mock technical language the way the speechlessness and lack of resources of desire may be a welcome but anxious breakdown of the rhythm of person, speaking to "you," but in the midst of flickering arrhythmia, and added to this the paradox of sight and sound in "visual sonar." The speaker does not get past the crisis by saying something simple and direct, such as "I love/want you"; this speaker needs "uptake gradient" and "cognition" and Latinate prefixes that eloign person at the peak moment of feeling. A minor narrative of a possibly botched encounter of persons gains the precision of denotative science in the chromatin story, and gains also, at the end, the connotative literary reach of "homeric." It is built up into something strange by the clash and overlap of separate discourses.

This is yet another way detonation may disrupt the steadiness of person and narrative. The reader must continually make adjustments of discourse type in the midst of parsing difficult sentences, treading the minefield of scare-quotes, italics, parentheses containing quotations we know not from where, paradoxes such as *visual sonar*, allusions such as *homeric*. A minimal implied author requires a maximal implied reader.

Unforgiving in his demands, hieratic, Prynne is the Mallarmé of recent English poetry. There is no elimination of person according to what is all too easily believed of postmodern methods in verbal art. In fact, the habitual use of the trappings of scholarship and the abstractness of lexicon in Prynne has the same role as the preference for dramatic monologue in Browning—a place to hide an abundance of person, whose other more revealing emergence is in Prynne's fascination with physical and psychological wounding, everywhere in evidence.

Uncanny De-tonation

Uncanny de-tonation marks another shift, now into the most transgressive mode of writing. Very rarely does a novel or play reach this step, because those forms are necessarily too social; perhaps it occurs in those forms, as we have seen in an earlier chapter with Poe and Lovecraft, only at points where the writer needs to push beyond an ultimate barrier, corporeal, social, or theological.

Uncanny has its place in the OED between *uncandid* and *uncanonical*. Ghostly voice, sublime voice, mythological voice, gelatinous voice, voice from the grave, avant-garde voice from literature's future. Impossible voice, but still voice. If in de-tonation and strong de-tonation, person is the measure, now this can no longer be so. It is personless and placeless language, often without syntax as well. Uncanny detonation is apotheosis of the nominal phrase, clots of phrase. Sometimes theorized as a feminine zone of language (Stephen Paul Martin), an abandonment on principle of patriarchal meanings and hierarchies of most sorts, a writing that is "everything all the time" (Ron Sukenick). If a writing mingles the serious and the playful everywhere, it will be beyond the reach of irony because it is outside any determination of tone. Mixing genres will also be beyond the reach of genre—schizo writing, often highly erotic, pushing aleatory techniques like the Fibonacci series (Ron Silliman in *Tjanting*) beyond any schema of communication. It is repudiation of the transitivity of writing in favor of the pleasures of continuous transition, no initiation of utterance, no closure.

The more the author as person is abdicated, the more the reader as co-creator is necessary. Energy is transferred to the reader—ears open and eyes wandering. The reader's inattention and mistakes become the uncanny text.

The phantasm of immediacy has ceded itself utterly to the infinite indefinite mediation. In its purest form this is the category of "without," "outside," "repudiation," "beyond," "apotheosis," "no . . . no," "the more . . . the more," "utterly." Obviously a last instance is never reached in verbal art, but it is necessary to imagine a limiting case so that commentary may approach the mind of the avant-garde postmodern.

To present the category in its purest form, it would be necessary to quote extensively from a text we have no hope of being permitted to quote. Still, it is possible to list the poem's devices. This poem plays for all it is worth the method of word salad, a nonsyntactic or part-syntactic jamming of single words, single lines, nearly every line a new tone, a new idea, a new device, a new measure. The reader is continuously unsettled by changes of pace and emphasis, floating wisps of meaning and coherence. A rough tally of devices includes ambiguous pronoun reference, impossible grammar, macaronic language with German and Spanish, part words, taboo words, portmanteau words, obscure sexual or bodily content, unexplained cultural allusions, imitations of stuttering, neologism and nonsense terms, suspension dots, but otherwise no punctuation, deixis gestures but not toward persons or things, nouns not as subjects, verbs not as agents, applying the animate performative verbs to inanimate subjects and the reverse, and capitalized words on the average of one every six lines calling attention to themselves but not producing any syntagmatic meaning of their own when read without the intervening matter.

Admirable uncanny de-tonation we have already analyzed in the work of Paul Celan, one of the most difficult twentieth-century poets who is also one of the greatest. The same could be said, has been said by Roman Jakobson, of Velemir Khlebnikov. We take writings by Michael Palmer and Ron Silliman, splendid poets from the Language group, to show examples of works which abominate voice and try to push it over into text. Their intention, in part, seems to be to play with and against ordinary logic, and to force the materiality of language to the forefront of aesthetic experience.

MICHAEL PALMER: "NOTES FOR ECHO LAKE 8 (FOR ONE TO SEVENTY-SEVEN VOICES)". This is number eight in a series poem whose segments are interwoven between other poems in Palmer's book *Notes for Echo Lake* (1981). It is set up in short double-spaced lines, here seventy-seven lines which may each be a voice on its own, according to the subtitle—or may be voiced by one person, or less plausibly by anywhere from two to seventy-six voices. The poem starts with Steining:

> Abragrammatica
> He she will or did
> Had had having been
> Yes
> Would will it yes
> Is if it's given
> Is as it's given him
> Is if if if if and when if and when
> If if if he is[17]

We hear about Kzenia and a blue answer and a small red car and other things by way of standard postmodern pseudonarrative, with a certain amount of yes and no and tense-shifting from past to present, and nearing the end we have one very unusual lyrical line, logically a jumble but plainly a voice never heard before in this poem or indeed in the rest of Palmer's book:

> Wood, water, knot, word, water, knot, collar and forehead and wrist, bayberry, bare stalk, leonine, cirrate, blue hill (51)

In context, this is in its rhythm and sounds and range of meanings a gorgeous misfit, a fashion model in a congress of logicians, impertinent. The poem ends:

There is writing like a wooden fence
There is writing now and when
There are letters on forehead and wrist

There's a word at each end of it
There is exactly what is said
There is this and what resembles it
There is a certain distance (52)

As rhythm this has diminished eventfulness because of the heavy balance produced by the anaphora and syntactic parallelism. The appeal to the thoughtful reader is to take this as enactment of writing-as-value, and as statement about writing as such—about multiple voice and unreliable narrative.

In the book *Notes*, as a whole, Palmer's lexicon is dominated by words like *same/different, is/isn't, if, or, as, while, stand for, silence, name, said, thought, color, seven, idea,* and notably by a cluster of terms cognate to his central value, *writing*: namely, *letter, grammar, word, poetry, poem, text, book.* If writing can mean *every line a new voic*e, reading cannot represent that by performing aloud, unless reading is a collective act, and unless every poem requires a chorus of different size. But a line is an artificial division, like a word, or an artwork's beginning and ending; so perhaps, pushing this beyond Palmer's subtitle premise, one might have a new voice at many variable-length units within the poem, making random the entry point of new voices.

So seventy-six lines appear to be spoken in one voice; and one line, with the words *leonine, cirrate,* appears to be spoken in another voice. The premise of seventy-seven has resolved into two. That is entirely consonant with Palmer's design: to decertify "voice" as value and turn it into endless enquiry.

RON SILLIMAN: *TJANTING* (1981). This poem, set up as usually unparagraphed prose sentences over 202 pages, is a whole book but also one part of a series of writings in a long-range project. Its sections are organized by the Fibonacci series, so this example, like the Hejinian and Palmer, has an impersonal constraint upon structural features, principally upon overall length, but also upon the relative length of segments. In Silliman's case few sentences extend longer than ten or twelve words, and few have the special type of complexity given by subordination, nesting of clauses, periodicity. This makes for a punchy statemental recording tone, but it also prevents the stylistic choice of surprising the reader by switching from a run of long, compound sentences to a short one, or the opposite. Diary-like, the sentences keep changing perspective, attitude, topics, but as with Hejinian there are recurrent issues, writerly, political, perceptual, and so on, and also some recurrent fixed phrasings such as "Not this." The paragraph opening on page seventy-eight begins:

> This house, my home, merely postpones movement. Pistols hence. A zoo coughs he coughs. Falls tart. Rain in the airshaft shifts light, no it doesn't. Thru the building, dim corridor residence hotel, the shadow went, silently checking each door to see if it was lockd. Dialectic is the ecological response to catastrophe/intervention, we're the only species that requires it. Circadi. An orderly distribution of rain on the window, more dense toward the bottom. Dawn patches begin to cloud up between the pre-blue show. Drops connect, convert to streams. Truce tart. Language extends memory's limits. Seam colord cleaners. Always wires & pipes extending up sides of houses. Awe enables apples. Pink tail of a white kite. The dog extends & a paw sits. Fever is the other inhabiting the body. A grunt around a crag of cruises crowed. From the tip of rabbit ears grey feather dangles. A writing-crew way of wrecking. Your brain doesn't just happen to you. Eight buy gum crowns. String of bells hangs from a dis-used hinge. Call that one in an egg nog all it art lived abstraction, it. I sat in the ghetto of the bus. Amid puffs & bursts of the audience whoops droplets of bombs plummeting over the destroyer, then rise cheers, anti-aircraft fire & gull-jet swoop. Small men in long cars wear hats. When I saw, I lookd again, the museum guard was holding onto an old lollipop. Garage doors on rollers. Logic to the sand & quik. Afterwards, rows of empty garbage cans with their lids off. New smell of toxic paint. My teeth crunchd into the caviar. Lots the poem P. Dead coleus in a clay pot. Proposd speech blur as roar. Inner organs swell with food, press on one another. Not this. Gelatin caps melt in the mouth. Chicken beef in almond hot sauce. More to Mephistopheles than a red acrylic tail. An inn dented swerve. Each word has its own arc.[18]

Ron Silliman makes discoveries: for example, the segmentation that makes a pun out of *Falls tart* and *truce tart*, phrasings separated in textual space but connected in meaning and method. The coleus plant, mentioned at intervals in decline in earlier sections of the poem, now definitively dies. The I speaker notices striking things about ordinary experience and about language. The sentences are sturdy and make up a diary of memories, perceptions, events in the present tense; the sentences have a variety of constructions, short as they are. Read, however, over more than twenty pages of recurrent topics and phrases, the poem de-tones by flattening out all the information to make it seem the same, a kind of equalized "chanting" to employ the pun embedded in the title: equal in length of units, repeating themes and phrases, moral and political facts. For fifty pages the reader with some interest in an agile well-stocked mind may track Silliman through his many turns. At that length *Tjanting* would be as long as *My Life*; but at four times fifty pages the eye-wandering effect Silliman knows about and expects will come to play. De-tonation here is an effect of the sentences and their sameness and brevity, miniaturization at the local level; but also an effect of the ensemble—gigantism of Silliman's project.

Both of the uncanny examples are from Language poets, a group that represents a growing fraction of recent American work. As a group they are loosely affiliated and do not always agree about the aims and languages of poetry. As a group they specialize in de-tonation, but only a fraction of this fraction moves all the way across the scale to the category of the uncanny. Of the two examples analyzed here, Silliman's poem employs full grammatical sentences of a certain length and type; Palmer's poem shows little interest in the form of the sentence as such, but does use free-verse lines of, usually, a certain length and type, and Palmer's poem also plays out, often by running them into trouble, certain lines of logic. The uncanniness in both examples is sufficient radically to destabilize the reader's perceptions of person, world, and language, but does not make a show of abandoning these modalities. More thoroughgoing examples might have been used: Gertrude Stein's *Tender Buttons* (1910) for disrupted syntax and for metaphors that offer a vehicle without a plausible tenor; Frank O'Hara's 1950s word salad and mix of high and low cultural allusions in the fifteen-page poem "Biotherm"; P. Inman's 1980s lettrism which breaks words into their components and deletes and suggests meaning by withdrawing markers like juncture, punctuation, and standardized line placement on the page. Already there exists a body of admirable readings of these and similar opaque writings, analyzing the devices that diversify, mask, or obliterate person.

Accompanying uncanny practice is an array of commentary, beginning with the original journal *L=A=N=G=U=A=G=E* and continuing with other journals such as *This, Hills,* and *Poetics Journal*. Barrett Watten, Ron Silliman, Steve McCaffery, and Charles Bernstein have published collections of essays, and the group contains formidable scholars and polemicists such as Lyn Hejinian, Bruce Andrews, Michael Davidson, and David Bromige.[19] Silliman's anthology of the group's poems, *In the American Tree* (1986), has 477 pages of poetry and over 130 pages of commentary on method.[20] Insofar as the group shares an aesthetic, the basic manifesto would emphasize fragmentation of person, skepticism about speech and voice, need to inquire into the materiality of language, reference and communication held at arm's length or further, sensitivity toward syllogism and logic since thinking makes poetry and prosody (not lines, rhymes, meters, sounds), the reader as co-creator.

Marjorie Perloff's 1981 book on indeterminacy and the Rimbaud tradition points toward this aesthetic, but then withdraws from the most radical practice and theory by closing with an account of a narrative and autobiographical poet, David Antin—and by a last-page speculation that when aleatory nonreferential writing reaches a limit, it will curve back to person, story, rhythm. Rather than pulling back from this limit, Stephen-Paul Martin pushes up against it in his book on the politics of reading in twentieth-century innovative writing, *Open Form and the Feminine Imagination* (1988).[21] Martin argues that when temporal sequence and hierarchical perception are abandoned, words become "vibraphonic entities" and sentences are to be defined by negatives: sentences do not cluster around a consistent personal subject, do not interact with each other, do not come from any point of view. Hence this writing is not easily consumed. Such writing, say in Djuna Barnes, Susan Howe, Ron Silliman, eludes the masculine left-brain approach to language, cannot be employed to serve a patriarchal system of "impregnable language," and so in reading it we enter into a "feminine zone of language" (171). We cease to become readers and become collaborators, Martin argues, and this in turn means a subversive political shift in discourse and our relation to it. Skeptical of Martin's textual and gender politics, we defer until below the question of what kind of politics there can be without some concept of a subject who can will and act, and without temporal sequence and hierarchical perception. Enough to have come to where, in recent theory, person as voice and voice as person have arrived at a virtual vanishing point. Enough to have shown that one leading edge of recent practice takes as a method the radical eloignment of voice. Here literary voice as such all but absconds.

For the Subject[22]

Our story is complete with the presenting of the so-far-furthest reach of uncanny detonation in the Language poets and those like them who emphasize disruptions of perceptual activity and logic. Their repudiation of sloppy, absorptive, organic-form, autobiographical, reference-driven ideas of "voice" obliges them to be adepts of printed language itself, as art's material medium. In the heart of their project these writers are researchers, like Derrida, into the writing that is in speaking, rather than the speaking that is in writing. Emphasizing, as this influential minority does, the materiality of writing, their tendency in practice and theory is to relish the obscurity of artifice—not the clarity of communication. To the degree that they place text over speech, they are like Roland Barthes in his midcareer preference for the knowledge-discovering, imaginative, *scriptible* writing, over the staid status quo of *lisible* writing. To the degree that they make voice the equivalent of speech, something empirical and not in itself discoverable in both text and speech, their position is identical with that of Derrida who devised a polemical grammatology to offset twenty centuries and more of misplaced trust in the *phoné*. Their speaking subject is supremely, drastically syncopated. And yet, like Derrida, while they have been stressing "the ways in which the subject was no longer identical with itself," there never has been with them any "intent to destroy or cancel the subject. Deconstruction and reconstruction go together."[23] Still, we would question whether a heavy emphasis on the materiality of language does not, like Derrida's anti-phonocentrism, make a decision about something that ought to have been left undecided, given their own premises.

In chapter 2, we argued that the place of the subject is mediation between the here and the there. We used the metaphor of oscillation. Now we would strengthen the metaphor to one of interference, which implies (1) no one warring entity, text, or speech, without the other; (2) each side trying to turn the other into something material and dead, like Beckett's fictional and actual selves in the fourth of the *Stories and Texts for Nothing*, quoted in chapter 1; and (3) continuous cohabitation and struggle in the words of the literary voice. A decision either for text or speech will, perhaps fatally for that text, call truce in an interference that is by the strictest logic both necessary and interminable. Of course, if those who decide for printed text would privilege the material side of an interference, that may well be one kind of current literature, defined as an anti-literature; it would mean the vanishing of literary voice as defined in this book, and of double-voicing as defined by Bakhtin.

Bakhtin's large-scale demonstrations of social heteroglossia in novels, driven by an integral theory of human culture in terms of dialogic communication, afford the most comprehensive account we know of the many-voiced text, including also the poetic text, for Bakhtin ought to be read against his own mistaken notion of 'poetry as monologic'. Nevertheless, there is a voice Bakhtin cannot hear or perceive: indeterminate voice, the literature of de-tonation. This salient limit in Bakhtin is perhaps related to his rootedness in Russian language theory with its theological basis, his isolation from currents of modern literary experimentation. Bakhtin cannot hear what we have called "textual voice," the voice that exempts itself from social registers, the nods and hints that come from intentionality based on gender, class, and other markers. Unplaceable voice is not theorized in Bakhtin's system. Bakhtin cannot imagine that there would be a kind of voice that tried to drop out of dialogue, to pretend that it was one of a kind, without tone or partner, the emanation of language itself as a power. In his account, even monologism is a social beckoning to an audience. It is true that voice in Bakhtin never has full self-presence because there will always be quotations from those absent and responses from those present, our partners in dialogue; but there is a speaking subject in place at all times, defined as one-half of a dialogue, or one member of the chorus of the heteroglossia. Textual voice has not that ontological, ultimately theological basis. So Bakhtin has no terms with which to recognize a significant and growing part of modern and postmodern writing. And yet his blindness is possible because of a total, social faith in the community, imaged as a struggle of consciousnesses within the work and between the work and its readers. What prevents him from recognizing is also what permits his philosophy of dialogism and answerability to make a critique-in-advance of interference dissolving methods based in the material text.[24]

Still, it would be a mistake to think of Bakhtin as an essentially modernist philosopher with a Russian Orthodox language theory. This is because dialogism is endless, and so Bakhtin's "meaning" is also an unfixing of meaning, his speaking subject sometimes private, sometimes common property. For this reason he is also one sponsor of postmodern uncertainty: a writer who has managed to be "For the Subject" but also, through his profoundly relational vision, to show a route out of the old dilemmas of the philosophy of the subject.

Language poets, along with writers of the textual voice, have theorized an extensive role for the reader of difficult texts, a reader able to make those willing surrenders in the area of understanding Jerome Rothenberg calls for, but also able to float from the page, get bored and drop out, mingle fantasies with the book's language, supply gaps, follow false leads, put the work together, and so on. Theirs is a "perceiver centered" aesthetic of reception, with a reader who can pay attention to the smallest as well as the largest change in the sequence and sound of writing. This attention to the reader's attention is empowering and gives many cues as to the frame of mind and actual techniques necessary for living in and with the *scriptible* text. But is the reader now taking over the abdicated position of the writer, acting not only as the co-creator, but also as the object of imitation and the construing subject? Without an inscribed image of the sender in a text, can it be that there is no inscribed image of the receiver either? An excerpt from Anne Mack and J. J. Rome in their dialogue on Ron Silliman follows:

> **Mack:** The social contract of writer and reader in Silliman . . . means that *The Alphabet*'s "flood of details" is not the possession of "Ron Silliman." The text is thickened by other readers and users, for whom "the same" word, phrases, and lines will never be "the same"—for themselves, for "Ron Silliman," for anyone else.
>
> **Rome:** Yes, of course—but I think one would get closer to the "meaning" of *The Alphabet* if we forgot about its "meanings" and paid more attention to its procedures. . . . *The Alphabet*'s chief distinction . . . lies in its having found a way to escape the control of a governing and a priori principle of order. Most apparent here is [its] refusal to allow "Ron Silliman" the customary (lyrical and romantic) privilege of authorial control.[25]

To enter into dialogue with this typical commentary, it is not churlish to reassert the forgotten question of communication. It is possible that if we stay with procedural shifts we lose larger Bakhtinian issues of voluntary association and of the social and dialogic context; and once we are immersed in fragments and perspectives, as signaled by the scare-quotes in the Mack-Rome passage, we may begin to see these fragments and perspectives as a means of escape from a bad social totality and lose the will to attack these as precisely *effects* of totality.

In an era of computer writing, virtual reality prostheses, and the deliberate (albeit temporary) forgetting of meaning, it is not easy to be for the subject, but as we have seen, there are dilemmas for those who would radically fragment or abandon the subject.[26] That is why the logic of the undecidable, in its strong form of interference, is appropriate to such an era: to be found as the basis of Ronald Schleifer's study of postmodern discourse theory (1990), whose argument moves between the two options of language considered as communicative and language considered as significative; the basis of Chantal Mouffe's call for "a new form of individuality that would be truly plural and democratic," her response to neo-Capitalist hegemonies; and the basis of Don E. Wayne's principled claim that "new historicism [as an emergent scholarly field], and postmodernism in general, constitute the prerequisites of an ethos that is struggling to emerge. And an ethos implies a relation to what we once confidently termed the 'self.'" Wayne goes on: "Like many of their contemporaries, new historicists have been justly resistant to notions of subjectivity in terms of *identity*. What some of these critics sense is the need for an ethics based on the acknowledgement of [historical and social] difference, but also on the principle of relationship."[27] Like many others, Wayne, Mouffe, and Schleifer understand that the radical relativism of much postmodern thought is not compatible with, in Wayne's words, our "roles, not as originary authors and agents, but as willful, deliberate and articulate participants in a present historical process that can disturb and disrupt (even if it cannot fully subvert) existing power structures" (803). Over many years Meschonnic in his historical anthropology of language has propounded a similar wish that we estimate, and employ, the transitivity of writing—always arguing that the impersonal is not the nonsubject. It is the work and outcome of a subject and that a complete elimination of the subject of speech ends in an idolatry of language.[28] Apparently, mere resistance to the call for communication is not enough, but must be countered by another kind or intensity of communication. Derrida is right: "Deconstruction and reconstruction go together," but they go together in a rapport of interference, like text/ speech, signify/communicate, individual/plural, difference/ relation, observe/act.

In this final chapter, reading has been our practice and our problematic. We are struck, at the last, by the convergence of an ethics of reading with de Certeau's gregarious theology of interlocution: "Subjects supposed to believe," de Certeau wrote, "are, in fact, the condition of belief."[29] What may seem the most isolating and personal act, praying or reading, may be reformulated as the most reassuringly social act, depending on how we hear the call.

Heidegger, Ronell aptly reminds us, immediately answered the call when the Nazis asked him to be Rector at Freiburg. His was didactic obedience, an automatic, direct following of commands and directions coming from an authority. By contrast, what we will call "ethical obedience" involves delay, detour, a long and wonderful voyage where miraculous and threatening things happen—like Jonah's escape from Yahweh which jeopardizes his life but demonstrates the solidarity of people when sailors try to save his life. This is where beings are not classifiable and go beyond good and evil. And yet the delay, the gap created between the command and the obedience, creates human unintended meanings, indeed a dialogic ethics of speech and response. When we read the Book of Jonah as a dialogue, clearly one of the purposes of Yahweh is to make Jonah more skeptical of his own teaching ability, more aware of human limitation. Even then the didactic call was a terrible thing, to be approached in awe!

Only through having collaborated in the partition-sharing of voice and on voice, is it fully clear to us that the meaning of the story is what goes on between Yahweh and Jonah in a space that is sonorous, ethical, ontological—and pedagogical. We can now confirm Jean-Luc Nancy's thesis that the logos is not a semantic *phoné* or a sense. The logos is what spaces the voices; the logos articulates itself in the space between silence and the voice. (*"NOUS sommes le sens, dans le partage de nos voix,"* writes Nancy; and Henri Meschonnic: *"Jona, c'est moi. C'est-à-dire toi."*) Jonah had certain advantages: the Nation was there as a full-faith community levered against the others, who included Nineveh; Jonah went toward divine particular places, Joppa, Nineveh, the sea bottom and the whale's belly, and Nancy is correct in this also—there were, perhaps still are, divine places; Yahweh spoke to Jonah, made him aware of his teacher's calling as a sacred life or death duty. Jonah also had the good fortune not to have to be the interpreter of the trauma of Jonah and the meanings of the spacings between Yahweh and himself. If this is a satire, as some scholars sense when they read a tone of broad exaggeration when Jonah moans inside the whale, and a tone of finger-wagging humor when Yahweh corrects Jonah at the end, there is division and multiplication of voice reaching into the interior of the book. If it is satire, Jonah's voice is partitioned, but Yahweh's is too. Presumably, though Yahweh knew this, Jonah did not. Knowing it ourselves, now, we may claim to understand something Jonah did not. Nonetheless, Jonah's refusal and trauma, his being punished by a storm and by being tossed overboard from a ship and being taken up into a whale's belly—these experiences will not seem unfamiliar to persons with a calling as professors of reading.

NOTES

Following the first reference for full identification, subsequent references to frequently cited books are given as page numbers inside parentheses within the Chapters. When translators are not mentioned in the Notes, translations into English are by the authors.

1. Toward a Philosophy of Literary Voice

1. Henri Meschonnic, *Jona et le signifiant errant* (Paris: Gallimard, 1981), p. 133.

Here we would like to state that remarks from an anonymous reader for the press have reminded us of the constitutive work on voice of Walter J. Ong. We address this in the Dedication and in certain additions, and by our deletion from our very first sentence of the hasty assertion that this is "not a book about something phonic or physiological." (Chapter 2 is all about physiology, and chapter 6 is quietly a protest against a writing that substitutes text for sound. Throughout, one intent of our argument is to struggle against the "chirographic and typographic bias" in the structuralist/Derridian enterprise, something already tactfully resisted in Ong's work since the mid-1970s). What we in fact most admire in Ong and try to develop is his central insight that "words remain at root always sounds," and that texts "must be recycled back through sound to have meaning" (*Interfaces of the Word: Studies in the Evolution of Consciousness and Culture* [Ithaca, NY: Cornell University Press, 1977], pp. 164, 310.) Taken as a whole, from his path-breaking book on Ramus (1958) to his magisterial foreword to Paul Zumthor's *Oral Poetry* (1990), Ong's work delivers what he claims is impossible—a history of voice that accounts for changes in personality structure and in social institutions.

2. Peter Dews, *Logics of Disintegration* (London and New York: Verso, 1987), p. 244.

3. David Carroll, *The Subject in Question: The Languages of Theory and the Strategies of Fiction* (Chicago: University of Chicago Press, 1982); Geoffrey H. Hartman, *Saving the Text: Literature/Derrida/Philosophy* (Baltimore and London: The Johns Hopkins University Press, 1981).

4. Dennis Potter, "Some Sort of Preface," in *Waiting for the Boat: On Television* (London and Boston: Faber and Faber, 1984), p. 12.

5. Gilles Deleuze, *Spinoza et le problème de l'expression* (Paris, Éditions du Minuit, 1968), p. 299.

6. John Cage, *Silence* (Cambridge, MA: MIT Press, 1966), p. 260.

7. Such as *Mureau*, a combination of music and Thoreau which is "a mix of letters, syllables, words, phrases, and sentences. I wrote it by subjecting all the remarks of H. D. Thoreau about music, silence, and sounds he heard . . . to a series of *I Ching* operations": John Cage, *Writing '67–72* [Middletown, CT: Wesleyan University Press, 1974], p. 1).

8. To speak of the bardic in the post-deconstructive era must mean talking in a digressive mode. Any other rhetorical choice would locate a critique of the bardic in the center, in the mainstream of discourse—where homogeneity may reign. If one wants to practice the reflection founded upon heterogeneity and discontinuity, then one will have to move toward the margins and peripheries of discourse. The bardic element, even if it is grounded in specific localities, brings them over toward the national, central, "healthy" language of the "tribe"; if it does present the drama of small villages, they are but a local stage upon which a much more general drama is being played. The periphery in the bardic is nothing else but a displaced and scattered center.

The bardic voice must necessarily be entrenched in history, as—in the final count—it is history that is always right in the bardic world. And yet the contemporary predicament of the speaking subject seems to consist in the subject's obligation to historicize the antihistorical; we know that history understood as continuity and its mortal lessons fails us miserably, and yet we are only groping our way toward opening possibilities of a new sense of history as a vertigo where the future materializes now building up its realm with the blocks of the past—like a postmodernist building which, playfully, becomes a folly in which a Gothic arch supports a steel and glass ceiling.

Thus we locate our speaking subject in this agonistic position in which he or she disrupts the historical continuity and sees that the present cannot be explained as a mere result of the past and a transition toward the future, and yet he or she has somehow "historically" to account for such a situation. Walter Benjamin described just this in his sixteenth thesis on the philosophy of history, when he spoke about "blasting open the continuum of history."

Hence our critique of the bardic in chapter 4 implies the near exhaustion of a certain mode of understanding human temporality and the tone of human voice taken as a certain "expression." We imply therefore that

1. the new bardic voice will be possible when thought of not as a celebration of history but as its dismantling. (As Anne Janowitz puts it in her reading of William Blake: "[The poet's] task is to dismantle the oppression of that [national] history and make something new out of it" (Anne Janowitz, *England's Ruins: Poetic Purpose and the National Landscape* [Oxford: Basil Blackwell, 1990], p. 174). The bardic is possible only as coming from within its own apocalypse, as an explosion and a de-tonation of the voice of the bard.
2. Continuity and density of events can no longer be viewed as guarantors of the bardic, since especially in the debate over the nature of causes and effects which has taken place in philosophy and physics at least since the mid-seventeenth century, "continuity, conceived as a chain of causes and effects, is unidirectional, an enslavement to steady attrition" (V. A. de Luca, *Words of Eternity, Blake and the Poetics of the Sublime* [Princeton, NJ: Princeton University Press, 1991], p. 58).
3. The crisis of the bardic voice is then the crisis of "unidirectionality," and hence our critique must necessarily hinge on the notions of heterogeneity and plurality which
4. can be controlled on a minimal, peripheral scale by the subject who no longer, like the bard, "expresses" the flux of events serving as their medium but changes his or her point of view momentarily. In this way the speaking subject "controls" a tiny section, a periphery, of events, remaining spectacularly and consciously helpless as far as wider chains or arrangements of events are concerned.

To use a pictorial example, the subject we are arguing for in this book could not, even if it wanted to salvage its bardic avatar, be visualized in the now classic 1817 painting by John Martin. What is at stake is not only a change of painterly conventions but, first of all, an impossibility of such an immediate and direct linking of the speaking subject with its past, as well as representation of the world as homogeneously solid and reliable. (In the painting, the link with the past is evident in the landscape and the old castle, both clearly alluding to the historical and natural greatness of Wales, and the image of King Edward in the distance, come to bring English rationality and root out bardic superstition; and the solid and reliable is manifested in the materiality of rocks—also in the direction of the bard's glance, for evidently the bard redeems the earth by means of the heavens, and the miserable present by the glorious future.) By contrast, we would illustrate the position of our subject with a painting by Salvador Dali, who in his 1940 *Slave Market with the Disappearing Bust of Voltaire* shows how history of art, politics, philosophy, and literature becomes fluid and loses contours through the image of Houdon's sculpture of Voltaire. It both gains and loses reality—loses through dreamlike scenery, gains through images of women in seventeenth-century costume—images of the slave market, images of subjection. And yet these images make up the image of Voltaire the philosopher with a reputation as a champion of freedom! Here is Dawn Ades's description of the Dali: "The seated figure of Gala on the left gazes at the group of figures, including two men dressed in black and white, in the style of Seventeenth Century Spain. They, together with the gaping arch in the ruined building behind them, form the bust of Voltaire . . . their faces become his eyes, their gloved and ruffled hands and arms his jaw, the glowing sky through the arch his domed head. Dali places a third woman similarly dressed at the right rear of the group, which resists any alternative reading" (Dawn Ades, *Dali* [London: Thames and Hudson, 1982], p. 136).

9. George Steiner, "The Distribution of Discourse," *On Difficulty and Other Essays* (New York: Oxford University Press, 1978).

10. See Michel de Certeau on St. Teresa, *La fable mystique: XVI–XVII siècle* (Paris: Gallimard, 1982), pp. 257–73, and his related article on a fourth-century holy woman, "Folies deliées: séductions de l'autre," *Traverses* 18 (Paris: Pompidou Center, February 1980):37–54.

11. M. H. Abrams' schema has "the work of art, the thing to be explained, in the center" of a triangle, whose points are universe, artist, and audience: *The Mirror and the Lamp: Romantic Theory and the Critical Tradition* (New York: Norton Books, 1953), p. 6. Wai-lim Yip's scheme for multicultural discussion of critical theories is a detailed diagram, explained by his article "The Framing of Critical Theories: A Reconsideration," *in Studies in Language and Literature* 2 (Taipei, 1986): 1–11, now reprinted as epilogue to Yip's *Diffusion of Distances: Dialogues between Chinese and Western Poetics* (Berkeley: University of California Press, 1993).

12. Michel de Certeau, "Utopies Vocales: Glossolalies," *Traverses* 20 (Paris: Pompidou Center, November 1980):26–37.

13. Samuel Beckett, *Stories and Texts for Nothing* (New York: Grove Press, 1967). The quotation is approximately the first quarter of the unparagraphed text 4. Writing on Beckett's play *Endgame*, Dina Sherzer argues that disruption of ordinary language rather than disintegration and decay is Beckett's game: "The cruel, ridiculous, laughable, thin deeds of the characters . . . are performed with talk, on and in language. . . . Their talk is far from meaningless. . . . Such an enterprise may be called signifying with impotence" ("Beckett's *Endgame*, or What Talk Can Do," *Modern Drama* 22, 5 [1979]:301–302).

14. Kaja Silverman, in *The Subject of Semiotics* (New York: Oxford University Press, 1983), offers the best survey of the stages by which, since Ferdinand de Saussure, the autonomy and the identity of the human subject comes in question. Also pertinent is her book *The Acoustic Mirror: The Female Voice in Psychoanalysis and Cinema* (Bloomington and Indianapolis: Indiana University Press, 1988), where chapter 2 on the soundtrack is an exposé of Hollywood's "diegetic containment of the female voice" (45).

The recent book closest to our own in its meditation on prophetic voice, spectral voice, multiple voice, "ear-fear," is Geoffrey Hartman's *Saving the Text: Literature/Derrida/Philosophy* (Baltimore and London: The Johns Hopkins University Press, 1981). Hartman dedicates his book "For the Subject." We too are for the subject and would affiliate with recent scholarship that makes reference to the discourses of power—legal, bardic-national, gender and genre—through which the subject receives and makes meaning.

15. Michel de Certeau, "Le corps et les masques de l'esprit," interview with Guitta Pessis-Pasternak in *Le Monde*, 19–20, January 1986.

16. Julia Kristeva, "The Ruin of a Poetics," was first published in Paris in 1970; the English version here is quoted from *Russian Formalism*, ed. Stephen Bann and John E. Bowlt (New York: Barnes & Noble, 1973), p. 109. "The Speaking Subject," first printed in *Times Literary Supplement* in 1973, is reprinted in *The Kristeva Reader*, ed. Toril Moi (New York: Columbia University Press, 1986); see p. 32. In the late sixties and early seventies, Kristeva first published her *Revolution of Poetic Language*, with many of the early pages on the concept of the 'speaking subject' (Paris, 1974; partial English version, New York, 1984), and two essays, also directly pertinent to the notion of the speaking subject, now collected in *Desire in Language: A Semiotic Approach to Literature and Art*, ed. Leon S. Roudiez, trans. T. Gora, A. Jardine, and L. Roudiez (New York, Columbia University Press, 1980): "Word, Dialogue, and Novel" (1969), and "The Ethics of Linguistics" (1974).

17. Toril Moi, ed., *Kristeva Reader*, introduction by Moi, 13. For related work see Tsvetan Todorov, *Mikhail Bakhtin: The Dialogical Principle*, trans. Wlad Godzich (Minneapolis: University of Minnesota Press, 1984). The same aporia of the speaking subject is reached through religious routes by Michel de Certeau and Emmanuel Levinas, through Saussurean linguistics by Émile Benveniste and through therapeutic dialogue by Jacques Lacan, whose linguistic supplement to Freud has it that the unconscious is structured like a language, the discourse of the other which in turn produces the "subject." "We are 'speakings,'" Lacan says, "a word that could substitute for the unconscious" ("Conférence," *Scilicet* 6–7 (1977):49).

A crucial Russian-French connection exists through Benveniste, whose use of Roman Jakobson on pronouns develops an account of subjectivity in language that Jakobson himself was unable to give: Émile Benveniste, "The Nature of Pronouns" and "Subjectivity in Language," in *Problems in General Linguistics*, trans. Mary Meek (Coral Gables, FL: University of Florida Press, 1971). Louis Althusser used Benveniste in his own study of how subjectivity is "interpellated" in specific ideological contexts: Marxist studies that explicitly thematize the human subject may take their proximate starting point with Althusser's "Ideology and Ideological State Apparatuses" in *Lenin and Philosophy* (New York: Monthly Review Press, 1971). These follow and modify: Fredric Jameson, "Imaginary and Symbolic in Lacan: Marxism, Psychoanalytic Criticism, and the Problem of the Subject," *Yale French Studies* 55/56 (1977); Chantal Mouffe, "Radical Democracy: Modern or Postmodern?" and Stanley Aronowitz, "Postmodernism and Politics," in Andrew Ross, ed., *Universal Abandon? The Politics of Postmodernism* (Minneapolis: University of Minnesota Press, 1988); Keith C. Pheby, *Interventions: Displacing the Metaphysical Subject* (Washington, DC: Maisonneuve Press, 1988); Paul Smith, *Discerning the Subject* (Minneapolis: University of Minnesota Press, 1988).

18. Stephen M. Ross's splendid phrase about a human yet nonpersonal referent is generated in a passage summarizing the dialogism of Mikhail Bakhtin in Ross's book *Fiction's Inexhaustible Voice: Speech and Writing in Faulkner* (Athens, GA, and London: University of Georgia Press, 1989), p. 10.

19. Michael McCallion, *The Voice Book (for actors, public speakers, and everyone who wants to make the most of their voice)* (London: Faber, 1988).

20. Peter Elbow, *Writing with Power* (Oxford: Oxford University Press, 1981).

21. Jack Goody and Ian Watt, "The Consequences of Literacy," *Comparative Studies in Society and History* 5 (1963):344. See also Jack Goody, *The Domestication of the Savage Mind* (Cambridge, England, and New York: Cambridge University Press, 1977), and Jack Goody, *The Interface between the Written and the Oral* (Cambridge, England, and New York: Cambridge University Press, 1987). Both more thoughtful and more truly multicultural than Goody is Paul Zumthor, *Oral Poetry: An Introduction* (Minneapolis: University of Minnesota Press, 1990).

22. Don Ihde, *Listening and Voice: A Phenomenology of Sound* (Athens: Ohio University Press, 1976), pp. 184–85.

23. This paragraph summarizes and responds to Hayden White's lecture discussion on the role of the middle voice in literary modernity: Department of Literature, University of California, San Diego, spring 1992.

24. Eric Griffiths, *The Printed Voice of Victorian Poetry* (Oxford: Oxford University Press, 1989).

25. Geoffrey Hartman, *Saving the Text: Literature/ Derrida/ Philosophy* (Baltimore and London: The Johns Hopkins University Press, 1981); Garrett Stewart, *Reading Voices: Literature and the Phonotext* (Berkeley and Los Angeles: University of California Press, 1990); Jonathan Goldberg, *Voice Terminal Echo: Postmodern and English Renaissance Texts* (New York and London: Methuen, 1986); Stephen M. Ross, *Fiction's Inexhaustible Voice: Speech and Writing in Faulkner* (Athens, GA, and London: University of Georgia Press, 1989); Charles O. Hartman, *Jazz Text: Voice and Improvisation in Poetry, Jazz and Song* (Princeton, NJ: Princeton University Press, 1991).

26. George Steiner, *Real Presences* (Chicago: University of Chicago Press, 1989).

27. Jean-Luc Nancy, *Le partage des voix* (Paris: Éditions Galilée, 1982), p. 67. See also Nancy's related meditation "Of Divine Places," *Paragraph* 7 (March 1986):1–52.

28. Martin Heidegger, *Being and Time*, trans. John Macquarrie and Edward Robinson (New York: Harper & Row, 1962), p. 72.

29. Jacques Derrida, *The Post Card: From Socrates to Freud and Beyond*, trans. Alan Bass (Chicago: University of Chicago Press, 1987), p. 478.

30. Walter J. Ong, *The Barbarian Within, and Other Fugitive Essays and Studies* (New York: Macmillan, 1962), p. 60.

31. For texts by de Certeau, see above, notes 10 and 12.

32. Walter J. Ong, *The Presence of the Word: Some Prolegomena for Cultural and Religious History* (New Haven and London: Yale University Press, 1967); page numbers in the text refer to this edition.

33. Mark Poster, *The Mode of Information: Post-structuralism and Social Context* (Chicago: University of Chicago Press, 1990); Avital Ronell, *The Telephone Book: Technology, Schizophrenia, Electric Speech* (Lincoln and London: University of Nebraska Press, 1989).

34. Sentences here on cyborgs (cybernetic biological organisms) summarize points made by N. Katherine Hayles in "Cyborg Subjectivity," a presentation at the Literature and Philosophy Conference, University of California, Berkeley, April 30 to May 2, 1992.

35. Henri Meschonnic, "L'écriture de Derrida," *Le signe et le poème: essai* (Paris: Gallimard, 1975), p. 492.

36. Henri Meschonnic, *Voyageurs de la voix* (Paris: Verdier, 1985).

37. Henri Meschonnic, "La situation d'un langage poétique," *Poésie sans réponse* (Pour la poétique, 5) (Paris: Gallimard, 1978), p. 22.

38. Gabriella Bedetti, "Henri Meschonnic: Rhythm as Pure Historicity," *New Literary History* 23, 2 (Spring 1992):431–32.

39. David Appelbaum, *Voice* (Albany: State University of New York Press, 1990).

2. Fish and Bird: Minimal Articulation

1. Avital Ronell, *The Telephone Book: Technology, Schizophrenia, Electric Speech* (Lincoln and London: University of Nebraska Press, 1989), p. 240. In passing, this chapter refers to two rewritings of the Jonah story: *Paul Goodman: Three Plays* (New York: Random House, 1965), and Robert Nathan, *Jonah, or the Withering Vine* (New York: Knopf, 1934).

2. David Appelbaum, *Voice* (Albany: State University of New York Press, 1990), p. 20.

3. William Blake, "Nurse's Song," *The Poetry and Prose of William Blake*, ed. David V. Erdman, commentary by Harold Bloom (New York: Doubleday and Company, 1965), p. 15.

4. Charles O. Hartman, *Jazz Text: Voice and Improvisation in Poetry, Jazz and Song* (Princeton, NJ: Princeton University Press, 1991).

5. Martin Heidegger, "...Poetically Man Dwells...," in: *Poetry, Language Thought*, trans. Albert Hofstadter (New York: Harper & Row, 1971), p. 222.

6. H. P. Lovecraft, "The Statement of Randolph Carter," in *At the Mountains of Madness* (and Other Tales of Terror) (New York: Ballantine Books, 1971).

7. Martin Heidegger, *Being and Time*, trans. John Macquarrie and Edward Robinson (New York: Harper & Row, 1962). Quotations in this order from 106/140 and from 107/142; quotation in next sentence from 107/141. Abbreviation: SZ.

8. Edgar Allan Poe, "The Facts in the Case of M. Valdemar," in *Collected Works of Edgar Allen Poe*, volume 3, Tales and Sketches 1843–1849, edited by Thomas Ollive Mabbott (Cambridge, MA, and London: Harvard University Press, 1978).

9. Martin Heidegger, *Introduction to Metaphysics* [1935], trans. Ralph Manheim (New York: Anchor Books, 1961).

10. William Richardson, "The Place of the Unconscious in Heidegger," *Review of Existential Psychology and Psychiatry* 5 (Fall 1965):265–90.

11. Jacques Maritain, *Creative Intuition in Art and Poetry* (New York: Pantheon Books, 1953), all references to pp. 91–92.

12. Edgar Allan Poe, "The Imp of the Perverse," in *Collected Works of Edgar Allan Poe*, volume 3, Tales and Sketches 1843–1849, edited by Thomas Ollive Mabbott (Cambridge, MA, and London: Harvard University Press, 1978).

13. Emmanuel Levinas, *Noms propres* (Paris: Fata morgana, 1976), p. 61.

14. Paul Celan, *Poems: A Bilingual Edition*, Selected, translated, and introduced by Michael Hamburger (London: Anvil Press Poetry, 1988), p. 79. Celan's German is quoted in the original from Paul Celan, *Die Niemandsrose* (Frankfurt am Main: S. Fischer Verlag, 1964): "ES WAR ERDE IN IHNEN," p. 9; "RADIX, MATRIX," p. 37; reprinted by permission of S. Fischer Verlag, copyright 1963.

15. E. M. Cioran, *Drawn and Quartered*, trans. Richard Howard (New York: Seaver Books, 1983), pp. 67–68. All references to Cioran in parenthetical pages numbers in the text of chapter 2 refer to this volume.

16. John Clare, *Poems*, ed. Eric Robinson and David Powell (Oxford: Oxford University Press, 1984), p. 415.

17. Friedrich Nietzsche, *Early Greek Philosophy and Other Essays*, trans. Maximilian A. Mugge (New York: Russell and Russell, 1964), p. 31.

18. Friedrich Nietzsche, *Historisch-Kritische Gesamtausgabe* (Munich: 1937), 5, p. 205.

19. Erich Heller, *The Importance of Nietzsche* (Chicago and London: University of Chicago Press, 1988), p. 174.

20. Friedrich Nietzsche, *Sämtliche Werke: Kritische Studienausgabe in 15 Banden*, ed. Colli and Montinari (Berlin: de Gruyter, 1980), 10, p. 39.

21. E. M. Cioran, *The Temptation to Exist*, trans. Richard Howard (Chicago: Quadrangle Books, 1968), p. 190.

22. Danielle André-Carraz, *Expérience intérieure d'Antonin Artaud* (Paris: Le Cherche Midi, 1973), p. 140.

23. Nietzsche, *Sämtliche Werke*, 13, p. 55.

24. Edmund Burke, *A Philosophical Enquiry into Our Ideas of the Sublime and the Beautiful*, ed. J. T. Boulton (London: Routledge and Kegan Paul, 1958), p. 57.

25. Peter de Bolla, *The Discourse of the Sublime: Readings in History, Aesthetics and the Subject* (Oxford: Blackwell, 1989), p. 295.

26. Blake's proverb comes from *The Marriage of Heaven and Hell*, in Erdman, p. 35; Nietzsche's from *The Birth of Tragedy*, trans. Walter Kauffmann (New York: Random House, 1967), p. 47.

27. Emmanuel Levinas, "Phenomenon and Enigma," in *Collected Philosophical Papers*, trans. Alfonso Lingis (Dordrecht: Martin Nijhoff, 1987), pp. 69–71.

28. E. M. Cioran, *Drawn and Quartered*, p. 112.

29. John Clare, "The Landrail," *Poems*, pp. 233–35.

30. John Clare, "The Robins [sic] Nest," *Poems*, p. 223.

31. Annie Dillard, *Pilgrim at Tinker Creek* (New York: Harper and Row, 1974), p. 217.

32. Allan Cruickshank, *The Pocket Guide to Birds* (New York: Dodd, Mead, 1953), p. 32.

33. Henri Meschonnic, *La Rime et la vie* (Paris: Verdier, 1989), p. 51.

34. Immanuel Kant, *Critique of Judgement*, trans. Werner Pluhar (Indianapolis: Hackett, 1987), p. 94.

35. Meschonnic, *La Rime et la vie*, p. 274.

36. Ibid., p. 275.

37. Uvedale Price, *Essays on the Picturesque* (1810; rpt. London: J. Mawman, 1971), pp. 111–12.

38. Jacques Derrida, *Writing and Difference*, trans. Alan Bass (Chicago and London: University of Chicago Press, 1978), p. 188.

39. The need to clarify and unify in songs is imperious; however, "It does not follow that what is said . . . by the words of songs is unimportant. It can be profoundly important" despite the simplifications (Mark W. Booth, *The Experience of Songs* [New Haven: Yale University Press, 1981], pp. 13–14).

40. Bob Robert Hodge is correct to state that "popular songs do not exist till they are performed" (*Approaches to Popular Culture*, ed. C. W. E. Bigsby [London: Edward Arnold, 1976], p. 125). Compare what Walter J. Ong says of song in his foreword to Paul Zumthor, *Oral Poetry: An Introduction*, trans. Kathryn Murphy-Judy (Minneapolis: University of Minnesota Press, 1990): "The culmination of voice is not merely any use of language, but song." Zumthor's book is far more than an introduction on these matters of voice and song.

41. Meschonnic, *La Rime et la vie*, p. 207.

42. Adam Mickiewicz, *Dzieła* (Warsaw: Społdzielnia Wydawnicza—Czytelnik, 1955), 1 [*wiersze*], p. 259.

43. Julian Klaczko, "La Crimée Poétique" in *La Revue Contemporaine*, rep. in *Szkice i rozprawy literackie* (Warsaw: 1904), p. 240. For more recent scholarship on Crimea and Caucasus in Mickiewicz, see Molly Wesling, "Pushkin, Mickiewicz and the South," in *Slava Orientalis* 41 (Warsaw, 1992), pp. 3–10.

44. Adam Mickiewicz, *Dzieła*, 1, 263. The English version is a drastic modification of the one in *Poems by Adam Mickiewicz*, ed. George Rapall Noyes (New York: Polish Institute of Arts and Sciences in America, 1944), p. 155.

45. See also Jacques Derrida, *Psyche* (Paris: Galilée, 1987), p. 628: "The law of the double. Knot and caesura, obligation and breaking-off: that's rhythm. Is not rhythm a double—and reciprocal—law?"

46. Derrida, *Psyche*, p. 630.

47. Meschonnic, *La Rime et la vie*, p. 41.

3. Early Modern Speaking Subjects

1. Emmanuel Levinas, *Le Temps et l'autre* (Paris: Presses Universitaires de France, 1979), p. 63.

2. René Descartes, *The Philosophical Works of Descartes*, trans. Elizabeth S. Haldane and G. R. T. Ross (Cambridge: Cambridge University Press, 1969), 1, 189. All subsequent page references are to this edition and volume.

3. Samuel van Hoogstraten is quoted in Svetlana Alpers, *The Art of Describing: Dutch Art in the Seventeenth Century* (Chicago and London: University of Chicago Press, 1983), p. 141.

4. John Donne, "The Triple Fool," *The Complete Poetry of John Donne*, ed. John T. Shawcross (New York: Doubleday, 1967), pp. 98–99.

5. Compare Jean-Luc Nancy: "The human being is thus a subject that cannot name itself, that cannot situate itself as such. It is the subject that cannot subject itself" (*Ego Sum* [Paris: Flammarion, 1979], p. 154).

6. Joseph Salmon is quoted in Nigel Smith, *Perfection Proclaimed: Language and Literature in English Radical Religion, 1640–1660* (Oxford: Oxford University Press, 1989), p. 62.

7. John Donne, "The Legacie," *Complete Poetry of John Donne*, pp. 102–3.

8. We find useful on these matters John Hollander, *The Figure of Echo: A Mode of Allusion in Milton and After* (Berkeley and London: University of California Press, 1981).

9. *The Works of George Herbert*, ed. F. E. Hutchinson (Oxford: Oxford University Press, 1941), p. 188.

10. Compare Jean-François Lyotard on the law in *Le différend* (Paris: Editions du Minuit, 1983), p. 9: "As distinguished from a lawsuit, a disagreement would be a case of conflict between at least two parties, which could not be settled equitably, short of a rule of judgment applicable to both sides of the argument. That the one should be lawful wouldn't entail that the other isn't as well. . . . A wrong [*dommage*] results from an injury done to the rules of a genre of discourse, and is redressed according to those rules."

11. Jacques Derrida, "On a Newly Arisen Apocalyptic Tone in Philosophy," originally published in *Semeia* 23 (1982), then in *The Oxford Literary Review* 6, 2 (1984). We quote from the John Leavey, Jr., translation as published in Peter Fenves, ed., *Raising Tone of Philosophy: Late Essays by Immanuel Kant, Transformative Critique by Jacques Derrida* (Baltimore and London: The Johns Hopkins University Press, 1993), p. 166.

12. L. Elaine Hoover, *John Donne and Francisco de Quevedo: Poets of Love and Death* (Chapel Hill: University of North Carolina Press, 1978), p. 90.

13. Richard Crashaw, "The Weeper," *The Complete Poetry of Richard Crashaw*, ed. G. W. Williams (New York: Anchor Press, 1970), p. 264.

14. *This Dialogue of One: The Songs and Sonnets of John Donne* (University: University of Alabama Press, 1982), p. 141.

15. Andrew Marvell, "Eyes and Tears," *The Complete Poems of Andrew Marvell*, ed. Elizabeth Story Domo (Harmondsworth: Penguin Books, 1972), pp. 52–54.

16. Charles Cotton, "Laura Weeping," in *The Poems of Charles Cotton*, ed. John Beresford (New York: Boni and Liveright, n.d.), p. 189.

4. Bardic Voice: Vestiges of the Oral and the National

1. Robert B. Reich is quoted in *The New York Times*, 12 April 1990, p. C1.

2. Jürgen Habermas, *Strukturwandel der Öffenlicheit* (1962), English trans. *The Structural Transformation of the Public Sphere*, trans. Thomas Burger with Frederick Lawrence (London: Polity Press, 1989); "The Public Sphere: An Encyclopedia Article [1964]," *New German Critique* 3 (Fall 1974):49–55.

3. Jean-Luc Nancy, "Of Divine Places," *Paragraph* 7 (March 1986):1–52.

4. Joseph Fontenrose (Berkeley and London: University of California Press, 1978). Also pertinent by Fontenrose: *Didyma: Apollo's Oracle, Cult, and Companions* (Berkeley and London: University of California Press, 1988). In 1972 the publisher Benjamin Blom of New York republished Rev. T. Dempsey's *The Delphic Oracle: Its Early History, Influence and Development* (Oxford: Blackwell, 1918), with its sexist statement on the Pythia: "The fasting . . . the chewing of the laurel leaves . . . might in a guileless, uneducated soul—especially a woman—produce such an abnormal psychic state. . . of trance and agitation, such as were associated with the Delphi priestess." Compare the prizing of woman's vatic voice in H. D. and in American womn poets since 1970. Absolutely essential in these contexts is Eric A. Havelock's *Preface to Plato* (1963), which forever changed the study of voice for the Socratic period in Greek thought.

5. We quote from *The New Scofield Reference Bible: Holy Bible, Authorized King James Version* (New York: Oxford University Press, 1967). We accept the phrasing of the King James translation, and we of necessity base all interpretation on this mediating language.

6. John Miles, "Laughing at the Bible: Jonah as Parody," *Jewish Quarterly Review* 65 (January 1975). See also Adele Berlin's rejoinder to Miles in the April 1976 issue of *JQR*; for her the Book of Jonah is not a parody. Also pertinent: Baruch Halpern and Richard Elliott Friedman, "Composition and Paronomasia in the Book of Jonah," *Hebrew Annual Review* 4 (Columbus: Ohio State University Press, 1980):79–92. We thank Richard Elliott Friedman for personally informing us of Yahweh's delphic pun on the passive verb *NHPKT*, used when Yahweh tells Jonah of the coming fate of Nineveh. *NHPKT* can mean either "destroy" or "have a change of heart," so Yahweh's reversal of himself is contained within his statement of what will happen to the city. What we call Yahweh's "repentance" is repentance only from a human point of view.

7. Thomas Gray, "The Bard," *Selected Poems of Thomas Gray and William Collins*, ed. Arthur Johnson (Columbia: University of South Carolina, 1967), p. 77.

8. William Blake, "To the Muses," in *The Poetry and Prose of William Blake*, ed. David V. Erdman (New York: Doubleday, 1965) pp. 408–9.

9. Alfred Tennyson, "Ode on the Death of the Duke of Wellington," *The Poems of Tennyson*, 2nd edn., ed. Christopher Ricks (Berkeley and London: University of California Press, 1986), 2, p. 481. The distorted spelling is our joke of printed voice, not in Tennyson's original.

10. *The Cambridge History of Poland*, W. F. Redaway et. al., eds. (Cambridge, England: Cambridge University Press, 1950), p. 311.

11. Jan Lechoń, *O literaturze polskiej* (New York: Wydawn. Tygodnika Polskiego, 1946), p. 113.

12. This diagnosis is confirmed by the super-exile of the Polish romantic emigration, Cyprian Norwid, in his 1876 letter to Bronislaw Zaleski (our translation; Norwid's emphasis): "Emigration has robbed me of everything: youth, strength, personal friends, value, almost of the name and dignity of my forefathers. And has there been a reason for this? I wouldn't be surprised and would respect it. But they did it for *nothing*, because they did *nothing, nothing at all!* except for a few Jewish and antechamber fortunes and personal successes, which I am not able to feel envious of, nor would I lower myself to such an act" (Cyprian Norwid, *Pisma wierszem i proza*, ed. Juliusz W. Gomulicki [Warsaw: Państwowy Instytut Wydawniczy, 1970], p. 388).

13. See Martin Heidegger, *Being and Time*, trans. John Macquarrie and Edward Robinson (New York: Harper, 1962), p. 103. Useful commentators on this and other Heideggerian concepts are David Halliburton, *Poetic Thinking: An Approach to Heidegger* (Chicago: University of Chicago Press, 1981); Robert Magliola, *Phenomenology and Literature: An Introduction* (West Lafayette, IN: Purdue University Press, 1977); George Seffler, *Language and the World: A Methodological Synthesis of the Writings of Martin Heidegger and Ludwig Wittgenstein* (Atlantic Highlands, NJ: Humanities Press, 1974).

14. The phrasing in this explanation is Seffler's, p. 39.

15. Jan Lechoń has written: "*Pan Tadeusz* is indeed a poem of memory. Proust's memory was stimulated by illness; Mickiewicz's by exile and by his realization that the world of his childhood had gone for ever." See Lechoń's "Adam Mickiewicz," in *Adam Mickiewicz, 1798–1855: Selected Poems*, ed. Clark Mills, with a critical appreciation by Jan Lechoń (New York: Noonday, 1956), p. 46.

16. On the difference between gesture and gesticulation, see Jacques Derrida's analysis of Rousseau's *Essay on the Origin of Languages*: "Rousseau clarifies [the question of a supplementary return toward a greater naturalness] . . . by distinguishing between gesture and gesticulation: the former, which sketches the shadow of presence, silently governs the first metaphor; the latter is an indiscreet and cumbersome adjunct of speech. It is a bad supplement" (*Of Grammatology*, trans. G. Spivak [Baltimore: The Johns Hopkins University Press, 1976], p. 236).

17. Geoffrey Hartman, "Words, Wish, Worth: Wordsworth," in *Deconstruction and Criticism*, ed. Geoffrey Hartman (New York: Seabury, 1979), p. 193.

18. Kazimierz Wyka's comment may be found in his *Pan Tadeusz*, 2 (Warsaw: 1963), p. 26.

The monumental collected works (*Dzieła*, 1955) of Mickiewicz prints the epilogue after the poem, as does the Kenneth Mackenzie English translation. These are the two versions employed in the present essay, in order to quote from the original and to show the meaning in reasonably good English verse. Henceforth, quotations from Adam Mickiewicz, *Dzieła*, 4, ed. Julian Krzyżanowski (Warsaw: Czytelnik, 1955), will be followed by book and line number citations; quotations from *Pan Tadeusz, or the Last Foray in Lithuania*, trans. Kenneth Mackenzie (London: J. M. Dent, 1966; and New York: Dutton, Everyman's Library, 1966), will be followed by "Mack. tr." and the page number citation in the Mackenzie translation.

It is worth noting that the other English translations, by George Rapall Noyes (1930; prose) and by Watson Kirkconnell (1962; verse), both mistakenly print the epilogue before the poem, as a prologue.

19. On saying and speaking, see Heidegger, *Poetry, Language, Thought*, trans. Albert Hofstadter (New York: Harper and Row, 1971), p. 11.

20. Mickiewicz, *Dzieła*, 5, p. 119.

21. Hegel's account of the social conditions of epic may be found in his *Philosophy of Fine Art*, trans. F. P. B. Osmaston (London: G. Bell, 1920), 4, esp. p. 120. Using Hegel's concepts, we could claim that fatherland as voiced by the bard is "the relations of ethical life" *("die Verhältnisse des sittlichen Lebens")* in which organizational forms "cannot as yet have assumed the settled forms of regulations . . . and laws independent in their validity of the direct personal and private activities of the individual" (4, 120).

22. Describing this internalized form of law, Hegel proclaims it "the intuitive sense of right and fairness, the moral habit" (4, 120); and in his consideration of the difference between Roman and Greek ideas of virtue, Hegel specifies the Greek model as one in which "personality is a law to itself without any further subjection to a law, judgment, and tribunal of independent subsistence" (1, 250). So the internalization of fatherland and its transformation into a value sign is paralleled by the internalization of law. The "moral habit" (*die Sitte, das Gemüt*) of the bardic world is protected against anarchy by the idea of order, pattern, well-preserved model of life—something not imposed, but rather the outcome of the bond between the human and the world.

23. "Free from the restrictions of the written medium," we have written. Hence the importance in the poem of the verb *gadać*, an untranslatable word describing a relatively free, unstructured way of speaking rather by the physiology of the body of the speaker, than by rhetorical arrangement of arguments or sequential line of events. The word returns in a parodistic version of Polish oracular culture in the works of Witold Gombrowicz (1904–1969).

24. The phase is Heidegger's from *Being and Time*, p. 87/120.

25. This is the translation in the essay by Joseph J. Kockelmans, "Language, Meaning, and Existence," in *On Heidegger and Language* ed. and trans. Kockelmans (Evanston, IL: Northwestern University Press, 1972), p. 9.

26. Wolfgang Iser expresses it concisely: "What the language *says* is transcended by what it *uncovers*, and what it uncovers represents its true meaning" (Wolfgang Iser, *The Act of Reading: A Theory of Aesthetic Response* [Baltimore: The Johns Hopkins University Press, 1978], p. 142).

27. This is the interpretation of *Rede* offered by Magliola, p. 58.

28. The passage from Heidegger's *Holzwege* (Frankfurt am Main: Klostermann, 1977), p. 179, is quoted and translated by Magliola, p. 70.

29. Adam Mickiewicz, *Dzieła*, 8, pp. 174–75.

30. Wyka, *Pan Tadeusz*, 1, p. 28.

31. Ibid., 2, pp. 361, 363.

32. Ibid., 2, p. 363.

33. Adam Mickiewicz, *Dzieła*, 9, p. 292.

34. Friedrich Schlegel, *Dialogue on Poetry and Literary Aphorisms*, trans. Ernst Behler and Roman Struc (University Park: Pennsylvania State University Press, 1968), p. 151.

35. Letter from Czeslaw Milosz to one of the authors, 17 February 1982. The phrase is consistent with his excellent account of *Pan Tadeusz* in his *History of Polish Literature*, 2nd edn. (Berkeley: University of California Press, 1983), pp. 227–29.

36. On Scott and Mickiewicz, see J. Krzyżanowski, "Z dziejów walter-skotyzmu polskiego. W setną rocznicę śmierci Waltera Scotta," in *Przegląd współczesny*, No. 130 (1933), p. 172; also Wyka, *Pan Tadeusz*, 1, pp. 52–3, 183–220. An English writer who has dealt with the connexion is Donald Davie in *The Heyday of Walter Scott* (London: Routledge and Kegan Paul, 1961).

37. Wiktor Weintraub has capably explored the relation between human and outer nature in the poem's imagery: *The Poetry of Adam Mickiewicz* (The Hague: Mouton, 1954), p. 224 ff.

38. Adam Mickiewicz, *Dzieła*, 8, p. 206.

39. Weintraub, *The Poetry of Adam Mickiewicz*, p. 223.

40. Some data on population from Gąsiorowska may be useful. In 1791 a partitioned Poland had 8.8 million inhabitants; that makes 931 people per square mile (England had 3160; France 2668; Prussia 1613; European Russia 325). The stratification was landed gentry 8 percent; clergy 0.6 percent; Christian (gentile) middle class (burghers) 6.8 percent; Jews (mostly burghers)

10.2 percent; and peasants (serfs) 72.7 percent (Natalia Gąsiorowska, "Historia społeczno-gospodarcza Polski," *Wiedza o Polsce*, 1–3 [Warsaw: Wydawnictwo Wiedza o Polsce]).

Stefan Kieniewicz claims that in 1810 the grand duchy of Warsaw had 300,000 Jews, namely 7 percent of the population (*Historia Polski 1764–1864*, 2, part 1, ed. Stefan Kieniewicz and W. Kula [Warsaw: Państwowe Wydawnictwo Naukowe, 1958]).

41. Wyka, *Pan Tadeusz*, 2, p. 368.

42. Donald Davie, last stanza of "Or, Solitude," in *Collected Poems 1950–1970* (London: Routledge and Kegan Paul, 1972), p. 202.

43. Robert Graves, *The White Goddess: A Historical Grammar of Poetic Myth*, amended and enlarged edn. (London: Faber and Faber, 1952), p. 24.

44. Vachel Lindsay, *Collected Poems* (New York: Macmillan, 1913, 1925); "Yankee Doodle" starts on p. 378, and "Above the Battle's Front," is on p. 383. Page numbers of passages quoted refer to this edition.

5. De-tonation: Another Mode of the Minimal

1. *The Collected Works of Edgar Allan Poe*, ed. T. O. Mabbott (Cambridge, MA: Harvard University Press, 1969), 3, p. 191.

2. Henri Meschonnic, *Critique du rythme: anthropologie historique du langage* (Paris: Verdier, 1982), p. 73. Quotation in next sentence from same text, p. 710.

3. Stanislaw Brzozowski, *Kultura i Życie* (1905; Warsaw: Panstwowy Istytut Wydawniczy, 1973;), pp. 150, 149.

4. Cyprian Norwid, "Slowotwór," *Dzieła Zebrane*, ed. Juliusz W. Gomulicki (Warsaw: Czytelnik, 1966), p. 1.

5. Carol Jacobs traces a similar process in Antonin Artaud, in whose *Heliogabal* we witness a steady movement toward the inarticulate. The subject, in Artaud, exists in a series of "intestinal rumblings" in which "the tone is put forth by a series of sounds whose relationship is not precisely mutual destruction but rather a subtraction of each from the next, a limitless marking of difference that produces an indefinable *détimbrage*, approximated by, but not equivalent to, absolute silence and emptiness" (*The Dissimulating Harmony: The Image of Interpretation in Nietzsche, Rilke, Artaud, and Benjamin* [Baltimore: The Johns Hopkins University Press, 1978], p. 80).

6. Cyprian Norwid, "Pieśni społecznej cztery strony," *Dzieła*, ed. Tadeusz Pini (1848; Warsaw: 1934), p. 508.

7. Brzozowski, *Kultura i Życie*, p. 158.

8. In a long philosophical poem, "Rzecz o wolności słowa" ("A treatise on the freedom of the word"), written and, what is particularly noteworthy, delivered orally in Paris (13 May 1869), Norwid adds another element to this philosophy. As if in the wake of Hegel's meditation on master and slave, Norwid will claim that it is precisely the weakness of Poland, a lack of political tone, that will help to redeem the nation. The pair "Slav" and "word" *(stowianin/stowo)* acquires a third element, "weak" *(słaby)*:

Słabi . . . i Sławni—i słowo, to cała
Jest treść jak dziejów oś się obracała.
(*Dzieła Zebrane*, 1966, 3., p. 611)

[Weak . . . famous—and a word: this is the whole
Contents showing how the world's axis was revolving.]

Here de-tonement, a seeming weakening and deprivation of the subject, be it individual or national, turns out to be a source of new power and life. What is needed is not doubt concerning the existence of the subject, but rather the subject's positioning and characterization along new lines.

9. Jacques Derrida, *Speech and Phenomena*, trans. David B. Allison (Evanston, IL: Northwestern University Press, 1973), p. 96.

10. Ibid., p. 97.

11. Jacques Derrida, *Marges de la philosophie* (Paris: Éditions du Minuit, 1972), p. ix.

12. When Nietzsche was shown to students of psychiatry in Binswanger's Jena Clinic, he revealed "the soft tone of the pleasant voice" by which "one recognized the man of best education" (S. Simchowitz, quoted in *Conversations with Nietzsche: A Life in the Words of His Contemporaries*, ed. Sander Gilman, trans. D. Parent [Oxford: Oxford University Press, 1987], p. 225). The implication is that Nietzsche's contemporary combines education with the tone rather than the substance of the voice, and he considers tone as the shelter where the individual defies the attacks of madness. By this account, in the tone of voice is stored a person's integrity and past.

13. *Human, All Too Human*, trans. M. Faber and S. Lehmann (Lincoln: University of Nebraska Press, 1984), p. 181.

14. *The Gay Science*, trans. K. Reinhardt (New York: Fredrick Unger, 1960), p. 142.

15. *Basic Writings of Nietzsche*, ed. Walter Kaufmann (New York: Modern Library, 1966), both passages on p. 352.

16. *The Will to Power*, trans. Anthony M. Ludovici (New York: Russell and Russell, 1964), 2, p. 255.

17. Jacques Derrida, *Schibboleth* (Paris: Éditions Galilée, 1986), p. 44.

18. Hans-Georg Gadamer, *Philosophical Hermeneutics* (Berkeley and London: University of California Press, 1973), p. 13.

19. Jacques Derrida, *Speech and Phenomena*, p. 104.

20. Jacques Derrida, *L'écriture et la différence* (Paris: Éditions du Seuil, 1967), p. 353.

21. Jacques Derrida, *De la grammatologie* (Paris: Editions de Minuit, 1967), p. 213.

22. Jacques Derrida, *La dissemination* (Paris: Éditions du Seuil, 1972), p. 194.

23. Émile Benveniste, "Subjectivity in Language," in *Problems in General Linguistics*, 226.

24. James Beattie, *The Theory of Language* (1788; Menston: The Scholar Press, 1961), pp. 147–48.

25. Wilhelm von Humboldt, *On Language: The Diversity of Human Language. Its Structure and Its Influence on the Mental Development of Mankind* (1836), trans. Peter L. Heath (Cambridge: Cambridge University Press, 1988), p. 63.

26. See Jacques Derrida, "On a Newly Arisen Apocalyptic Tone in Philosophy," trans. John P. Leavey, Jr., in Peter Fenves, ed., *Raising the Tone of Philosophy: Late Essays by Immanuel Kant, Transformative Critique by Jacques Derrida* (Baltimore and London: The Johns Hopkins University Press, 1993); this is a major point throughout, but see esp. pp. 156–57.

27. Jacques Derrida, University of California, Irvine Conference on Postmodernism and Beyond: Architecture as the Critical Art of Contemporary Culture, October 26–28, 1989. The absent Derrida's communication to the conference was a fifteen-page letter in French to architect Peter Eisenman. Quotation from p. 15 of the typescript.

28. Derrida, "On a Newly Arisen Apocalyptic Tone," p. 151. Next quoted passage from same text, same page.

29. Ibid., p. 166. Next quoted passage is from same text, same page.

30. Quoted from Wolfram Ax, *Laut, Stimme, und Sprache: Studien zur drei Grundbegriffen der antiken Sprachtheorie* (Göttingen: Vandenhoeck and Ruprecht, 1986), p. 16.

31. Derrida, "On a Newly Arisen Apocalyptic Tone," p. 165.

32. Humboldt, *On Language*, p. 55.

33. Even in Humboldt voice, although markedly privileged, is already flawed by its mediating force. At one moment in his analysis, Humboldt in *On*

Language describes sound as a veil intervening between person and reality: "As the individual sound stands between him and the object, so the entire language steps in between him and the nature" (60).

34. Victorianus in Ax, *Laut, Stimme, und Sprache*, p. 33; Probus in Ax, p. 28.

35. Jacques Derrida, *Ulysse gramophone. Deux mots pour Joyce* (Paris: Galilée, 1987), p. 16.

36. Ibid., p. 17.

37. Steven L. Bindeman, *Heidegger and Wittgenstein: The Poetics of Silence* (Lanham, MD: University Press of America, 1981), p. 97.

38. Beattie, *Theory of Language*, p. 16.

39. Derrida, *Ulysse gramophone*, p. 16.

40. Humboldt, *On Language*, p. 54.

41. Charles Winquist, *Epiphanies of Darkness: Deconstruction in Theology* (Philadelphia: Fortress Press, 1986), pp. 25, 30.

42. Marshall McLuhan, *Understanding Media: The Extension of Man* (New York: Signet, 1964), p. 264.

43. Henri Meschonnic, *Voyageurs de la voix* [poems] (Paris: Verdier, 1985), p. 35.

44. Henri Meschonnic, *Modernité, Modernité* (Paris: Verdier, 1988), p. 255. The next two quotations are from the same book, same page.

45. Henri Meschonnic, interview with Gabriella Bedetti, *Diacritics* (Fall 1988), p. 103.

46. Meschonnic, *Modernité*, p. 282. The next three quotations are from the same book, pp. 283, 284, 10.

47. Henri Meschonnic, *Critique du rythme: anthropologie historique du langage* (Paris: Verdier, 1982), p. 83.

48. Meschonnic, Modernité, p. 11.

49. Meschonnic, *Critique du rythme*, pp. 285, p. 705.

50. Henri Meschonnic, *La Rime et la vie* (Paris: Verdier, 1989), p. 275.

51. Meschonnic, *Voyageurs de la voix*, p. 33.

52. Meschonnic, *La Rime et la vie*, p. 246.

53. Meschonnic says, "The discovery-role . . . reserved to Saussure, Benveniste, Humboldt" (*La Rime et la vie*, p. 315); on pronouns and subjectivity: "The 'I' is the impersonal form of the subjective; as such, beyond the first person, the exchange of the function of the subject—something quite other than the non-person, the absent, hidden 'he'" (*Critique du rythme*, p. 102).

54. Walter J. Ong, *The Presence of The Word* (New Haven and London: Yale University Press, 1967), p. 324.

55. Meschonnic, *La Rime et la vie*, p. 235.

56. We are quoting Walter J. Ong from respectively, "Literacy and Orality in Our Times," *Profession* 79 (New York: Modern Language Association, 1979), p. 3, and "The Writer's Audience Is Always a Fiction," *Interfaces of the Word* (1977), p. 80.

57. Meschonnic, *La Rime et la vie*, p. 236. The next quoted passage is from the same book and page.

58. Henri Meschonnic, *Le Signe et le poème* (Paris: Gallimard, 1975), p. 247. The next quoted passage is from the same book, p. 245.

59. Meschonnic, *Critique du rythme*, pp. 84, 705.

60. Henri Meschonnic, "La Nature Dans La Voix," a long introductory essay to Charles Nodier, *Dictionnaire des onomatopées françaises* (1808) (Mauvezin: Trans-Europ-Repress, 1984), p. 39.

61. Meschonnic, interview in *Diacritics*, p. 106.

62. Meschonnic, *La Rime et la vie*, p. 190.

63. Meschonnic, *Critique du rythme*, p. 72. The next two quotations are from the same book, pp. 73, 179.

64. Meschonnic, *La Rime et la vie*, p. 275.

6. Reading the De-toned Text

1. Quotations in this paragraph come from Stephen Barker, "Textual Person and the Paramodern Self-Text," presentation at the Philosophy and Literature Conference, University of California, Berkeley, April 30 to May 2, 1992.

2. See Eric Griffiths, *The Printed Voice in Victorian Poetry* (Oxford: Oxford University Press, 1989), p. 55.

3. Jacques Derrida, "On a Newly Arisen Apocalyptic Tone in Philosophy," in Peter Fenves, ed., *Raising the Tone of Philosophy: Late Essays by Immanuel Kant, Transformative Critique by Jacques Derrida* (Baltimore and London: The Johns Hopkins University Press, 1993), pp. 167, 168.

4. *The Complete Poems of Robert Frost* (New York: Holt, 1949), p. 404.

5. The distinction between mimetic and textual voice is described by Stephen M. Ross in "'Voice' in Narrative Texts: The Example of *As I Lay Dying*," *PMLA* 94, 2 (March 1979):300 ff.

6. Federico García Lorca, "Theory and Function of the *Duende*," in *Lorca*, ed. J. L. Gili (Harmondsworth: Penguin Books, 1960), p. 131 (translation modified).

7. John Ashbery, quoted in Richard Nason's footnotes to Canto 3, *A Modern Dunciad* (New York: The Smith, 1978).

8. *Times Literary Supplement* for 3 November 1973 has a summary of a lecture on "Tone in Eliot's Poetry" given by Christopher Ricks. Eliot deliberately left lines toneless, says Ricks (p. 1345).

9. Jerome Rothenberg, interview with Barry Alpert, *Vort* 7 (Silver Spring, MD: 1975), p. 148.

10. Delmore Schwartz, "The Isolation of Modern Poetry," quoted in David Lehman, "Delmore, Delmore: A Mournful Cheer," *Parnassus: Poetry in Review* (Spring/Summer 1979), p. 219.

11. Marjorie Perloff, *The Poetics of Indeterminacy: Rimbaud to Cage* (Princeton, NJ: Princeton University Press, 1981).

12. Longinus, *On Sublimity*, trans. D. A. Russell (Oxford: Oxford University Press, 1965), p. 47.

13. Dennis Potter, *The Singing Detective* (New York: Vintage Books, 1988 [first United Kingdom copyright, 1986]), pp. 14–15.

14. William Gibson, *Neuromancer* (New York: Ace Books, 1984), p. 5.

15. Lyn Hejinian, *My Life*, second, expanded edition (Los Angeles: Sun & Moon Press, 1991 [first published 1980]), pp. 41–42.

16. J. H. Prynne, *Poems* (Edinburgh and London: Agneau, 1982), p. 307. "Chromatin," below, is on p. 223. Admirable commentary which pursues the Prynne-Celan connection may be found in Geoffrey Ward, "Nothing but Mortality: Prynne and Celan," in A. Easthope and J. O. Thompson, eds., *Contemporary Poetry Meets Modern Theory* (Brighton: Harvester, 1991), pp. 139–52.

17. Michael Palmer, "Notes for Echo Lake 8 (for one to seventy-seven voices)," *Notes for Echo Lake* (San Francisco: North Point Press, 1981), pp. 48, 51, 52.

18. Ron Silliman, *Tjanting* (Berkeley, CA: The Figures, 1981), pp. 78–79.

19. To list only the published collections of essays: Barret Watten, *Total Syntax* (Carbondale: Southern Illinois University Press, 1984); Ron Silliman, *The New Sentence* (New York: Roof Books, 1987); Steve McCaffery, *North of Intention: Critical Writings 1973–1986* (New York: Roof Books, 1986); Charles Bernstein, *Content's Dream: Essays 1975–1984* (Los Angeles: Sun & Moon Press, 1986).

20. *In the American Tree*, ed. Ron Silliman (Orono, ME: National Poetry Foundation, 1986).

21. Stephen-Paul Martin, *Open Form and the Feminine Imagination: The Politics of Reading in Twentieth-Century Innovative Writings* (Washington, DC: Maisonneuve Press, 1988).

22. Reminder: the title of this final section of our book is Geoffrey H. Hartman's Dedication to *Saving the Text* (1981). We too are "For The Subject," especially the kind of subject whose lineage is traced by Charles Taylor in *Sources of the Self: The Making of the Modern Identity* (Cambridge, MA: Harvard University Press, 1989). Taylor argues that "agents are constituted by exchange": "once we see that. . . we understand that [in addition to instrumental domination of object by subject] reason also advances in another dimension, that of the rational search for consensus through argument" (509)

23. Jacques Derrida, presentation at Oxford University in March 1992, *Times Literary Supplement*, 1992 April 3, p. 13.

24. In *Mikhail Bakhtin: Creation of a Prosaics* (Stanford: Stanford University Press, 1990), Gary Saul Morson and Caryl Emerson show that "even before Bakhtin turned his attention to language, tone was a central category of his thought" (133). And tone, they show, was for Bakhtin always evaluative and ethical (see pp. 133–35). On Russian language theory, an admirable study is Steven Cassedy's *Flight from Eden: The Origins of Modern Literary Criticism and Theory* (Berkeley: University of California Press, 1990), esp. chapters 2 and 5; on Bakhtin, see pp. 119–20.

25. Anne Mack and J.J. Rome, "*The Alphabet*, Spelt from Silliman's Leaves: A Conversation on the American Longpoem," *South Atlantic Quarterly* 89, 4 (Fall 1990): 737–59.

26. "Computer writing is the quintessential postmodern linguistic activity. . . . a machine for constituting non-identical subjects" (Mark Poster, "Derrida and Electronic Writing," *The Mode of Information* [Chicago: University of Chicago Press, 1990], p. 128). We have written of the human subject with the metaphors of mediation, oscillation, and interference. In an age of electronic writing, we might also use "conduction": the subject as the flow of energy through a circuit, an idea from Gregory Ulmer, *Teletheory: Grammatology in the Age of Video* (London and New York: Routledge, 1989), p. 63. Another formula for our being for the subject comes from terms for deterritorialization in recent writings of Gilles Deleuze and Felix Guattari. We have tried to read the dominating sedentary subject through the potential of the nomadic which it covers up. Our syncopated subject is the in-passage, pilgrim subject of holes, gaps, and unexpected turns.

27. Ronald Schleifer, *Rhetoric and Death: The Language of Modernism and Postmodern Discourse Theory* (Urbana and Chicago: University of Illinois Press, 1990); Chantal Mouffe, "Radical Democracy: Modern or Postmodern?" in *Universal Abandon? The Politics of Postmodernism* (Minneapolis: The University of Minnesota Press, 1988), esp. p. 44; Don E. Wayne, "New Historicism," *Encyclopedia of Literature and Criticism*, ed. Martin Coyle, et al. (London: Routledge, 1990), p. 803.

By now it should be evident that we have arrived, at the last, speaking for the subject in the mood of negative assurance Paul de Man discusses when he takes up the difference between "rhetorization of grammar" and "grammatization of rhetoric": "the former ends up in indetermination . . . , but the latter seems to reach a truth, albeit by the negative road of exposing an error, a false pretence. . . . We seem to end up in a mood of negative assurance that is highly productive of critical discourse" (*Allegories of Reading* [New Haven and London: Yale University Press, 1979], p. 16).

28. Henri Meschonnic's positions on the subject in twentieth-century language theory and in avant-garde writing are well summarized in his interview for the journal *Esprit*, published as "Poétique et politique," *Les états de la poétique* (Paris: PUF, 1985): 50–67.

29. Michel de Certeau, "The Jabbering of Social Life," *On Signs*, ed. Marshall Blonsky (Baltimore and London: The Johns Hopkins University Press, 1985), p. 202. De Certeau goes on: "In order for there to be belief, belief must be somewhere—not believable objects (that only constitute the object of exchange) but a positing of the subject (or quasi-subject) who is 'straight' and does not deceive."

We find a similar drawing-together of the ideas of belief, reading, and subject-construction in Edith Wyschogrod's revisioning of moral philosophy, *Saints and Postmodernism* (Chicago: University of Chicago Press, 1990), p. 149: "the hagiographic text lays hold of the reader so that the hermeneutics of reading . . . [of the saint's story] is transformed into a struggle of writing. . . . The addressee must reinscribe, not merely re-present, the narrative in her/his own story. In the process of reinscription a new life is shaped."

Finally, we would mention two recent studies which harmonize with our Voice: Seàn Burke, *The Death and Return of the Author: Criticism and Subjectivity in Barthes, Foucault, and Derrida* (Edinburgh: Edinburgh University Press, 1992), and Fabian Goudas and Michael Davidson, "Voice" in *The New Princeton Encyclopedia of Poetry and Poetics*, ed. Alex Preminger and T. V. F. Brogan (Princeton, NJ: Princeton University Press, 1993).

Index